CODING
AND
INFORMATION
THEORY

CODING
AND
INFORMATION
THEORY

RICHARD W. HAMMING

Adjunct Professor in Computer Science
Naval Postgraduate School

Prentice-Hall, Inc., Englewood Cliffs, New Jersey   07632

Library of Congress Cataloging in Publication Data

HAMMING, RICHARD WESLEY, 1915–
    Coding and information theory.

    Bilbliography: p. 233
    Includes index.
    1. Coding theory   2. Information theory.   I. Title.
QA268.H35   519.4   79-15159
ISBN 0-13-139139-9

Editorial/production supervision and interior design
    by Gary Samartino
Cover design by Frederick Charles Ltd.
Manufacturing buyer: Gordon Osbourne

Printed in the United States of America
10 9 8 7 6 5

PRENTICE-HALL INTERNATIONAL, INC., *London*
PRENTICE-HALL OF AUSTRALIA PTY. LIMITED, *Sydney*
PRENTICE-HALL OF CANADA, LTD., *Toronto*
PRENTICE-HALL OF INDIA PRIVATE LIMITED, *New Delhi*
PRENTICE-HALL OF JAPAN, INC., *Tokyo*
PRENTICE-HALL OF SOUTHEAST ASIA PTE. LTD., *Singapore*
WHITEHALL BOOKS LIMITED, *Wellington, New Zealand*

Contents

3 Error-Correcting Codes *35*

4 Variable-Length Codes—Huffman Codes *51*

5 Miscellaneous Codes 79

6 Entropy and Shannon's First Theorem *101*

10 Shannon's Main Theorem 179

11 Algebraic Coding Theory 195

Appendix A: Bandwidth and the Sampling Theorem 219

Preface

This book combines the fields of coding and information theory in a natural way. They are both theories about the representation of abstract symbols. The two fields are now each so vast that only the elements can be presented in a short book.

Information theory is usually thought of as "sending information from here to there" (transmission of information), but this is exactly the same as "sending information from now to then" (storage of information). Both situations occur constantly when handling information. Clearly, the encoding of information for efficient storage as well as reliable recovery in the presence of "noise" is essential in computer science.

Since the representation, transmission, and transformation of information are fundamental to many other fields as well as to computer science, it is time to make the theories easily available. Whenever and wherever problems of generation, storage, or processing of information arise, there is a need to know both how to compress the textual material and how to protect it against possible mutilation. Of the many known encoding methods, we can indicate only the more important ones, but hopefully the many examples in the text will alert the student to other possibilities.

The text is designed to cover the fundamentals of the two fields and to give examples of the use of the ideas in practice. The amount of background mathematics and electrical engineering is kept to a minimum. The book uses, at most, simple calculus plus a little probability theory, and anything beyond that is developed as needed. Techniques that have recently arisen in computer science are used to simplify the presentation and the proofs of many results. These techniques are explained where they are used so no special knowledge of computer science is required. Many other proofs have been greatly simplified, and, when necessary, new material has been developed to meet current technological needs. An effort has been made to arrange the material, especially the proof of Shannon's main result, so that it is evident *why* the theorems are true, not just that they have been proved mathematically.

Chapter 11, on algebraic codes, develops the needed mathematics of finite fields. Because of its mathematical difficulty, this chapter is placed last and out of logical order. It can follow Chapter 3, if desired. There is deliberate repetition in the text; important ideas are usually presented at least twice to ensure that the reader understands them.

The text leaves out large areas of knowledge in the belief that it is better to master a little than to half know a lot. Thus, more material may easily be added (at the discretion of the teacher) when it seems appropriate for the class.

I have followed custom in referring to *Hamming codes* and *Hamming distance*; to do otherwise would mislead the student and be false modesty.

ACKNOWLEDGMENTS

It is difficult for the author to recall all his indebtedness to others, since he has known about the material from many years of working at the Bell Laboratories. Teaching a course at the Naval Postgraduate School, based on N. Abramson's elegant, small book, *Information Theory and Coding* [A], rearoused this author's interests in the two fields. Short courses on the topic at other places further developed many of the simplifications, elaborations, and examples, and the help of many students is gratefully acknowledged. The assistance of Albert Wong is especially appreciated.

In the actual production of the book, Bostrom Management Corporation's computer produced various drafts, and the help of Ralph Johnson is especially appreciated. However, as always, all faults are to be assigned to the author.

R. W. HAMMING

CODING
AND
INFORMATION
THEORY

1

Introduction

1.1 A VERY ABSTRACT SUMMARY

Although the text uses the colorful words "information," "transmission," and "coding," a close examination will reveal that all that is actually assumed is an *information source* of symbols $s_1, s_2, \ldots, s_q$. At first nothing is said about the symbols themselves, nor of their possible meanings. All that is assumed is that they can be uniquely recognized.

Next we introduce the probabilities $p_1, p_2, \ldots, p_q$ of these symbols occurring. How these p_i are determined is not part of the abstract theory. For any discrete probability distribution there is the value of the *entropy function*:

$$H = \sum_{i=1}^{q} p_i \log \frac{1}{p_i}$$

The function H of the probability distribution p_i measures the amount of uncertainty, surprise, or information the distribution contains. This function plays a leading role in the theory and provides a lower bound on the average code length. Later we examine more complex probability structures involving the symbols s_i.

The problem of representing the *source alphabet* symbols s_i in terms of another system of symbols (usually the binary system consisting of the two symbols 0 and 1) is the main topic of the book. The two main problems of representation are the following:

1. How to represent the source symbols so that their representations are far apart in some suitable sense. As a result, in spite of small changes (noise) in their representations, the altered symbols can be discovered to be wrong and even possibly corrected.

2. How to represent the source symbols in a minimal form for purposes of efficiency. The average code length,

$$L = \sum_{i=1}^{q} p_i l_i$$

is minimized, where l_i is the length of the representation of the ith symbol s_i. The entropy function provides a lower bound on L.

Thus, in principle, the theory is simply an abstract mathematical theory of the representation of some undefined source symbols in terms of a fixed alphabet (usually the binary system). In this abstract theory there is no transmission, no storage of information, and no "noise is added to the signal." These are merely colorful words used to motivate the theory. We shall continue to use them, but the reader should not be deceived; ultimately, this is merely a theory of the representation of symbols.

1.2   HISTORY

The beginnings of both coding and information theory go far back in time. Many of the fundamental ideas were understood long before 1948, when the two theories were first established on a firm basis. In 1948 Claude E. Shannon published two papers on "A Mathematical Theory of Communication" in the *Bell System Technical Journal* (reprinted in Ref. [S]). They almost immediately popularized the field of information theory, and soon additional papers on information theory appeared in the journals and courses were taught on the subject in electrical engineering and other departments of various universities.

As in most fields that suddenly open up, many of the early applications were ill-advised; but how else are the limitations of a new field to be discovered? As a result of the overexpectations of what information theory could do there gradually set in a disenchantment and a decrease in the number of courses taught. Now, perhaps, a more just evaluation can be made, somewhere between the wild enthusiasm of the first days and the sad disappointment that slowly followed.

Information theory sets bounds on what can be done but does little to aid in the design of a particular system. The idea that it is therefore useless to know information theory is false, as the following analogy shows. Consider the theory of evolution as taught in biology. Few students will ever apply it directly in their lives, yet it is a valuable constellation of ideas. In spite of this lack of direct application, when the following ideas are mastered:

1. Small changes in the species (variations)
2. Survival of the fittest (selection)

then the ideas can profitably be used in many other situations, often far removed from biology. For example, when looking at a social institution, such as a computer science department, a university, a military organization, a banking system, a government, or even a family relationship, one asks: "How did the present situation arise?" and "What were the forces that selected this particular realization for survival?"

A little more appreciation of the power of the theory suggests the questions: "Given the present forces on the social institution, what are its possible variations (its ability to respond to the forces)?" and, "How will it evolve (what will survive)?" Thus the ideas in the theory of evolution can be used in many situations far removed from biology.

Similarly, information theory has ideas that are widely applicable to situations remote from its original inspiration. The applicability of the ideas is not exact—they are often merely suggestive—but the ideas are still very useful.

At about the same time as information theory was created, and in about the same place, coding theory was also created. The basic paper, however, was delayed by patent requirements until April 1950, when it also appeared in the *Bell System Technical Journal* (reprinted in Refs. [B2] and [B1a]). In the case of coding theory, the mathematical background was at first less elaborate than that for information theory, and for a long time received less attention from the theorists. With the passing of time, however, various mathematical tools such as group theory, the theory of finite fields (Galois theory), and even linear programming have been applied to coding theory. Thus coding theory has now become an active part of mathematical research (Refs. [B1], [Gu], [MS], [Mc], and [W]).

Most bodies of knowledge give errors a secondary role, and recognize their existence only in the later stages of design. Both coding and information theory, however, give a central role to errors (noise) and are therefore of special interest, since in real-life noise is everywhere.

Logically speaking, coding theory leads to information theory, and information theory provides the bounds on what can be done by suitable encoding of the information. Thus the two theories are intimately related, although in the past they have been developed to a great extent quite separately. One of the main purposes of this book is to show their mutual relationships. For further details on the history of coding theory, see Ref. [B2].

1.3 MODEL OF THE SIGNALING SYSTEM

The conventional signaling system is modeled by:

1. An information source.
2. An encoding of this source.
3. A channel over, or through, which the information is sent.
4. A noise (error) source that is added to the signal in the channel.
5. A decoding and hopefully a recovery of the original information from the contaminated received signal.
6. A sink for the information.

This model, shown in Figure 1.3-1, is the one that we will use for our signaling system. It has many features of signaling systems now in use. Often the ENCODE is divided into two stages, one the encoding of the source and the other the further encoding to fit the channel. The DECODE is then, of course, similarly divided into two stages. We will begin at the ends of the system and gradually work our way to the middle.

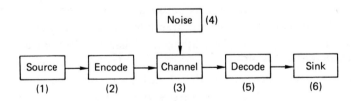

FIGURE 1.3-1 STANDARD SIGNALING SYSTEM

1.4 INFORMATION SOURCE

We begin with the *information source*. The power of both coding and information theory is to a great extent due to the fact that we *do not define* what information is—we *assume* a source of information, a sequence of symbols in a *source alphabet* $s_1, s_2, \ldots, s_q$. When we get to Chapter 6 we will find that information theory uses the entropy function H as a *measure of information*, and by implication this defines what is meant by "the amount of information." But this is an abstract definition that *agrees only partly* with the commonly accepted ideas concerning information. It is probably this appearance of treating what we mean by information that made information theory so popular in the early days; people did not notice the differences and thought that the theory supplied the proper meaning in all cases. The implied definition does give the proper measure to be used for information in many situations (such as the storage and transmission of data) and people hoped that their situation was one of these (they were often wrong!). Information theory *does not* handle the *meaning* of the information, it treats only the *amount* of information.

The source of information may be many things: for example, a book, a printed formal notice, and a company financial report are all information sources in the conventional alphabetic form. The dance, music, and other human activities have given rise to various forms (symbols) for representing their information, and therefore can also be information sources. Mathematical equations are still another information source. The various codes which we next turn to are merely particular ways of representing the information symbols of a source.

Information also exists in continuous forms; indeed, nature usually supplies information in that form. But modern practice is to sample the continuous signal at equally spaced intervals of time, and then to digitize (quantize; Ref. [J]) the amount observed. The information is then sent as a stream of digits. Part of the reason for this use of digital samples of the analog signal is that they can be transmitted more reliably than can the analog signal. When the inevitable noise of the transmission system begins to degrade the signal, the digital pulses can be sensed (detected), reshaped, and amplified to standard form *before* relaying them down the system to their final destination. At the destination the digital pulses may, if necessary, be converted back to analog form. Analog signals cannot be so reshaped, and hence the farther the signal is sent and the more it is processed, the more degradation it suffers from small errors.

A second reason that modern systems use digital methods is that integrated circuits are now very cheap and provide a powerful method for flexibly and reliably processing and transforming digital signals.

Although information theory has a part devoted to analog (continuous) signals, we shall concentrate on digital signals both for simplicity of the theory and because, as noted above, analog signals are of decreasing importance in our technical society. Almost all of our large, powerful computers are now digital, having displaced the earlier analog machines almost completely in information-processing situations. There are still a few large, general-purpose hybrid systems left (1979). Most of our information transmission systems, including the common telephone, are also rapidly going to digital form.

1.5 ENCODING A SOURCE ALPHABET

It is conventional to represent information (digital signals or more simply symbols) as being in one of two possible states; a switch up or down, on or off, a hole punched or not, a relay up or down, a transistor conducting or not conducting, a magnetic domain magnetized N-S or S-N, and so on. At present devices with two states, called *binary devices,* are much more reliable than are multistate devices. As a result, binary systems dominate all others. Even decimal information-processing systems such as hand calculators are usually made from binary parts.

It is customary to use the symbols "0" and "1" as the names of the two states, but any two distinct symbols (marks) such as a circle and a cross will do. It is sometimes useful not to think of the 0 and 1 as numbers but only as a pair of arbitrary symbols.

First, we consider merely the problem of representing the various symbols of the source alphabet. Given two binary (two-state) devices (digits) we can represent four distinct states (things, symbols):

$$00$$
$$01$$
$$10$$
$$11$$

For three binary digits we get $2^3 = 8$ distinct states:

000	100
001	101
010	110
011	111

For a system having k binary digits—usually abbreviated as *bits*—the total number of distinct states is, by elementary combinatorial theory,

$$2^k$$

In general, if we have k different devices, the first having n_1 states, the second n_2 states, . . . , the kth having n_k states, then the total number of states is clearly the product

$$n_1 n_2 \ldots n_k$$

For example, if $n_1 = 4$, $n_2 = 2$, and $n_3 = 5$, then we can represent $4 \times 2 \times 5 = 40$ distinct items (states).

This is the number of source symbols we can represent *if all we consider* is the number of distinct states. We will later (Chapter 4) discuss how to take advantage of the probabilities of the source symbols occurring. For the present we merely consider the number of distinct states—and this is the same as assuming that all the source symbols are equally likely to occur.

We have emphasized two-state devices with two symbols; other multi-state devices exist, such as a "dead center switch," with three states. Some signaling systems also use more than two states, but the theory is easiest presented in terms of two states. We shall therefore generally use a binary system in the text and only occasionally mention systems with r states.

Human beings often attribute meanings to the sequences of 0's and 1's, for example in the ASCII code (Table 1.7-1). The computer (or signaling system), however, merely regards them as sequences of 0's and 1's. In particular, a digital computer is a processor of streams of the two symbols—it is the user (or possibly the input or output equipment) that assigns meanings; the computer merely combines 0's and 1's according to how it is built and how it is programmed. *The logic circuits of a computer are indifferent to the meanings we assign to the symbols; so is a signaling system.*

This is the reason that information theory ignores the meaning of the message, and by so doing it enables us to understand what the equipment does to messages; the theory provides an intellectual tool for understanding the *processing* of information.

Typically, the encoding of the message for the channel increases the redundancy (to be defined accurately later), as shown in Chapters 2 and 3. The source encoding (mentioned at the end of Section 1.3) usually decreases the redundancy, as shown in Chapters 4 and 5.

We need to think of the source as a random, or stochastic, source of information, and ask how we may encode, transmit, and recover the original information. Specific messages are, of course, actually sent, but the designer of the system has no way of knowing which of the *ensemble* of possible messages will be chosen to be sent. The designer must view the particular message to be sent as a random sample from the population of the class of all possible messages, and must design the system to handle any one of the possible messages. *Thus the theory is essentially statistical*, although we will use only elementary statistics in this book.

Exercises

1.5-1   Compute the number of license plates of the form "number number number letter letter letter."

1.5-2   How many instructions can there be in a computer with eight binary digits for each instruction?

1.6   SOME PARTICULAR CODES

The binary code is awkward for human beings to use. Apparently, people prefer to make a single discrimination among many things. Evidence for this is the size of the usual alphabets, running from around 16 to 36 different letters (in both upper- and lowercase) as well as the decimal system, with 10 distinct symbols. Thus for human use it is often convenient to group the binary digits, called *bits*, into groups of three at a time and call them the *octal code* (base 8). This code is given in Table 1.6-1.

TABLE 1.6-1   Octal Code

Binary	Octal
000	0
001	1
010	2
011	3
100	4
101	5
110	6
111	7

When using the octal representation numbers are often enclosed in parentheses with a following subscript 8. For example, the decimal number 25 is written in octal as

$$(31)_8$$

Thus, in America, Christmas is Halloween:

$$\text{Dec } 25 = \text{Oct } 31$$

$$(25)_{10} = (31)_8$$

As an example, in Table 1.7-1 of the ASCII code in the next section we have written the octal digits in the left-hand column rather than the binary digits. The translation from octal to binary is so immediate that there is little trouble in going either way.

Occasionally, the binary digits are grouped in fours to make the *hexadecimal code* (Table 1.6-2)

Since computers usually work in *bytes*, which are usually 8 bits each

TABLE 1.6-2   Hexadecimal Code

Binary	Hexadecimal
0000	0
0001	1
0010	2
0011	3
0100	4
0101	5
0110	6
0111	7
1000	8
1001	9
1010	A
1011	B
1100	C
1101	D
1110	E
1111	F

(there are now 9-bit bytes in some computers), the hexadecimal code fits into the machine architecture better than does the octal code, but the octal seems to fit into the human's psychology better. Thus neither code has a clear victory over the other in practice.

Exercises

1.6-1   Since $2^8 \simeq 3^5$, compare base 2 and base 3 computers.

1.6-2   Make a multiplication table for octal numbers.

1.6-3   From Table 1.6-2, what is the binary representation of D6?
Answer. 11010110

1.7   THE ASCII CODE

Given an information source, we first consider an encoding of it. The standard ASCII code (Table 1.7-1), which represents alphabetic, numeric, and assorted other symbols is an example of a code.

Basically, this code uses seven binary digits. Since (as noted already) computers work in *bytes* which are usually blocks of 8 bits, a single ASCII symbol often uses 8 bits. The eighth bit can be set in many ways. Sometimes it is always set as a 1 so that it can be used as a timing source. It is usually set so that the total number of 1's in the eight positions is an even number (or else an odd number—see Chapter 2). Finally, it may be left arbitrary and no use made of it. To convert to the modified ASCII code used by the LT33 8-bit teletype code, use 7-bit ASCII code $+ (200)_8$.

The purpose of the even number of 1's in the eight positions is that then any single error, a 0 changed into a 1 or a 1 changed into a 0, will be detected since after the change there will be an odd number of 1's in all the eight positions. Thus we have an error-detecting code which gives some protection against errors. *Perhaps more important*, the code enables the maintenance to be done much more easily and reliably since the presence of errors is determined by the machine itself, and to some extent the errors can be actually located by it.

We shall frequently use the check of an even (or odd) number of 1's. It is called *a parity check*, since all that is checked is the parity (the evenness or oddness) of the number of 1's in the message. Many computers have the very useful instruction to count the parity of the contents of the accumulator.

We are now in a better position to understand the ASCII code (Table

TABLE 1.7-1   Seven-Bit ASCII Code

Octal Code	Char.	Octal Code	Char.	Octal Code	Char.	Octal Code	Char.
000	NUL	040	SP	100	@	140	`
001	SOH	041	!	101	A	141	a
002	STX	042	''	102	B	142	b
003	ETX	043	#	103	C	143	c
004	EOT	044	$	104	D	144	d
005	ENQ	045	%	105	E	145	e
006	ACK	046	&	106	F	146	f
007	BEL	047	'	107	G	147	g
010	BS	050	(	110	H	150	h
011	HT	051	)	111	I	151	i
012	LF	052	*	112	J	152	j
013	VT	053	+	113	K	153	k
014	FF	054	,	114	L	154	l
015	CR	055	-	115	M	155	m
016	SO	056	.	116	N	156	n
017	SI	057	/	117	O	157	o
020	DLE	060	0	120	P	160	p
021	DC1	061	1	121	Q	161	q
022	DC2	062	2	122	R	162	r
023	DC3	063	3	123	S	163	s
024	DC4	064	4	124	T	164	t
025	NAK	065	5	125	U	165	u
026	SYN	066	6	126	V	166	v
027	ETB	067	7	127	W	167	w
030	CAN	070	8	130	X	170	x
031	EM	071	9	131	Y	171	y
032	SUB	072	:	132	Z	172	z
033	ESC	073	;	133	[	173	{
034	FS	074	<	134	\	174		
035	GS	075	=	135	]	175	}
036	RS	076	>	136	^	176	~
037	US	077	?	137	_	177	DEL

1.7-1). The ASCII has a source alphabet of

$$2^7 = 128$$

possible characters (symbols). These characters are represented (encoded) inside a computer in the binary code. An even-parity check can be used to set the eighth position of the 8-bit bytes of the ASCII code. The three printed symbols of Table 1.7-1 are in the octal code. As an example,

$$127 = 1 \quad 010 \quad 111$$

(where we have dropped the first 2 bits of the first octal symbol). For an even parity this would be $127 = 11 \quad 010 \quad 111$.

Exercises

1.7-1   Write the letters P and p in binary.

1.7-2   To what does 01   010   011 correspond?

1.7-3   Using base 4 code, write out the lowercase ASCII alphabet

1.7-4   Write out the uppercase ASCII alphabet in base 16.

1.8   SOME OTHER CODES

Another familiar code is the *Morse code*, which was once widely used. Part of the code is given in Table 1.8-1. The dash is supposed to be three times the length of the dot. Although the Morse code may appear to be encoded into a binary code, it is, in fact, a ternary (radix 3, $r = 3$) code, having symbols dot, dash, and space. The space between dot and dashes in a single letter is one unit of time, between letters it is three time units, and between words it is six time units.

We now make a brief digression to introduce a notation. We will continually need the binomial coefficients

$$C(n, k) = \frac{n!}{k!(n-k)!}$$

They count the number of ways a set of k items can be selected from a set of n items. We have adopted the old-fashioned notation $C(n, k)$ because it is easily produced on a typewriter, it is easily set in print, and it can be gracefully handled by most computers. The currently popular notation

$$\binom{n}{k}$$

is difficult for most equipment to handle and is awkward when it appears in running text.

TABLE 1.8-1   Morse Code

A	.—
B	—...
C	—.—.
D	—..
E	.
F	..—.
G	——.
H	....
I	..
J	.———
K	—.—
L	.—..
M	——
N	—.
O	———
P	.——.
Q	——.—
R	.—.
S	...
T	—
U	..—
V	...—
W	.——
X	—..—
Y	—.——
Z	——..

The Morse code is clearly a *variable-length code* which takes advantage of the high frequency of occurrence of some letters, such as "E," by making them short and the very infrequent letters, such as "J," relatively longer. However, the problems that arise when trying to recognize the words of a variable-length code are great enough in this case to cause the almost complete replacement of the Morse code by the van Duuren code, which uses three out of seven positions filled with 1's and the other four with 0's. There are $C(7, 3) = 35$ possible words in this code, and as with the 8-bit ASCII code, the van Duuren code enables the receiver to detect many types of errors since he knows exactly the number of 1's that should be in the received message unit of seven time slots.

Another widely used simple code is the *2-out-of-5 code*. As the name implies two of five positions are filled with 1's. In this code there are, very conveniently, $C(5, 2) = 10$ possible symbols. One of the many ways of associating the code symbols with the numerical values of the decimal digits is the *01247 code*, which merely means that we attach weights 0, 1, 2, 4, and 7 to the successive columns of the code and the corresponding decimal digit is the sum of the weights where the 1's occur, with the sole exception that the combination 4, 7 is taken as 0. The code is given in Table 1.8-2.

TABLE 1.8-2   The 2-out-of-5 Code

0 1 2 4 7	Decimal	Corresponds to
1 1 0 0 0	1	$0 + 1$
1 0 1 0 0	2	$0 + 2$
0 1 1 0 0	3	$1 + 2$
1 0 0 1 0	4	$0 + 4$
0 1 0 1 0	5	$1 + 4$
0 0 1 1 0	6	$2 + 4$
1 0 0 0 1	7	$0 + 7$
0 1 0 0 1	8	$1 + 7$
0 0 1 0 1	9	$2 + 7$
0 0 0 1 1	0	$4 + 7$

Again, any single error in a message can be recognized because it will have an odd number of 1's in it.

Exercises

1.8-1   Table 1-8.2 is one assignment of number values to the 10 possible symbols of the 2-out-of-5 code; how many possible 2-out-of-5 codes can there be?

1.8-2   Write 125 in the 2-out-of-5 code.

1.8-3   How many odd-parity symbols are not used in the van Duuren code?
Answer. 29

1.9   RADIX *r* CODES

As noted earlier, most systems of representing information in computers (and other machines) use two states, although the Morse code is an example of a signaling system with three symbols in the underlying alphabet. The reason for the dominance of two-symbol signaling systems is that two-state devices tend to be more reliable than are multistate devices. On the other hand, people clearly work better with multistate systems—witness the letters of the alphabet, along with the various punctuation symbols and the decimal digits. Thus it is necessary at times to consider codes with r symbols in their alphabets. For the Morse code, $r = 3$.

The English language alphabet uses 26 letters, both upper- and lowercase, plus miscellaneous punctuation marks. Occasionally, one sees a system in which there are exactly the 26 letters, the 10 decimal digits, and a space, a total of 37 symbols. We will examine this important code in Section 2.7.

In more abstract notation we assume a source alphabet S, consisting of q symbols $s_1, s_2, \ldots, s_q$. These are, in turn, represented in some other symbols, say the binary code. We may, therefore, either think of the ASCII code as having $r = q = 2^7 = 128$ symbols $s_1, s_2, \ldots, s_{128}$, or we may think of each symbol as being a block of eight binary digits with 1 extra bit appended to the 7 necessary bits.

1.10   ESCAPE CHARACTERS

When sending information it is usually necessary to control from the source end the remote equipment that is being used. For example, we have to tell the equipment what to do with the information that is being sent. Therefore, it is necessary to have a number of *reserved symbols* to which the remote equipment responds. "End Of Transmission" is such a symbol; another might be "Carriage Return"; another a "Shift Type Font" from lower- to uppercase or back again, and still another might be "Repeat Last Message." In the ASCII code the whole first column of the table is devoted to special characters.

How can this control be done if we do not wish to restrict the information that can be sent through the system? If, for example, we were using binary digits as numbers in our message, how do we avoid those combinations of bits that are control symbols for the remote equipment? If by chance our stream of binary numbers happened to contain such a reserved symbol, the equipment would respond to the reserved symbol when we did not want it to do so. Evidently, some kind of restriction on what can be sent is necessary, but the question is: "How can this be done with the least pain to the user of the system?"

One way this could be done is to add an extra binary digit to each block of digits, using, say, a 0 if it is message and a 1 if it is a control instruction. As can be seen, this will waste a good deal of channel capacity *if* the control words are rarely used. It does *not* solve the problem of relaying control words through one piece of equipment to another piece of equipment.

There are other ways to accomplish this goal of getting any message we want through the terminal equipment without the terminal responding to it. One popular way is to put any reserved symbols in quotes (") and arrange that the terminal equipment does not respond to what is in quotes but merely strips off the quote marks. In order to get quote marks themselves through the system they must in their turn be put in quotes. This approach is often used in computers, but can get a bit confusing at times. FORTRAN, for example, uses this method of quotes.

In FORTRAN the appearance of a quote symbol removes the quote from the stream of symbols and copies the next symbol, regardless of whether or not it is a quote. If this next symbol is not a quote, the text is copied until another quote occurs which is then deleted and takes the system out of the state of "copy next symbol." If this next symbol is a quote, the machine, (program), having already copied the quote, returns to its normal state. Thus a single quote mark can be gotten through by writing it twice. To get a message like

"Message"

through the system we write

""""""Message""""""

"Message" can contain any reserved symbols other than " (see Figure 1.10-1).

Another somewhat equivalent method of getting the reserved symbols through the system is to design the remote equipment to go to the proper state of obeying every special symbol every time it sees one, but before executing the action look to see if the next symbol is the same as the current

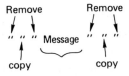

output is therefore

"Message"

FIGURE 1.10-1   DELETING QUOTE MARKS

special symbol. If it is, then the equipment merely transmits that symbol and goes back to the normal state. If it is not the same symbol, then the equipment executes the special instruction. Thus this process strips off one copy of each reserved symbol and lets the second one through. If the original message contains the same reserved symbol twice in a row, then two more such symbols must be inserted into the sent message, and the terminal equipment strips off the first and third.

This sounds like a complex program to execute in the computer software, but the finite-state automata theory points the way to a fast solution (see Figure 1.10-2). The initial state reads the next symbol and if it is a special symbol, the program stores it in a register and transfers to the special state program. The special state program reads the next symbol and compares it with the stored symbol. If the two symbols are the same, then the special symbol is copied and deleted from the input stream; otherwise, the program executes the special state instruction. Finally, control is returned to the initial state.

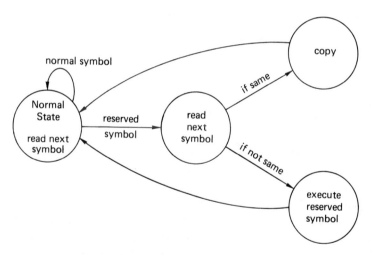

FIGURE 1.10-2   RESERVED SYMBOL AUTOMATA

In the field of logic this problem is known as the *metalanguage problem*— how does one talk about the language itself, especially when one has to use essentially the same language to do the talking? In practice we use voice accents (quote marks) to indicate that we are talking about the language itself and leave them out when we are merely talking. There are other formal devices for solving this common problem that arises in computer science and in other fields of information handling and processing, and these may also be adapted to this common, vexatious problem.

In controlling a digital computer the failure to distinguish between the various levels of metalanguages is a source of constant confusion. A FORTRAN program and the instruction to COMPILE it are in different languages. The end of the program requires two end marks, one for the metalanguage level of COMPILE to indicate the end of the source program, and one for the actual FORTRAN program to be used at RUN TIME.

Exercises

1.10-1   Describe in detail, using a state diagram, how

'''''Message'''''

would get through the FORTRAN-type system described in the text.

1.10-2   How would you send

DLE   (delete)

through the "duplicate special symbols" system? Put it in a stream and follow out the details.

1.11   OUTLINE OF THE COURSE

We have introduced the main topics as well as a number of codes with varying properties, and now have a basis for discussing the material the course is to cover.

Chapters 2, 3, and 11 will look at ways of encoding information (messages, sources of symbols) so that any errors, up to a given level, may be detected and/or corrected at the terminal end without recourse to the source. For a detected but uncorrectable error, we might call for a repeat of the message, hoping to get it correct the next time. In general, the error-detecting and -correcting capability will be accomplished by adding some digits to the message, thus making the message slightly longer. The main problem is to achieve the required protection against the inevitable errors (noise) without paying too high a price in adding extra digits. Typically, this is encoding for the channel.

The compression of messages is important for efficiency. In transmission through space the shorter message will use the signaling equipment for a shorter time; for storage problems less storage will be needed for the compressed code. This is source encoding. Chapters 4 and 5 will look at this side of the problem, and examine ways to reduce the amount of information being sent. We do this by examining the structure of the messages being sent. When there is a great deal of structure in the information being sent, then a good deal of message compression can be achieved and hence greater efficiency results. Since there are so many properties that messages can have which allow message compression, we can look only at a few of the most common ones. We restrict our attention to general methods and neglect the many special, trick methods which are often fairly easy to invent.

Chapter 6 introduces the central concept of the *entropy* of a source of information and shows how it is connected with the concept of the maximum amount of information that can be sent through a given channel. Thus we get a bit closer to the concept of exactly what information is. The first of Shannon's encoding theorems is for a noiseless channel, and is fairly easy to prove. The second theorem, presented in Chapter 10, discusses sending information through a noisy channel and is much more difficult to prove. Fortunately, the simple *binary symmetric channel* is the realistic case, and for this case the proof is easy to understand. The proof in the more general case is harder, and is only sketched.

Shannon's two theorems set bounds on what encoding can accomplish. Unfortunately, the second of his theorems is somewhat nonconstructive and does not tell us how in practice to achieve the bounds indicated. The result is not useless since it indicates where we can expect to achieve large improvements in a signaling system and where we can expect at best only small improvements.

The definition of a channel in information theory is often not a practical one and we need other ways of assessing this central concept of channel capacity. Therefore, Appendix A looks briefly at how, in practice, we measure the channel capacity of a signaling system.

We remind the reader that while we often use the language of "signaling from here to there," all of it is applicable to "signaling from now to then" through some storage medium. In this case it is often the first of Shannon's theorems (the noise-free one) that is important.

Traditionally, the development of both coding and information theory is done in as elegant and general a way as possible—usually highly abstract, with many fancy mathematical symbols, and devoid of practical aspects. This approach is not necessary, and we shall regularly pause to show how what we are talking about is reflected in common sense and in actual practice, and how it suggests going about the design of future systems. We shall also try to make the proofs of the results as intuitively obvious as possible rather than merely mathematically elegant. Along the way we shall introduce many small, practical details that are important when designing a whole system.

But let us be clear about the approach we are adopting. When there are so many different signaling systems now in use, and so many new ones over the immediate horizon, it is impractical to take them up one at a time. It is necessary to take an overview approach and concentrate on the fundamentals that seem most likely to be relevant for understanding both the past and the future signaling systems. Indeed, this is the only reasonable approach to any rapidly changing field of knowledge. The approach through special cases simply leaves the student surprised by tomorrow's system. Thus, of necessity, the treatment is often abstract and avoids many of the messy details of current systems.

2

Error-Detecting Codes

2.1 WHY ERROR-DETECTING CODES?

Experience shows that it is not easy to build equipment that is highly reliable. By "highly reliable," consider how much computing a modern computer does in 1 hour. At one operation per microsecond it does 3.6 billion (10^9) operations in 1 hour (and each operation involves many individual components). By comparison there are less than 3.16 billion seconds in 100 years (more than your probable lifetime). Similarly, reliable transmission systems require very high reliability of their individual components. Reliability in the transmission of words of human languages is one thing; for transmission of computer programs it is something else! Hence the importance of detecting errors. Furthermore, as already noted, error detection is a great aid in high-quality maintenance.

Whenever repetition is possible, very frequently it is sufficient merely to detect the presence of an error. When an error is detected we simply repeat the message, the operation, or whatever was being done, and with reasonable luck it will be right the second (or even possibly the third) time (see Section 2.5).

It is not possible to detect an error if every possible symbol, or set of symbols, that can be received is a legitimate message. *It is only possible to catch errors if there are some restrictions on what is a proper message.* The problem is to keep these restrictions on the possible messages down to ones that are simple. In practice, "simple" has tended to mean "easily computable." In this chapter we will investigate the problem of designing codes such that *at the receiving end* any single, isolated error can be detected. In Chapter 3 we will consider correcting at the receiving end the errors that occur in the message.

2.2   SIMPLE PARITY CHECKS

The simplest way of encoding a binary message to make it error detecting is to count the number of 1's in the message, and then append a final binary digit chosen so that the entire message has an even number of 1's in it. The entire message is therefore of even parity. Thus to $(n - 1)$ message positions we append an nth parity-check position. At the receiving end the count of the number of 1's is made, and an odd number of 1's in the entire n positions indicates that at least one error has occurred.

Evidently in this code a double error cannot be detected. Nor can any even number of errors be detected. But any odd number of errors can be detected. If (1) the probability of an error in any one binary position is assumed to be a definite number p, and (2) errors in different positions are assumed to be independent, then for n much less than $1/p$, the probable number of single errors is approximately np. The probability of a double error is approximately $n(n - 1)p^2/2$, which is approximately one-half the square of single error. From this it follows that the optimal length of message to be checked depends on both the reliability desired (the chance of a double error going undetected) and the probability of a single error in any one position, p. For more details, see Section 2.4.

Counting the number of 1's and selecting an even number is equivalent to working in a *modulo 2 arithmetic*. "Modulo 2" means that every number is divided by 2 (the modulus) and only the remainder is kept. In this arithmetic (which counts 0, 1, 0, 1, ...) we count modulo 2 the number of 1's in the $(n - 1)$ message positions and then put this sum into the nth position. Thus there are an even number of 1's in the n positions sent. This *even-parity check* is generally used in the theory. In practice it is occasionally convenient to adopt an *odd-parity check* so that the message of all 0's is not a legitimate message. The changes necessary in the theory are sufficiently easy to make that we will continue to use even-parity checks throughout the theory.

To actually find the parity of a string of 0's and 1's we can use a two-state finite automaton (Figure 2.2-1). We start in the state 0, and each 1 in the message causes a change in the state. The final state at the end of the message gives the parity count.

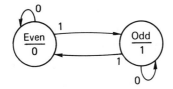

FIGURE 2.2-1   PARITY COUNT CIRCUIT

Many computers have an instruction that directly counts the number of 1's in the accumulator register. The right-hand digit of this sum is the required count modulo 2. If this, or some equivalent instruction, is not available, then *logically adding* (exclusive OR, XOR, see Section 2.8) one-half of the message to the other half preserves the parity count in the sum. Repeated use of this observation halves at each step the length of the message and will produce the required sum modulo 2 of all the 1's in the accumulator. Thus about "the first integer greater than or equal to $\log_2 n$" logical additions will be needed.

2.3   ERROR-DETECTING CODES

It is common practice to break up a long message in the binary alphabet into runs (blocks) of $(n - 1)$ digits each, and to append one binary digit to the run, making the block that is sent n digits long. The final block may need to be padded out with 0's. This produces *the redundancy* of

$$\frac{n}{n-1} = 1 + \frac{1}{n-1}$$

where the redundancy is defined as the number of binary digits used divided by the minimum necessary. The *excess redundancy* is $1/(n-1)$.

Clearly, for low redundancy we want to use long messages. But for high reliability short messages are better. Thus the choice of the length n for the blocks of message to send is a compromise between two opposing forces.

The 2-out-of-5 code mentioned in Section 1.8 is an example of an error-detecting code with $n = 5$ and using an even-parity check. The van Duuren 3-out-of-7 code is another such code but uses odd parity. Neither uses all the symbols it could. A variant is the word count occasionally used in sending telegrams.

Many other examples of this simple kind of encoding for error detection occur in practice. For example, when making a memory transfer to tape, drum, or disc, the *logical sum* of all the words being transferred is often appended as a check word. See Ref. [W] for hardware realizations.

2.4   INDEPENDENT ERRORS—WHITE NOISE

We have already mentioned the model usually assumed for errors in a message, namely (1) an equal probability p of an error in each position, and (2) an independence of errors in different positions. This is called "white noise," in (a poor) analogy with white light, which is supposed to contain uniformly all the frequencies detected by the human eye. The theory for this case is very easy to understand. But in practice there are often reasons for errors to be more common in some positions in the message than in others, and it is often true that errors tend to occur in bursts and not be independent (a common power supply, for example, tends to produce a correlation among errors; so does a nearby lightning strike), (see Section 2.6).

It is only fair to note that due to the rapid pace of technological change it is not possible at the design stage to have much idea about the noise patterns of errors that will actually occur, so that white noise is often a reasonable assumption.

For white noise the probability of no error in the n positions is

$$(1 - p)^n$$

The probability of a single error in the n positions is

$$np(1 - p)^{n-1}$$

The probability of k errors is given by the kth term in the binomial expansion:

$$1 = [(1 - p) + p]^n = (1 - p)^n + np(1 - p)^{n-1}$$
$$+ \frac{n(n - 1)p^2}{2}(1 - p)^{n-2} + \ldots + p^n$$

For example, the probability of exactly two errors is

$$\frac{n(n - 1)}{2}p^2(1 - p)^{n-2}$$

We can get the probability of an even number of errors (0, 2, 4, . . .) by adding the following two binomial expansions and dividing by 2:

$$1 = [(1 - p) + p]^n = \sum_{k=0}^{n} C(n, k)p^k(1 - p)^{n-k}$$

$$[(1 - p) - p]^n = \sum_{k=0}^{n} (-1)^k C(n, k)p^k(1 - p)^{n-k}$$

(The [ ] in the next equation means "greatest integer in.")

$$\frac{1 + (1 - 2p)^n}{2} = \sum_{m=0}^{[n/2]} C(n, 2m)p^{2m}(1 - p)^{n-2m} \qquad (2.4\text{-}1)$$

The probability of an odd number of errors (which will always be detected) is 1 minus this number.

The probability of no errors is the first term of the series (2.4-1). Therefore, to get the probability of an undetected error, we drop the first term of (2.4-1), to get

$$\sum_{m=1}^{[n/2]} C(n, 2m)p^{2m}(1 - p)^{n-2m} \qquad (2.4\text{-}2)$$

Usually, only the first few terms are of any importance in evaluating this formula.

Exercises

2.4-1 If $p = 0.001$ and $n = 100$, what is the probability of no error?

Answer. $\exp\left(-\frac{1}{10}\right)$

2.4-2 If $p = 0.001$ and $n = 100$, what is the probability of an undetected error?

2.4-3 If $p = 0.01$ and you want the probability of an undetected error to be 0.005, what is the maximum length n you can use?

Answer. $n = 10$ but almost $n = 11$

2.4-4 For small p and arbitrary n, do Exercise 2.4-1. *Answer.* $\exp(-np)$

2.5 RETRANSMISSION OF MESSAGE

When an error is detected, it is often possible to ask for a retransmission, a recomputation, or repeat of the process being done. For example, in the Bell Relay Computers the code used for representing the decimal digits was a 2-out-of-5 code, and whenever an error was detected, then a second, and even a third trial was requested. On the Model 6 Relay Computer, if after the third trial the message was still not acceptable, then the whole problem was dropped and the next one taken up, in the hope that the defective part would not be used in the new problem.

When reading magnetic tapes it is the custom to use at least an error-detecting code and to call for repeated readings of the tape if the parity checks are violated. How many repetitions to use depends on your model for the error. If you think that it is a slight loss of magnetization, then with luck a subsequent trial will read the tape correctly; but if you think it is due to a more permanent failure, then repetitions will likely occur until another, independent error occurs so that the parity check is met. You will therefore get a message with two errors in it rather than the right message! Thus the strategy of "detect an error and if one is found, call for one or more repetitions" is sound *only if* the type of error you expect is transient.

Parity checks have long been used in computers both in hardware and software Ref. [W]. For example, in the early days of unreliable drum storage, every WRITE on the drum was followed by the logical sum of all the registers being stored on the drum. This sum was then stored in a final register of the block on the drum. The drum was next read back and checked to see if the message was written properly. Only then was the information being stored released from the machine's storage registers. When later the drum was read, the parity check (the logical sum of *all* the registers being stored) was again computed to see if the sum was identically zero. If not, retrials were made to read it again. This method depends on the fact that $x + x = 0$ for logical addition.

2.6   SIMPLE BURST ERROR-DETECTING CODES

Noise (errors) often occur in bursts rather than in isolated positions in the received message. Lightning strikes, power-supply fluctuations, loose flakes on a magnetic surface are all typical causes of a burst of noise.

Suppose from measurements in the field that we agree on the maximum length L of any burst we are to detect. Suppose for ease in discussion (since the changes necessary to handle other cases are easy to invent) that the burst length L is the accumulator word length of the computer. We have only to select the appropriate error-detecting code (or error-correcting code of

Chapter 3), and instead of computing parity checks over the bit positions we compute parity word checks over the corresponding word positions. In effect, we work in words, not bits, and have L independent (interleaved) codes, one over each bit position in the word.

If a burst covers the end of one word and the beginning of another, still no two errors will be in the same code, since we *assumed* that any burst length k satisfied $(0 \leq k \leq L)$.

Thus we can send messages through noise that is "bursty" provided that we recognize the noise pattern and design for it. For reliable hardware, see Ref. [W].

Example. If the message is

Fall 1980

this can be encoded in ASCII in a burst code as follows (no parity check used here):

$$F = 106 = 01 \quad 000 \quad 110$$

$$a = 141 = 01 \quad 100 \quad 001$$

$$1 = 154 = 01 \quad 101 \quad 100$$

$$1 = 154 = 01 \quad 101 \quad 100$$

$$sp = 040 = 00 \quad 100 \quad 000$$

$$1 = 061 = 00 \quad 110 \quad 001$$

$$9 = 071 = 00 \quad 111 \quad 001$$

$$8 = 070 = 00 \quad 111 \quad 000$$

$$0 = 060 = 00 \quad 110 \quad 000$$

$$\overline{\text{check sum} = 00 \quad 000 \quad 111} = \text{BEL}$$

The encoded message is therefore

Fall 1980BEL

where BEL is the single ASCII symbol 00   000   111.

Exercise

2.6-1   Given the message

$$
\begin{array}{ll}
101 & 01010 \\
011 & 00110 \\
000 & 11110 \\
110 & 00110 \\
111 & 10101 \\
\end{array}
$$

add the appropriate check to form a burst error-detecting code of word length 1 byte.

2.7   ALPHABET PLUS NUMBER CODES—WEIGHTED CODES

The codes we have discussed so far have generally assumed a simple form of "white noise." This is very suitable for many types of machines, although in serial transmission the loss of a symbol (or the insertion of an extra one) is a common error in some systems, and is not caught by such codes, hence causes a loss of synchronization.

When dealing with people, another type of noise is more appropriate. Human beings have a tendency to interchange adjacent digits of numbers: for example, 67 becomes 76. A second common error is to double the wrong one of a triple of digits, two adjacent ones which are the same: for example, 667 becomes 677. It is merely a change of one digit. These are the two most common human errors in arithmetic. In a combined alphabet/number system, the confusion of "oh" and "zero" is very common.

A rather frequent situation is to have an alphabet, plus space, plus the 10 decimal digits as the complete set of symbols to be used. This amounts to $26 + 1 + 10 = 37$ symbols in the source alphabet. Fortunately, 37 is a prime number and we can use the following method for error checking. We *weight* the symbols with weights 1, 2, 3, . . . , beginning with the check digit of the message. We reduce the sum modulo 37 (divide by 37 and take the remainder) so that a check symbol can be selected that will make the sum 0 modulo 37. Note that "blank" at the end as a check symbol is *not* the same as nothing.

It is easy to compute that the interchange of adjacent digits will be detected, and that the doubling of the wrong digit (which is the changing of a single symbol) will also be detected. Many other interchanges can also be caught. The interchange of "oh" and "zero" is the changing of a single symbol. Such a code is very useful when people are involved in the process. Notice that the length of the message being encoded is not fixed, and can exceed 37 symbols if necessary (although special precautions are then required). This kind of encoding can be used on credit cards, the names of some kinds of items in inventory, and so on. The probability that a random encoding will get through the input check is $\frac{1}{37}$. Thus by using this simple parity check, attempts at forgery will be caught about 97 % of the time.

To find the weighted check sum in an easy fashion, notice that if you compute the running sum of a set of n numbers, and then sum these again, you will have the first number entered into the final sum n times, the next number $n - 1$ times, the next $n - 2$ times, and so on, down to the last number, which will get into the final total only once. Thus you have the required weighted sum of the numbers which correspond to the symbols of the alphabet being used.

If this "summing the sum" seems mysterious consider the message *wxyz*.

Message	Sum	Sum of Sum
w	w	w
x	$w + x$	$2w + x$
y	$w + x + y$	$3w + 2x + y$
z	$w + x + y + z$	$4w + 3x + 2y + z$

and we see the weighted sum emerging. This is sometimes known as "progressive digiting."

Example. If $0 = 0, 1 = 1, 2 = 2, \ldots, 9 = 9, A = 10, B = 11, \ldots,$ $Z = 35, b1 = 36$, then encode

A6   7

We proceed as follows:

	Sum	Sum of Sum
A = 10	10	10
6 = 6	16	26
bl = 36	52	78
7 = 7	59	137
x = x	59 + x	196 + x

$$\begin{array}{r} 5 \\ 37\overline{)196 + x} \\ 185 \\ \hline 11 + x \end{array}$$

Since $11 + x$ must be divisible by 37, it follows that

$$x = 26 = Q$$

The encoded message is therefore

$$A6 \quad 7Q$$

To check at the receiver that this is a legitimate encoded message, we proceed as follows:

A	$10 \times 5 = 50$
6	$6 \times 4 = 24$
bl	$36 \times 3 = 108$
7	$7 \times 2 = 14$
Q	$26 \times 1 = 26$

$$\text{Sum} = 222 = 37 \times 6 \equiv 0 \quad \text{modulo } 37$$

Exercises

2.7-1   If $0 = 0, 1 = 1, \ldots, 9 = 9, A = 10, B = 11, \ldots, Z = 35, b1 = 36$, then encode

$$B23F \quad mod \quad 37$$

Answer. B23F9

2.7-2   In the same code as Example 2.7-1 is

$$K9K9$$

a correct message?

2.8   REVIEW OF MODULAR ARITHMETIC

Because we are going to use parity checks many times, we need to get a firm grasp on the arithmetic of the corresponding manipulations. We have seen that mod 2 addition ("mod" is an abbreviation for "modulo") is the arithmetic that the simple binary parity checks use and is the same as logical addition (exclusive OR, XOR). The rules for addition are

$$0 + 0 = 0$$
$$0 + 1 = 1$$
$$1 + 0 = 1$$
$$1 + 1 = 0$$

There are no other numbers than 0 and 1 in the system. If we choose to work in normal arithmetic, then we merely divide the result by 2 and take the remainder. When we later come to the algebra of linear equations and polynomials where the coefficients are from the mod 2 number system, we will have the same table for addition. For multiplication we have the rules

$$0 \times 0 = 0$$
$$0 \times 1 = 0$$
$$1 \times 0 = 0$$
$$1 \times 1 = 1$$

Thus, multiplication is the logical AND of computing.

Occasionally, we will work modulo some number other than 2. For example, in the previous section we used numbers modulo 37. Generally, the theory in any prime base p (such as 37) is very much like that of base 2, and we need not go into the details here. One has only to read the previous paragraph and make simple changes to understand the corresponding arithmetic and algebra. For addition and subtraction mod p, we divide every number by p and take the positive remainder.

For multiplication mod m (not a prime) we have to be more careful. Suppose that we have the numbers a and b congruent to a' and b' modulo the modulus m. This means that

$$a \equiv a' \quad \text{mod } m$$
$$b \equiv b' \quad \text{mod } m$$

or

$$a = a' + k_1 m$$
$$b = b' + k_2 m$$

for some integers k_1 and k_2. For the product ab we have

$$ab = a'b' + a'k_1 m + b'k_2 m + k_1 k_2 m^2$$
$$ab \equiv a'b' \quad \text{mod } m$$

Now consider the particular case

$$a = 15 \qquad b = 12 \qquad m = 10$$

We have

$$a' = 5 \qquad b' = 2$$

and

$$ab \equiv a'b' \equiv 0 \quad \text{mod } 10$$

But neither a nor b is zero! Only for a prime modulus do we have the important property that if a product is zero, then at least one factor is zero. Hence the importance of a prime modulus. Now we see why 37 was so convenient a number in Section 2.7.

Modular arithmetic should be clearly understood, especially the need for a prime modulus, because in Chapter 11 we will face the problem of constructing a corresponding modular algebra. We will therefore give yet another example of this type of encoding in the next section.

2.9 ISBN BOOK NUMBERS

The International Standard Book Number (ISBN) now appears on most textbooks. It is (usually) a 10-digit code that publishers assign to their books. A typical book will have

$$0\text{-}1321\text{-}2571\text{-}4$$

although the hyphens may appear in different positions. (The hyphens are of no importance.) The 0 is for United States and some other English-speaking countries. The 13 is Prentice-Hall, the publishers. The next six digits, 21-2571, are the book number assigned by the publisher, and the final digit is the weighted check sum as in Section 2.6. Modulo 10 will not work, since 10 is a composite number. Thus they use the check sum modulo 11 and are forced to allow an X if the required check digit is 10.

Searching around, I found the ISBN number

$$0\text{--}1315\text{--}2447\text{--}\mathbf{X}$$

To check that this number is a proper ISBN number we proceed as follows:

Code		
0		
1	1	1
3	4	5
1	5	10
5	10	20
2	12	32
4	16	48
4	20	68
7	27	95

$$X = 10 \quad 37 \quad 132 = (11) \times (12) \equiv 0 \quad \text{modulo 11}$$

It checks!

Here again we see a simple error-detecting code designed for human use rather than for computer use. Evidently, such codes have wide applicability.

Exercises

2.9-1   Check the ISBN 0–13165332–6.

2.9-2   Check the ISBN 0–1391–4101–4.

2.9-3   Consider the ISBN 07–028761–4. Does it make sense?

2.9-4   Check your current textbooks.

3

Error-Correcting Codes

3.1 NEED FOR ERROR CORRECTION

Frequently simple error detection with repetition is not enough. The immediate question is, "If a computer can find out that there is an error, why can it not find out where it is?" The answer is that indeed by proper encoding this can be done. For example, we can write out or do each thing three times, and then take a vote. But, as we shall see, much better methods are available. As an example of the use of an error-correcting code, when information is sent from Mars to Earth the signaling time is so long that by the time an error can be discovered, the source may have long since been erased. At present (1979) a code is used that will correct up to eight errors in one block of digits in this particular signaling system.

Error correction is also very useful in the typical storage (memory) system. The U.S. Census Bureau, for example, stores much of its information on magnetic tapes. Over the years the quality of the recording gradually deteriorates, and the time comes when some of it cannot be read reliably. When this happens, often the original source of the information is no longer available and the information stored on the tape is lost forever. If some error-correction ability is incorporated into the encoding of information, then the corresponding types of errors can be corrected.

The error correction can be incorporated into the hardware. For example, the NORC computer had a simple type of error correction for isolated errors that occurred on its cathode-ray-tube storage device. Often it is only the storage device that uses the error correction. The STRETCH computer that IBM built "to *stretch* the state of the art" had single error correction and double error detection (Section 3.7) throughout much of the computer. On the STRETCH acceptance test it has been claimed that an error in a circuit developed in the first few minutes and the error-correcting circuits fixed up the errors for the rest of the hour. Among current (1979) computers the Eclipse computers have some error correction in the hardware. The CRAY 1 computers have error correction as an optional feature of memory. See Ref. [W] for hardware checking.

The error correction can be in the software, as the Census Bureau is now doing when they record information on tapes. We have earlier mentioned the error-detection programs for drum storage as being in the software. Error correction could also be used there. In many other places, correcting codes are built into the software. The software approach has the advantage that the error correction can more easily be put on the important parts of the information and omitted from the less important parts. Furthermore, only as experience reveals the weaknesses of the computer system is it known where error protection is most needed as well as how much is needed. Only after simulation of error protection in software has proved that it handles the problem should it be added to the system in the form of hardware.

3.2   RECTANGULAR CODES

The first, and simplest, error-correcting codes are the *triplication codes*, where every message is repeated three times and at the receiving end a majority vote is taken. It is obvious that this system will correct isolated single errors. However, it is also obvious that this encoding system is very inefficient. Three computers in parallel with the associated "compare and interrupt if necessary circuits" is expensive. Therefore, we look for better methods of encoding information so that a single error can be corrected.

The next simplest error-correcting codes are the *rectangular codes*, where the information is arranged, in principle, although not necessarily in fact, in the form of an $m - 1$ by $n - 1$ rectangle (Figure 3.2-1). A parity-check bit is then added to each row of $m - 1$ bits to make a total of m bits. Similarly, for each of the columns a check bit is added. Whether or not the final corner bit is used has little importance; for even parity checking, the parity sum of its row and its column are both the same. Thus the original code of $(m - 1)(n - 1)$ bits of the rectangle becomes an array of mn bits. The redundancy is therefore $1 + 1/(m - 1) + 1/(n - 1) + 1/(m - 1)(n - 1)$. For a given size mn, the redundancy will be smaller the more the rectangle

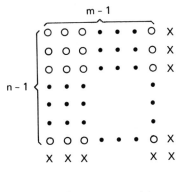

O = message position
X = check position

FIGURE 3.2-1   RECTANGULAR CODES

approaches a square. For square codes of side n, we have $(n - 1)^2$ bits of in formation and $2n - 1$ bits of checking along the sides.

A rectangular code, for example, was the code that the NORC computer used for its cathode-ray storage tubes. Rectangular codes often are used on tapes (Refs. [B2] and [W]). The longitudinal parity checks are on the individual lines, and an extra line is put at the end of the block to form the vertical parity check. Unfortunately, the machine designer rarely lets the user get at the parity-check information so that by using suitable software programs the isolated error could be corrected.

Exercises

3.2-1   Discuss various possible rectangular codes for 24 message bits.

3.2-2   Discuss the use of the corner check bit. Prove that for even-parity checks, it checks *both* row and column. Discuss the use of odd-parity checks in this case.

3.3   TRIANGULAR, CUBIC, AND
n-DIMENSIONAL CODES

Thinking about the rectangular codes soon suggests a *triangular code* where each element on the diagonal (and there are only n of them if the entire triangle has n bits on a side) is set by a parity check covering *both* its own row and column (Figure 3.3-1). Thus for a given size we lower the redundancy we use. The triangular array of bits of information has $n(n - 1)/2$ bits with n bits added for the checks. Thus the redundancy is $1 + 2/(n - 1)$.

FIGURE 3.3-1   TRIANGULAR CODES

But remember that the triangle has a more favorable size n than the corresponding rectangular for a given amount of message.

Once we have found a better code than the simple rectangular ones, we are led to ask the question: "What is the best that we can do with respect to keeping the redundancy down?" For a cube we can check each plane in the three dimensions (Figure 3.3-2). The three intersecting edges of check bits use $3n - 2$ positions out of the n^3 total positions sent. The excess redundancy is roughly $3/n^2$ extra bits.

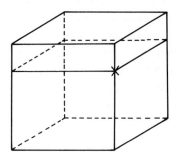

FIGURE 3.3-2   CUBIC CODE, SHOWING ONLY ONE PLANE AND ITS CHECK
POSITION

If the use of three dimensions is better than two dimensions, then would not going to still higher dimensions be better? Of course, we do not mean to arrange the bits in the three-dimensional or higher space, it is only that we will imagine them so arranged to calculate the proper parity checks. A little thought about checking over the three-dimensional planes in the four-dimensional space will lead to (approximately) an excess redundancy of $4/n^3$. We soon come to the conclusion that the highest possible dimensional space might be the best, and we want a total of 2^n bits of which $(n + 1)$ are checks. There would be, therefore, $(n + 1)$ parity checks. If they were suitably arranged, then they would give a number called the *syndrome*, which we would get by writing a 1 for each failure of a parity check, and a 0 when it is satisfied.

These $(n + 1)$ bits form an $(n + 1)$ bit number, and this number (the syndrome) can specify any of 2^{n+1} things—more than the n locations of the corresponding single error plus the fact that no error occurred. Notice that the check bits, as in the simple error-detecting codes, are *equally protected* with the message bits. All the bits sent enter equally—none is treated specially.

However, we see that there are more than enough states in the syndrome to indicate when the entire message is correct plus the position of the error if one occurs. Thus there is a loss of efficiency. Nevertheless, this suggests a new approach to the problem of designing an error-correcting code, which we take up in the next section.

Exercises

3.3-1   Make a triangular code of 10 message positions.

3.3-2   Discuss in detail the four-dimensional $2 \times 2 \times 2 \times 2$ code.

3.4 HAMMING ERROR-CORRECTING CODES

In this section we adopt an algebraic approach to the problem that was started in the previous section—finding the *best* encoding scheme for single error correction *for white noise.* Suppose that we have m independent parity checks. By "independent" we mean, of course, that no sum of any of the checks is any other check—remember that they are to be added in our modulo 2 number system! Thus the three parity checks over positions

$$1: \quad 1, 2, 5, 7$$
$$2: \qquad\;\; 5, 7, 8, 9$$
$$3: \quad 1, 2, \qquad 8, 9$$

are dependent checks since the sum of any two rows is the third. The third parity check provides no new information over that from the first two, and is simply wasted effort.

The *syndrome* that results from writing a 0 for each of the m parity checks which is correct and a 1 for each failure can be viewed as an m-bit number and can represent at most 2^m things. We need to represent the state of all the message positions being correct, plus the location of any single error in the n bits of the message. Thus we must have the inequality

$$2^m \geq n + 1 \qquad (3.4\text{-}1)$$

Can such a code be found? We will show how to build ones that exactly meet the equality condition. They represent a particular solution to the problem of designing a suitable code and are known as *Hamming codes*.

The simple, underlying idea of the Hamming code is that the syndrome shall give the actual position (location) of the error, with all 0's in the syndrome meaning no error. What should the parity checks be? Let us look at the binary representations of the position numbers (Table 3.4-1). Evidently, if the syndrome is to indicate the position of an error when it occurs, then every position that has a 1 in the last position of its binary representation must be in the first parity check (see the extreme right-hand column of the table). Think carefully why this must be true. Similarly, the second parity check must be tripped by those positions that have a 1 in the second lowest position in its binary representation; and so on.

TABLE 3.4-1   Check Positions

Position Number	Binary Representation
1	0001
2	0010
3	0011
4	0100
5	0101
6	0110
7	0111
8	1000
9	1001
10	1010
.	.
.	.
.	.

Thus we see that the first parity check covers positions 1, 3, 5, 7, 9, 11, 13, 15, ... The second covers 2, 3, 6, 7, 10, 11, 14, 15, ... The third parity check covers positions 4, 5, 6, 7, 12, 13, 14, 15, ... The next, positions 8, 9, 10, 11, 12, 13, 14, 15, 24, 25, . . . , and so on.

To illustrate what we have just said (see Table 3.4-2) let us design a simple error-correcting code for four binary digits. We must have $2^m \geq n + 1$ and we easily see that $2^3 \geq (4 + 3) + 1 = 8$. Therefore, we will need to have $m = 3$ parity checks and this gives $7 = n =$ total of message plus parity-check positions. The positions to use to set the parity checks will for convenience be picked as 1, 2, and 4. Thus the information message positions are 3, 5, 6, and 7. To encode the information message, we write it in these positions and compute the parity checks. Let this message be, say,

TABLE 3.4-2   Encoding a 4-Bit Message and Locating Error

Encode

1	2	3	4	5	6	7	Positions
–	–	1	–	0	1	1	Message
0	1	1	0	0	1	1	Encode
		×					Error
0	1	0	0	0	1	1	Receive

Locate error

Check 1:	1	3	5	7	
	0	0	0	1	fails ⟶ 1
Check 2:	2	3	6	7	
	1	0	1	1	fails ⟶ 1
Check 3:	4	5	6	7	
	0	0	1	1	correct ⟶ 0
syndrome =	0	1	1	=	3 ⟶ position of error

Correct

		1					Correct error
0	1	1	0	0	1	1	Corrected message

_ _1_011; the spaces are where the parity checks are to go. The first parity check which goes in position 1 is computed over positions 1, 3, 5, and 7, and looking at the message we see that position 1 gets a 0. We now have 0_1_011. The second parity check over positions 2, 3, 6, and 7 sets position 2 as a 1. We then have 011_011 as the partially encoded message. The third parity check is over positions 4, 5, 6, and 7, and looking at what we have we see that position 4 must get a 0. Thus the final encoded message is 0110011.

To see how the code corrects an isolated error, suppose that when the message 0110011 is sent, the channel adds a 1 in the third position from the left. The corrupted message is then 0100011. The receiving end applies the parity checks in order. The first, over positions 1, 3, 5, and 7, evidently fails, so the lowest-order digit of the syndrome is a 1. The second parity check over 2, 3, 6, 7 fails, so the second digit of the syndrome is 1. The third parity check over 4, 5, 6, and 7 succeeds, so the highest-order digit is a 0. Looking at the syndrome as a binary number we have the decimal number 3. Thus we change (logically add 1) the symbol in position 3 from the received 0 to a 1. The resulting sequence of 0's and 1's is now correct, and when we strip off the checking bits 1, 2, and 4 we have the original information message 1011 in positions 3, 5, 7, and 8.

Notice that the check positions are equally corrected with the message positions. The code is *uniform in its protection; once encoded there is no difference between the message and check digits.* The cute part of the Hamming code is the numerical ease of both the encoding and the code correction based on the syndrome at the received end. Also, notice that the syndrome indicates the position of the error *regardless* of the message being sent; logically adding a 1 to the bit in the position given by the syndrome corrects the received message, where, of course, the syndrome all 0's means the entire message has no errors.

The redundancy in the example of four message with 3 check bits seems high. But if we took 10 check bits, we have from equation (3.4-1) $2^{10} \geq 10 +$ message positions $+ 1$, or $1024 - 11 = 1013 \geq$ message positions. This shows that the excess redundancy rises like $\log_2$ of the number of message positions.

Exercises

3.4-1 Discuss the Hamming code using four checks.

3.4-2 Discuss the Hamming code for two checks.

Answer. Triplicate code

3.4-3 Show that 1111111 is a correct message.

3.4-4 Correct 1001111 and decode.

3.4-5 Locate the error in 011100010111110 where we have used four checks, as in Exercise 3.4-1. What is the correct message?

3.4-6 What is the probability that a random sequence of $2^m - 1$ 0's and 1's will be code word?

3.5 EQUIVALENT CODES

The example above is one way of encoding a message. There are many other equivalent codes. It should be obvious that any interchange of the positions of the code will leave us with a code that is only trivially different. Similarly, if we were to *complement* (change 0's to 1's and 1's to 0's) all the digits appearing in a certain position, then again we would have a trivially different code.

We can, if we wish, use this observation about the interchange of positions to move all the check bits to the end of the message. This makes the "masking" of the message to get the parity checks, and to make the correction, less simple in appearance, but it is exactly the same amount of work by the computer, since for each check bit we still mask the received message to get the check bit by the "parity sum." Where we place the check bit is also changed. Similarly, the meaning of the syndrome has its position changed, but the syndrome is still essentially the same and refers to a unique place. The position to logically add the correcting bit is therefore changed, but that can be found by either a formula or by a table lookup, which enters the table with the syndrome, and the entry in the table is the word with a 1 in the position to be corrected. Of course, for a long code a message might be two or more words long. The table size is proportional to n. The original Hamming code used computing power rather than table lookup, and in general for very long codes this is necessary.

Exercise

3.5-1 In the $n = 7$ code, discuss in detail the encoding and decoding if the three parity checks are moved to positions 5, 6, and 7.

3.6 GEOMETRIC APPROACH

We have just given an algebraic approach to error-correcting codes. A different, equivalent approach to the topic is from n-dimensional geometry. In this model we consider the string of n 0's and 1's as a point in n-dimensional space. Each digit gives the value of the corresponding coordinate in the n-dimensional space (where we are assuming that the encoded message is exactly n bits long). Thus we have a cube in n-dimensional space; each vertex is a string of n 0's and 1's. The space consists *only* of the 2^n vertices; there is nothing else in the space of all possible messages except the 2^n vertices. This is sometimes called a "vector space."

Each vertex is a possible received message, but only selected vertices are to be original messages. A *single* error in a message moves the message point along one edge of the imagined cube to an immediately adjacent point. If we require that every possible originating message be at least a *distance* of two sides away from any other message point, then it is clear that any single error will move a message only one side away and leave the received message as an illegitimate message. If the minimum distance between message points is three sides of the cube, then any single error will leave the received message *closer* to the original message than to any other message, and thus we can have single error correction.

Effectively, we have introduced a *distance function*, which is the minimum number of sides of the cube we have to traverse to get from one point to another. This is the same as the number of bits in the representations of the two points which differ. Thus the distance can be looked on as being the *logical* difference, or sum, of the two points. It is a legitimate distance function since it satisfies the three conditions:

1. The distance from a point to itself is 0.

2. The distance from point x to point y is the same as the distance from y to x and is a positive number.

3. The triangle inequality holds—the sum of two sides (distance from a to c plus the distance from c to b) is at least as great as the length of the third side (the distance from a to b).

This distance function is usually called the *Hamming distance*. It is the distance function for binary white noise.

Using this distance function we can define various things in the space. In particular, the *surface of a sphere* about a point is the set of points a given distance away. The surface of sphere of radius 1 about the point $(0, 0, 0, \ldots, 0)$ is the set of all vertices in the space which are one unit away, that is, all vertices which have only one 1 in their coordinate representation (see Figure 3.6-1). There are $C(n, 1)$ such points.

We can express the minimum distance between vertices of a set of message points in terms of the error correctability possible. The minimum distance must be at least 1 for uniqueness of the code (Table 3.6-1). A minimum distance of two gives single error detectability. A minimum distance of three gives single error correctability; any single error leaves the point closer to where it was than to any other possible message. Of course, this minimum-distance code could be used instead for double error detection. A minimum

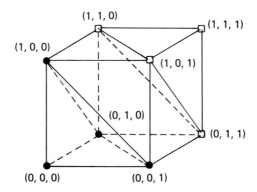

FIGURE 3.6-1   THREE-DIMENSIONAL SPHERES ABOUT $(0, 0, 0)$ AND $(1, 1, 1)$

TABLE 3.6-1   Meaning of Minimum Distance

Minimum Distance	Meaning
1	Uniqueness
2	Single error detection
3	Single error correction (*or* double error detection)
4	Single error correction plus double error detection (*or* triple error detection)
5	Double error correction
etc.	

distance of four will give both single error correction plus double error detection. A minimum distance of five would allow double error correction. *Conversely*, if the required degree of detection or correction is to be achieved, then the corresponding minimum distance between message points must be observed.

Taking the case of single error correction with the minimum distance of three, we can surround each message point by a unit sphere and not have the spheres overlap. The *volume* of a sphere of radius 1 is the center plus the n points with just one coordinate changed, a volume of $1 + n$. The total volume of the n-dimensional space is clearly 2^n, the number of possible points. Since the spheres do not overlap, the maximum number of message positions k must satisfy

$$\frac{\text{total volume}}{\text{volume of a sphere}} \geq \text{maximum number of spheres}$$

or

$$\frac{2^n}{n+1} \geq 2^k \qquad (3.6\text{-}1)$$

Since

$$n = m + k$$
$$2^{m+k} \geq 2^k(n+1)$$

or

$$2^m \geq n + 1$$

This is the same inequality as we derived from the algebraic approach, equation (3.4-1).

We can now see the restrictions for higher error correction. Thus for double error correction we must have a minimum distance of five, and we can put nonoverlapping spheres of radius two about each message position. The volume of a sphere of radius two is the center position plus the n positions a distance one away, plus those with two coordinates out of the n changed, which is the binomial coefficient $C(n, 2) = n(n-1)/2$. Dividing the total volume of the space, 2^n, by the volume of these spheres gives an upper bound on the number k of possible code message positions in the space

$$\frac{2^n}{1 + n + n(n-1)/2} \geq 2^k \qquad (3.6\text{-}2)$$

It does not mean that this number can be achieved, only that this is an upper bound. Similar inequalities can be written for larger spheres.

When the spheres about the message points completely exhaust the space of 2^n points, leaving no points outside some sphere, the code is called a *perfect code*. Such codes have a high degree of symmetry (in the geometric model each point is equivalent to any other point) and a particularly simple theory. In only a comparatively few cases do perfect codes exist. They require that the inequalities be equalities.

Exercises

3.6-1   Extend the bounds of (3.6-1) and (3.6-2) to higher error-correcting codes.

3.6-2   Make a table for the bound for double error correction of equation (3.6-2) ($n = 3, 4, 5, \ldots, 11$).

3.7   SINGLE-ERROR-CORRECTION PLUS DOUBLE-ERROR-DETECTION CODES

It is seldom wise to use only single error correction, because a double error would then fool the system in its attempts to correct, and the system would use the syndrome to correct the wrong place; thus there would be three errors in the decoded message. Instead, a single-error-correction plus double-error-detection code makes a reasonably balanced system for many (but not all) situations. The condition for the double detection is that the minimum distance must be increased by 1; it must be 4.

To make a double error-correcting code from a single error-correcting code, we add one more parity check (and one more position), this check over the whole message. Thus any single error will still produce the right syndrome and the added parity check will give a 1. A double error will now cause some nonzero syndrome but leave this added parity check satisfied. This situation can then be recognized as a double error; namely, some syndrome appears, but the extra parity check is still correct (Table 3.7-1). It is easy to see that two points which were at the minimum distance of three from each other in the original code had a different number of 1's in them, modulo 2. Thus

---

TABLE 3.7-1   Double Error Detection

Original Syndrome	New Parity Check	Meaning
0	0	Correct
0	1	Error in added position
Something	1	Original meaning
Something	0	Double error

---

their corresponding extra parity checks would be set differently, increasing the distance between them to four.

The argument we have just given applies to both the algebraic and geometric approaches, and shows how the two tend to complement each other. We have not yet given any constructive method for finding the higher error-correcting codes; we have only given bounds on them. Chapter 11 is devoted to the elements of their construction. The full theory for error-correcting codes has been developed over the years and is very complex, so we can only indicate the general approach.

Notice that the theory *assumes* that the correcting equipment is working properly; it is only the errors in the received (computed) message that are being handled.

Exercise

3.7-1 Show that the argument to get extra error detection can be applied to any odd minimum distance to get the next-higher (even) minimum distance.

3.8 APPLICATIONS OF THE IDEAS

In Section 1.2 we claimed that not only were the ideas in the text directly useful but they also had wider general application—we used evolution as an example.

The central idea of error detection and correction is that the meaningful messages must be kept far apart (in the space of probable errors) if we are to handle errors successfully. If two of the possible messages are not far enough apart then one can be carried by an error (or errors) into the other, or carried at least so close that at the receiving end we will make a mistake in identifying the source.

In assigning names to variables and labels in a FORTRAN, COBOL, ALGOL, PASCAL, and other high-level languages, the names should be kept far apart; otherwise, an intellectual "slip of the pen" or a typical error in keying in the name can transfer one name to another meaningful name. If the names are made to differ in at least two positions, then single typos will be caught by the assembler. Thus the use of short mnemonic names should be tempered by the prudent need to protect oneself against small slips.

The distance function in the Hamming codes is based completely on white noise. Sections 2.7 and 2.9 were included to emphasize that the proper distance function to use depends in some cases on the *psychological distance* between the names as well as more uniformly random keystroke errors.

3.9 SUMMARY

We have given the fundamental nature of error detection and error correction for white noise, namely the minimum distance between message points that must be observed. We have given methods for constructing codes for:

single error detecting   min. dist. $= 2$

single error correction   min. dist. $= 3$

1 error corr. $+$ 2 error det.   min. dist. $= 4$

Their design is easy, and they are practical to construct in software or in hardware chips. They can compensate for weak spots in a system or can be used throughout an entire system to get reliable performance out of unreliable parts. One need not put up with poor equipment performance, but the price is both in storage (or time of transmission) and equipment (or time) to encode and possibly correct. You don't get something for nothing! The codes also make valuable contributions to maintenance, since they pinpoint the error and repairmen will not try to fix the wrong things (meaning "fix" what is working right and ignore what is causing the error!).

A more widespread use of the idea of distance between messages was sketched in Section 3.8.

4

Variable-Length Codes— Huffman Codes

4.1 INTRODUCTION

The codes we have looked at so far have all used a fixed length, and they are called *block codes* from the fact that the messages are of fixed block lengths in the stream of symbols being sent. The Morse code mentioned in Chapter 1 is an example of a *variable-length* code. We now examine this class of codes in more detail. The advantage of a code where the message symbols are of variable length is that sometimes the code is more *efficient* in the sense that to represent the same information we can use fewer digits on the average. To accomplish this we need to know something about the statistics of the messages being sent. If every symbol is as likely as every other one, then the block codes are about as efficient as any code can be (see Section 4.6). But if some symbols are more probable than others, then we can take advantage of this feature to make the most frequent symbols correspond to the shorter encodings and the rare symbols correspond to the longer encodings. This is exactly what the Morse code does. The letter E in the English language occurs most frequently and corresponds to the encoded symbol "dot."

However, variable-length codes bring with them a fundamental problem; at the receiving end, how do you recognize each symbol of the code? In, for example, a binary system how do you recognize the end of one code word and the beginning of the next? If the probabilities of the frequencies of occurrence of the individual symbols are sufficiently different, then variable-length encoding can be significantly more efficient than block encoding.

In this chapter we will take advantage only of the frequencies of occurrence of the individual symbols being sent, and neglect any larger structure the messages may have. An example of a slightly larger scale structure is the fact that in English the letter Q is usually followed by the letter U—in Chapter 5 we will take advantage of such correlations in the message being sent.

Exercise

4.1-1   List advantages and disadvantages of variable-length codes.

4.2   UNIQUE DECODING

We need to make clear when we are talking about the symbols to be sent and when we are talking about the symbols used by the signaling system. We will refer to the *source symbols* when we refer to the symbols (such as the letters of the English alphabet) that are to be sent, and to the *code's alphabet* when we refer to the symbols used in sending (such as 0 and 1 in the binary system). In general, we will assume that the source alphabet being sent has q symbols, $s_1, s_2, \ldots, s_q$, and that the code's alphabet has r symbols (r for the radix of the system).

The first property that we need is *unique decodability*—the received message must have a single, unique possible interpretation. Consider a code in which the source alphabet S has four symbols, and they are to be encoded in binary as follows:

$$s_1 = 0$$
$$s_2 = 01$$
$$s_3 = 11$$
$$s_4 = 00$$

The particular received message 0011 could be one of these two:

$$0011 = \begin{cases} s_4, s_3 \\ s_1, s_1, s_3 \end{cases}$$

Thus the code is not uniquely decodable. While this property of unique decodability is not always absolutely essential, it is usually highly desirable. In order to get our thoughts clear we make a formal definition:

Definition. The nth extension of a code is simply all possible concatenations of n symbols of the original source code.

This is also called the nth *direct product* of the code. There are q^n symbols in the nth extension. The definition is necessary because the messages we send look to the receiver as concatenations of the encoded symbols of the source alphabet, and the receiver needs to decide which sequence of source symbols was sent. For unique decodability, no two encoded concatenations can be the same, even for different extensions. Clearly, only if every sequence is unique can we have a uniquely decodable signaling system. This is a necessary and sufficient condition, but it is hardly usable in this form.

Exercises

4.2-1   Is the code 0, 01, 001, 0010, 0011 uniquely decodable?

4.2-2   Is the code 0, 01, 011, 111 uniquely decodable?

4.3   INSTANTANEOUS CODES

Consider the following code:

$$s_1 = 0$$
$$s_2 = 10$$
$$s_3 = 110$$
$$s_4 = 111$$

Now consider how the receiver would decode messages sent in this code. It would set up what is equivalent to a *finite automaton,* or if you prefer, a *decision tree.* Starting in the initial state (Figure 4.3-1) the first binary digit received will cause a branch, either to a terminal state s_1 if the digit is 0, or else to a second decision point if it is a 1. For the next binary digit this second branch would go to the terminal state s_2 if a 0 is received, and to a third decision point if it is a 1. The third would go to the terminal state s_3 if the third digit is a 0, and to the terminal symbol s_4 if it is a 1. Each terminal state would, of course, emit its symbol and then return control to the initial state. Note that each bit of the received stream is *examined only once,* and that the terminal states of this tree are the four source symbols s_1, s_2, s_3, and s_4.

In this example the decoding is *instantaneous* since when a complete symbol is received, the receiver immediately knows this and does not have to

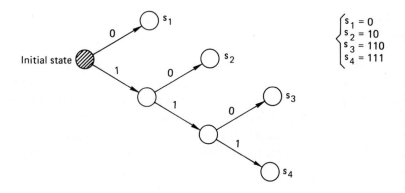

$$\begin{cases} s_1 = 0 \\ s_2 = 10 \\ s_3 = 110 \\ s_4 = 111 \end{cases}$$

FIGURE 4.3-1   DECODING TREE

look further before deciding what message symbol it has received. No encoded symbol of this code is a prefix of any other symbol. This particular type of code is what is called a *comma code*, since the binary digit 0 indicates the end of a symbol, *plus* the fact that in this case no symbol is longer than three digits.

The following code is uniquely decodable but is not instantaneous because you do not know when one symbol is over without looking farther:

$$s_1 = 0$$
$$s_2 = 01$$
$$s_3 = 011$$
$$s_4 = 111$$

(It is the previous code with the bits reversed.) We can see the trouble—some code words are *prefixes* of other words; that is, they are the same as the beginning part of some other symbol. Now consider the string

$$\underbrace{0111}_{s_4} \ldots \underbrace{1111}_{s_4}$$

It *can only* be decoded by first going to the end and then identifying runs of three 1's as each being an s_4 until the first symbol is reached. Only then can it be identified as s_1, s_2, or s_3. Thus the receiver cannot decide whether it has the word that corresponds to the prefix, or if it must wait until more is sent to complete the word. The simplest way to decode messages in this particular code is to always start at the back end of the received message! This puts a severe burden on the storage and also causes a time delay.

It is clearly both necessary and sufficient that an instantaneous code have no code word s_i which is a prefix of another code word s_j. If we had to deal with a noninstantaneous code, then the decision tree would have a structure which instead of returning to the start would, when it realized (finally) that it had received a complete word some time ago, emit the proper code word and then go to an appropriate place in the decision tree, not necessarily the start. As in the example above, the tree could require potentially infinite storage.

4.4 CONSTRUCTION OF INSTANTANEOUS CODES

It is clear that of all uniquely decodable codes, the instantaneous codes are preferable to ones that are not, and since it will turn out (Section 4.7) that they cost us nothing extra, it is worth concentrating on them. Let us, therefore, explore the problem of constructing them.

Given that we are to construct a code with five symbols s_i in the source code S, and that the code alphabet is the binary one, we can assign

$$s_1 = 0$$
$$s_2 = 10$$
$$s_3 = 110$$
$$s_4 = 1110$$
$$s_5 = 1111$$

to get an instantaneous (comma) code (Figure 4.4-1).

In this construction the use of the 0 for the first symbol reduced the number of possibilities available later. Instead of this, let us use two digits for the first two symbols, $s_1 = 00$ and $s_2 = 01$. We can now use $s_3 = 10$. With two symbols yet to go, we cannot use $s_4 = 11$; instead, we must try $s_4 = 110$, which leaves us with $s_5 = 111$. We get the code

$$s_1 = 00$$
$$s_2 = 01$$
$$s_3 = 10$$
$$s_4 = 110$$
$$s_5 = 111$$

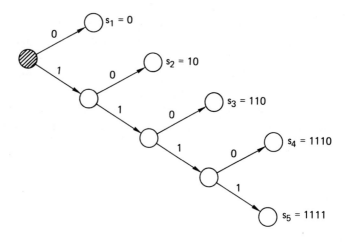

FIGURE 4.4-1   DECODING TREE

This code is clearly instantaneous, since no symbol is a prefix of any other symbol, and the decoding tree is easily constructed (Figure 4.4-2).

Which of these two codes is the better (more efficient)? This depends on the frequency of occurrence of the symbols s_i. By "better" we mean, of course, that the sent messages *on the average* will be shorter, more efficient. We will investigate this more closely in Section 4.8. Evidently "efficient" *must* depend

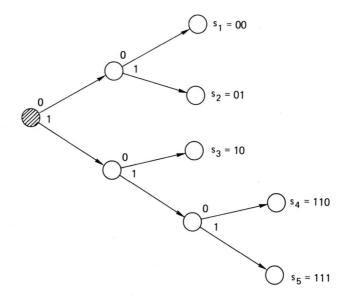

FIGURE 4.4-2   DECODING TREE

on the probability of the various symbols being used in the messages being sent.

Exercises

4.4-1   Devise a similar example using six words.

4.4-2   Find probabilities that favor one or the other of the two codes in this section.

Answer. $p_3 + p_4 + p_5$ vs. p_1

4.5   THE KRAFT INEQUALITY

The Kraft inequality, which we now examine, gives conditions on the existence of instantaneous codes; it tells when the *lengths* of the code words permit forming an instantaneous code, but it does not discuss the code itself.

Theorem. A necessary and sufficient condition for the existence of an instantaneous code S of q symbols s_i ($i = 1, \ldots, q$) with encoded words of lengths $l_1 \leq l_2 \leq l_3 \leq \ldots \leq l_q$ is

$$\sum_{i=1}^{q} \left(\frac{1}{r^{l_i}} \right) \leq 1 \qquad (4.5\text{-}1)$$

where r is the radix (number of symbols) of the alphabet of the encoded symbols.

It is easy to prove the Kraft inequality from the decoding tree, whose existence follows from the instantaneous decodability. We proceed by induction. For simplicity consider first the binary case (see Figure 4.5-1). For a tree whose maximum length is 1, we have either one or two branches of length 1. Thus we have either (for one symbol)

$$\tfrac{1}{2} \leq 1$$

or (for two symbols)

$$\tfrac{1}{2} + \tfrac{1}{2} \leq 1$$

We next assume that the Kraft inequality is true for all trees of length less than n. Now given a tree of maximum length n, the first node leads to a pair

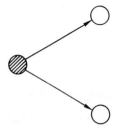

(a)   True for tree of length 1

(b)   Assume true for length n – 1

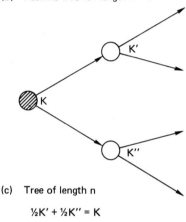

(c)   Tree of length n

$$\tfrac{1}{2}K' + \tfrac{1}{2}K'' = K$$

FIGURE 4.5-1   PROOF OF KRAFT INEQUALITY

of subtrees of length at most $n - 1$, for which we have the inequalities $K' \leq 1$ and $K'' \leq 1$, where the K' and K'' are the values of their respective sums. Each length 1_i in a subtree is increased by 1 when the subtree is joined to the main tree, so an extra factor of $\tfrac{1}{2}$ appears. We have, therefore,

$$\tfrac{1}{2}K' + \tfrac{1}{2}K'' \leq 1$$

For radix r instead of binary, we have at most r branches at each node—at most r subtrees, each with an extra factor of $1/r$ when joined to the main tree. Again the theorem is true.

When can an inequality occur? A moment's inspection shows that if every terminal node of the tree is a code word, then $K = 1$. It is only when some terminal nodes are not used that the inequality occurs. But if any terminal node is not used *for a binary-code alphabet*, then the preceding decision is wasted and that corresponding digit can be removed from every symbol that passes through this node in its decoding. Thus if the inequality holds, the code is inefficient, and how to correct for this is immediately evident for binary trees.

→   Note again that the theorem refers to the existence of such a code and does not refer to a particular code. A particular code may obey the Kraft inequality and still not be instantaneous, but there will exist codes which have the l_i and are instantaneous.

Let us see how the Kraft inequality applies to a binary block code where the 2^m words of the encoded message are all the same length, m. Direct substitution into the inequality shows (as it should) that the sum is exactly 1.

We next examine how comma codes satisfy the Kraft inequality. A comma code of r symbols (r is the radix) in its code alphabet has one reserved symbol, called the "comma," which is used to mark the end of each word, *except* the longest ones, for which the decoder can recognize their ending from their length alone.

There is one word, the comma itself, of length l; there are $r - 1$ words of length 2; there are $(r - 1)^2$ words of length 3; and so on. There are $(r - 1)^{k-2}$ words of length $k - 1$. Finally, there are $r(r - 1)^{k-1}$ words of length k. The Kraft expression becomes, when we group all the symbols which have the same length into one term,

$$\frac{1}{r} + (r - 1)\frac{1}{r^2} + (r - 1)^2\frac{1}{r^3} + \ldots + (r - 1)^{k-2}\frac{1}{r^{k-1}} + r(r - 1)^{k-1}\frac{1}{r^k}$$

The last two terms combine:

$$\frac{(r - 1)^{k-2}}{r^{k-1}}(1 + r - 1) = \frac{r(r - 1)^{k-2}}{r^{k-1}}$$

and we see one stage of the "telescoping" (collapsing) of the series down to

$$\frac{1}{r}\{r\} = 1$$

and the Kraft inequality is exactly satisfied for comma codes.

In the next two examples we will assume that only the code word lengths are given, since this is what matters in the theorem, not the actual code words. If the lengths when encoded in binary symbols are 1, 3, 3, and 3, then the

Kraft sum will be $\frac{1}{2} + \frac{3}{8} = \frac{7}{8}$, and an instantaneous code with those lengths is possible. One of the words of length 3 could be shortened to 2 bits. But if the lengths were 1, 2, 2, and 3, then the sum would be $\frac{1}{2} + 2(\frac{1}{4}) + \frac{1}{8} = \frac{9}{8}$, and such an instantaneous code could not exist.

Let us apply the theorem to yet another example. Suppose that we pick the radix $r = 3$ and want words of lengths 1, 2, 2, 2, 2, 2, 3, 3, 3, and 3. The Kraft inequality gives on the left side $\frac{1}{3} + 5(\frac{1}{9}) + 4(\frac{1}{27}) = \frac{28}{27}$, so we cannot hope to find an *instantaneous code* with these constraints. If we drop the last code word of length 3, then the sum would be exactly 1, and we can find such a code. To find an instantaneous code with these lengths, we proceed systematically; $s_1 = 0, s_2 = 10, s_3 = 11, s_4 = 12, s_5 = 20, s_6 = 21, s_7 = 220, s_8 = 221$, and $s_9 = 222$. In this construction we have followed the decoding tree (Figure 4.5-2) and have systematically increased the ternary (base 3) number equivalents of the codes so that the argument is easily followed.

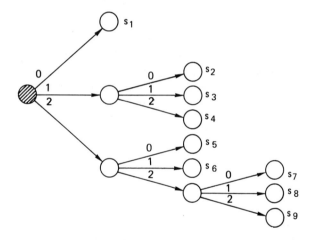

FIGURE 4.5-2   **DECODING TREE**

The reader should realize that the three symbols 0, 1, and 2 are arbitary and are not numbers. Thus any interchanges of the three symbols at any stage would leave the code essentially the same.

Exercises

4.5-1   Does the infinite-length comma code $l_1 = 1, l_2 = 2, \ldots, l_k = k$, ... satisfy the Kraft inequality? (Use $r = 2$.)

4.5-2   Generalize Exercise 4.5-1 to radix r.

4.6 SHORTENED BLOCK CODES

Returning for the moment to the earlier block codes, if we had exactly 2^m code words in a binary system (r^m in a radix system), then we could use m digits to represent each symbol. But suppose that we do not have an exact power of the radix. To see what can happen, consider the case of five symbols. Of the eight binary symbols

$$000$$
$$001$$
$$010$$
$$011$$
$$100$$
$$101$$
$$110$$
$$111$$

we can drop any three. But if we drop $001, 011$, and 101, we can shorten three branches of the decoding tree and still have instantaneous decodability. We will have

$$s_1 = 00$$
$$s_2 = 01$$
$$s_3 = 10$$
$$s_4 = 110$$
$$s_5 = 111$$

Figure 4.6-1a. Instead of this choice we can drop $001, 010$, and 011 and shorten only one branch of the tree to the code

$$s_1 = 0$$
$$s_2 = 100$$
$$s_3 = 101$$
$$s_4 = 110$$
$$s_5 = 111$$

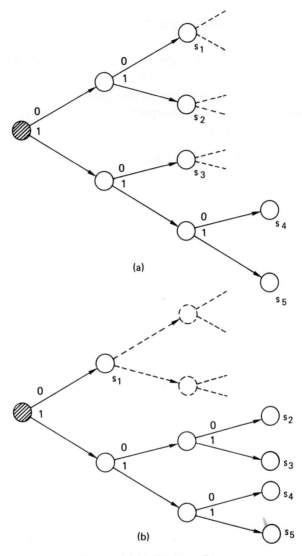

(a)

(b)

FIGURE 4.6-1 DECODING TREES

(Figure 4.6-1b). In both cases there now are no unused terminals and there-fore $K = 1$. We will call these *shortened block codes*; they are essentially block codes with small modifications.

Exercises

4.6-1   Discuss the case of two symbols in a ternary base.

4.6-2   Discuss the case of five symbols in the ternary base.

4.7 THE McMILLAN INEQUALITY

The Kraft inequality applies to instantaneous codes, which are a special case of *uniquely decodable codes*. McMillan showed that the same inequality applies to uniquely decodable codes. The underlying idea of the proof of the necessity is that very high powers of a number greater than 1 grow rapidly. If we can bound this growth, then we know that the number is not greater than 1. The proof of the sufficiency follows from the fact that we can do it for instantaneous codes, which are special cases of uniquely decodable codes.

The necessity part of the proof begins by taking

$$\left[\sum_{i=1}^{q} \frac{1}{r^{l_i}}\right]^n \equiv K^n$$

When we expand the term in the brackets we find that we have a sum of many terms to various powers; the exponents running from n, the lowest possible power, to nl, the highest, where l is the length of the longest symbol. Thus we have the expression

$$\sum_{k=n}^{nl} \frac{N_k}{r^k}$$

where N_k is the number of code symbols (of radix r) of length k. Since the code is uniquely decodable, N_k cannot be greater than r^k, which is the number of distinct sequences of length k in our code alphabet of radix r. Therefore, we have the bound

$$K^n \leq \sum_{k=n}^{nl} \frac{r^k}{r^k} = nl - n + 1 < nl$$

(The $+1$ comes from the fact that both end terms in the sum are counted.) This is the inequality we need, since for any $x > 1$ a sufficiently large n makes the number $x^n > nl$. Since n can be chosen as large as we please, it follows that the number K (the Kraft sum) must be ≤ 1.

From this we see that there is very little to gain from avoiding instantaneously decodable codes and using the more general uniquely decodable codes—both have to satisfy the same inequality on the lengths of the encoded symbols.

4.8 HUFFMAN CODES

Now for the first time we will make use of the *probabilities* of the various symbols being sent. As in the Morse code, we want the most frequent symbols to have the shortest encodings. If the probability of the ith symbol is p_i, and its length is l_i, then the average length of the code is

$$L_{av} = \sum_{i=1}^{q} p_i l_i$$

With no loss in generality the p_i may be taken in decreasing order. If the lengths l_i are not in the opposite order, that is, we do not have both

$$p_1 \geq p_2 \geq p_3 \geq \ldots \geq p_q$$

and

$$l_1 \leq l_2 \leq l_3 \leq \ldots \leq l_q$$

then the code is not *efficient* in the sense that we could have a shorter average length by reassigning the code representations of the symbols $s_1, s_2, s_3, \ldots , s_q$. To prove this assertion, suppose that for $m < n$ we have both conditions (for some m and n)

$$p_m > p_n \quad \text{and} \quad l_m > l_n$$

In computing the average length originally we have, among others, the two terms

$$\text{old:} \quad p_m l_m + p_n l_n$$

By interchanging the encoded symbols for s_m and s_n, we get the corresponding terms

$$\text{new:} \quad p_m l_n + p_n l_m$$

Subtracting the old from the new we have the change due to the reassignment

$$\text{new} - \text{old:} \quad p_m(l_n - l_m) + p_n(l_m - l_n) = (p_m - p_n)(l_n - l_m) < 0$$

From the assumptions above this is a negative number; we will decrease the average code length if we interchange the encoded symbols for s_m and s_n. We therefore assume that the two running inequalities both hold.

We begin our examination of Huffman coding with encoding into the binary alphabet. In Section 4.11 we will look at the base r alphabet. We will use "source symbol" for the input s_i and "code alphabet" for the alphabet we are encoding into.

The first thing to prove is that the two least-frequent source symbols of an efficient code have the same encoded lengths. For an instantaneous code we know that no encoded symbol is the prefix of another symbol, thus the encoded bits of the $(q - 1)$st code are not the same as the corresponding encoded bits of the qth code symbol. Therefore, any bits of the qth encoded symbol beyond those of the $(q - 1)$st can be dropped and no confusion will result in the decoding tree. Thus two of the longest encoded symbols have the same length and from the decoding tree they differ in the last digit.

The proof of the encoding properties, as well as the method of encoding, is a reduction at each stage to a shorter code. We simply combine the two least probable symbols of the source alphabet into a single symbol, whose probability is equal to the sum of the two corresponding probabilities. Thus we have to encode a source alphabet of one less symbol. Repeating this step by step we get down to the problem of encoding just two symbols of a source alphabet, which is easy, merely use 0 and 1. Now in going backward one of these two symbols is to be split into two symbols, and this can be done by appending a second digit 0 for one of them and 1 for the other. In the next stage of going back, one of these three symbols is to be split into two symbols in the same way. And so it goes. For one special case given below, Figure 4.8-1 shows the reduction process, and Figure 4.8-2 shows the corresponding splitting (expansion) process. The general case should be obvious from this.

How do we know that this process generates an efficient code? Suppose that there were a shorter code with code length L' with

$$L' < L$$

Let us compare the two decoding trees. In an efficient binary code, all the terminals are occupied and there are no "dead branches." (A dead branch would enable us to shorten the code by deleting the corresponding binary digit in all the terminals that pass through this useless decision point.)

If there are only two symbols of maximum length in a tree, then they must have their last decision node in common, and they must be the two least probable symbols. Before we reduce a tree, the two symbols contribute

$$l_q(p_q + p_{q-1})$$

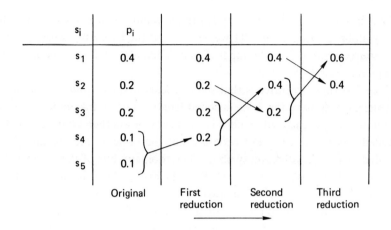

FIGURE 4.8-1 REDUCTION PROCESS

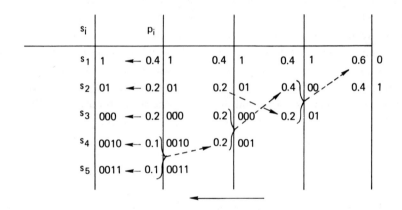

FIGURE 4.8-2 SPLITTING PROCESS

and after the reduction they contribute

$$(l_q - 1)(p_q + p_{q-1})$$

so that the code length is reduced by

$$p_q + p_{q-1}$$

If there are more than two symbols of the maximum length, then we can use the following proposition: symbols having the same length may be interchanged without changing the code length. Using this, we can bring the two least probable symbols so they share their final decision node. Thus after the reduction, we have shortened the code by the amount

$$p_q + p_{q-1}$$

Therefore, in either case we can shorten the code and decrease the code length by the same amount.

We apply this to both the decoding trees we are comparing. Since both are decreased by the same amount, the amount of inequality between their lengths is preserved.

Repeated application of this will reduce both trees to two symbols. In the Huffman code the length is 1; for the other it must be less than 1, which is impossible. Therefore, the Huffman code is the shortest possible code.

The encoding process is not unique in several respects. First, the assignment of the 0 or 1 symbols to the two source symbols at each splitting stage is arbitrary, but this produces only trivial differences. Second, when two probabilities are equal, it is a matter of indifference which we put above the other in the table, but the resulting codes can have different lengths of words. However, in both cases the average length of the encoding of messages in these codes will be the same.

As an example of two different Huffman encodings of the same source, let

$$p_1 = 0.4$$

$$p_2 = 0.2$$

$$p_3 = 0.2$$

$$p_4 = 0.1$$

$$p_5 = 0.1$$

If we put the merged states as low as possible, then in Figure 4.8-1 we get lengths (1, 2, 3, 4, 4), and the average length is

$$L = 0.4(1) + 0.2(2) + 0.2(3) + 0.1(4) + 0.1(4) = 2.2$$

On the other hand, if we push the merged states up as high as possible (Figure 4.8-3), we will get lengths (2, 2, 2, 3, 3) and the average length is

$$L = 0.4(2) + 0.2(2) + 0.2(2) + 0.1(3) + 0.1(3) = 2.2$$

Both codes have the same efficiency (average length) but not the same set of lengths of the symbols.

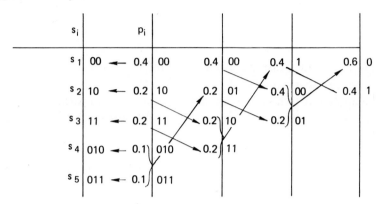

FIGURE 4.8-3   ALTERNATIVE ENCODING

Which one of these two codes should we choose? A very reasonable choice is the one whose average length would vary least over the ensemble of messages. We therefore compute the variances in the two cases:

$$\text{Var(I)} = 0.4(1 - 2.2)^2 + 0.2(2 - 2.2)^2 + 0.2(3 - 2.2)^2$$

$$+ \, 0.1(4 - 2.2)^2 + 0.1(4 - 2.2)^2 = 1.36$$

$$\text{Var(II)} = 0.4(2 - 2.2)^2 + 0.2(2 - 2.2)^2 + 0.2(2 - 2.2)^2$$

$$+ \, 0.1(3 - 2.2)^2 + 0.1(3 - 2.2)^2 = 0.16$$

Thus the second code has significantly less variability in use on finite-length messages and is therefore probably the preferable code. It seems highly probable that always moving a combined state as high as possible will give a minimum variance code.

Exercises

4.8-1   Give Huffman code for $p_1 = \frac{1}{2}$, $p_2 = \frac{1}{3}$, and $p_3 = \frac{1}{6}$.

4.8-2   Give Huffman code for $p_1 = \frac{1}{3}$, $p_2 = \frac{1}{4}$, $p_3 = \frac{1}{5}$, $p_4 = \frac{1}{6}$, and $p_5 = \frac{1}{20}$.

4.8-3   Give Huffman code for $p_1 = \frac{1}{2}$, $p_2 = \frac{1}{4}$, $p_3 = \frac{1}{8}$, $p_4 = \frac{1}{16}$, and $p_5 = \frac{1}{16}$.

4.8-4   Give Huffman code for $p_1 = \frac{27}{40}$, $p_2 = \frac{9}{40}$, $p_3 = \frac{3}{40}$, and $p_4 = \frac{1}{40}$.

4.9 SPECIAL CASES OF HUFFMAN CODING

There are a number of interesting cases of Huffman coding to look at. First, if all the symbols are equally likely, and if there are exactly $q = 2^m$ source symbols, then the (binary) Huffman code will be a block code with all symbols having the same length m (see Figure 4.9-1). If there are not exactly 2^m source symbols, then we will get a shortened block code (Section 4.6).

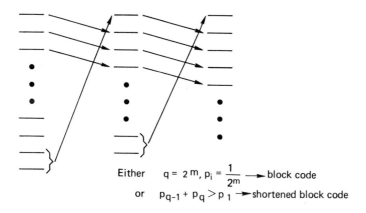

Either $q = 2^m$, $p_i = \dfrac{1}{2^m}$ ⟶ block code

or $p_{q-1} + p_q > p_1$ ⟶ shortened block code

FIGURE 4.9-1

The second case is more interesting. Suppose that the two least probable symbols have their probabilities such that their sum is greater than the most probable symbol; that is, $p_{q-1} + p_q > p_1$. In the Huffman process (see Figure 4.9-1) the corresponding symbol word will go to the top. It then follows that the next two least probable symbols will combine and will go to the top, and so on. If the number of original symbols q is an exact power of two, then the repeated combining process into the final code of two symbols will have each symbol go through *the same number* of splitting steps, and each symbol will acquire the same number of binary digits in the expansion process. Thus again we will have a block code. If q is not an exact power of 2, then, of course, there are small modifications to the above process, and we get a shortened block code (Section 4.6).

It is only when the probabilities of the source symbols of the message are very different that we get a significant economy from the Huffman encoding process. This is what we would expect if we but thought a bit—only when there are large differences in the probabilities of occurrence does the variable length of the code symbols pay off.

For example, if the probabilities p_i have great variability,

$$p_j \geq \frac{2}{3} \sum_{k=j+1}^{q} p_k \tag{4.9-1}$$

for all j, then a comma code will emerge. In words, equation (4.9-1) says that each probability is at least as great as two-thirds of the sum of all the probabilities that follow.

To prove this, we begin at the bottom of Figure 4.9-2. The sum $p_q + p_{q-1}$

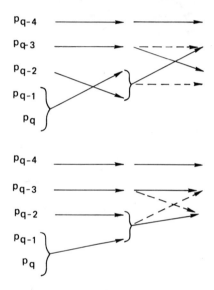

FIGURE 4.9-2   THE TWO POSSIBLE CASES

can be greater or less than p_{q-2}, but it cannot be greater than p_{q-3}. Thus at the next stage we get the sum

$$p_q + p_{q-1} + p_{q-2}$$

and p_{q-2} has been combined only once. Repeating this at each stage, we see that we can get a comma code. The code

$$p_1 = \frac{1}{2}$$

$$p_k = \frac{1}{2^k} \qquad (k < q)$$

$$p_q = \frac{1}{2^{q-1}}$$

is such a code and permits a comma-code realization.

Exercise

4.9-1   (*Difficult*) Discuss what happens in cases that lie between the two main results.

4.10   EXTENSIONS OF A CODE

In Section 4.2 we defined an extension of a code. We are now in a position to see why they are useful. Suppose that for the purposes of a concrete example, we have two symbols s_1 and s_2 with probabilities $p_1 = \frac{2}{3}$ and $p_2 = \frac{1}{3}$.

Encoding

$$s_1; p_1 = \tfrac{2}{3}, \qquad s_1 \longrightarrow 0$$
$$s_2; p_2 = \tfrac{1}{3}, \qquad s_2 \longrightarrow 1$$

The average code length is 1.

The second extension takes two symbols at a time:

Encoding

$$s_1 s_1; p_{1,1} = \tfrac{4}{9} \qquad s_1 s_1 \longrightarrow 1$$
$$s_1 s_2; p_{1,2} = \tfrac{2}{9} \qquad s_1 s_2 \longrightarrow 01$$
$$s_2 s_1; p_{2,1} = \tfrac{2}{9} \qquad s_2 s_1 \longrightarrow 000$$
$$s_2 s_2; p_{2,2} = \tfrac{1}{9} \qquad s_2 s_2 \longrightarrow 001$$

Here $p_{1,1}$ is four times as probable as $p_{2,2}$. The average length when normalized by dividing by 2, is $\frac{17}{18} = 0.94444\ldots$ for comparison.

The next extension takes three symbols at a time gives $\frac{76}{81} = 0.93827\ldots$
Taking four s_i at a time leads to the average code length $0.93827\ldots$

Thus we see that extensions increase the variability and hence allow Huffman coding to achieve some compression. We will show in Section 6.9 that a lower bound on what can be achieved for this example is $0.91830\ldots$

Exercise

4.10-1   Compute the average code length of the extensions given in this section.

4.11   HUFFMAN CODES RADIX *r*

The modifications of the radix *r* alphabet for the code are easy to make. We will, in general, be able to assign not two but *r* different symbols at each stage. But it is not necessarily true that we will always be able to find exactly *r* words to encode at the last stage unless we plan for it. The least loss in the average length of the code will occur with the least frequent symbols do not exactly fit *r* symbols, so we plan at the first splitting to assign *r* symbols (the top group of *r* symbols), the next *r* symbols, as long as we can, and let the last (bottom) splitting stage cover what is left. At each stage of reduction *r* symbols are replaced by 1 symbol, and we reduce the number of symbols by *r* − 1. We therefore divide the number of symbols by *r* − 1 and take the remainder. If the remainder is greater than 1, then we group this many as a single symbol; if the remainder is 1, we take *r* words in the first reduction; and if the remainder is zero, we group *r* − 1 symbols. At each subsequent stage the *r* symbols of least probability are again combined and replaced by a single symbol. Thus we come finally to exactly *r* symbols to be encoded.

s_i		p_i						
s_1	1	0.22	1	0.22	1	0.40	0	1.00
s_2	2	0.20	2	0.20	2	0.22	1	
s_3	3	0.18	3	0.18	3	0.20	2	
s_4	00	0.15	00	0.15	00	0.18	3	
s_5	01	0.10	01	0.10	01			
s_6	02	0.08	02	0.08	02			
s_7	030	0.05	030	0.07	03			
s_8	031	0.02	031					

FIGURE 4.11-1   HUFFMAN RADIX 4

With the r symbols to encode, we assign the code symbols $0, 1, \ldots, r - 1$. Figure 4.11-1 shows such an encoding for the base 4 applied to a particular case from Huffman's original paper.

For the proof of the efficiency of the encoding, we first, if necessary, add enough symbols of probability zero to the alphabet of symbols s_i so that at each stage r symbols can be combined. The tree will therefore have all its terminals filled, and we will be able to argue, as in the case of the binary trees, that no other encoding can be more efficient.

Exercise

4.11-1   Discuss adding symbols of probability zero so there are exactly $k(r - 1) + 1$ symbols.

4.12   NOISE IN HUFFMAN CODING PROBABILITIES

Suppose that the estimates of the probabilities p_i are not accurate. How much does the average code length suffer? In short, will small errors in the estimates greatly degrade (or improve) the system?

To answer this question, let the p_i be the original Huffman code design probabilities and

$$p_i' = p_i + e_i \tag{4.12-1}$$

be the probabilities for the source that is actually used. Clearly,

$$\frac{1}{q} \sum_{i=1}^{q} e_i = 0 \tag{4.12-2}$$

since both p_i and p_i' are probability distributions that sum to 1.

As one measure of the size of the errors e_i, we set

$$\frac{1}{q} \sum_{i=1}^{q} e_i^2 = \sigma^2 \tag{4.12-3}$$

Multiply (4.12-1) by l_i and divide by q to get the new average symbol length:

$$L' = \frac{1}{q} \sum l_i p_i' = \frac{1}{q} \sum l_i p_i + \frac{1}{q} \sum l_i e_i$$

$$= L + \frac{1}{q} \sum l_i e_i$$

The last term is the change in the average symbol length.

With the two conditions on the e_i (4.12-2) and (4.12-3), we resort to the method of Lagrange multipliers to find the *extreme* cases. The Lagrange expression is

$$\mathcal{L} = \frac{1}{q} \sum l_i e_i - \lambda \frac{1}{q} \sum e_i - \mu \left(\frac{1}{q} \sum e_i^2 - \sigma^2 \right)$$

The partial derivatives with respect to e_i are to be equated to zero; that is,

$$\frac{\partial \mathcal{L}}{\partial e_i} = \frac{1}{q}(l_i - \lambda - 2\mu e_i) = 0 \qquad (i = 1, 2, \ldots, q) \qquad (4.12\text{-}4)$$

We now sum these equations to get

$$\frac{1}{q} \sum_i l_i - \lambda = 0 \qquad (4.12\text{-}5)$$

which determines λ. Next we multiply the equations (4.12-4) by e_i and sum to get

$$\frac{1}{q} \sum_i l_i e_i - 2\mu \frac{1}{q} \sum_i e_i^2 = 0 \qquad (4.12\text{-}6)$$

which determines μ. Finally, we multiply the equations (4.12-4) by l_i and sum to get

$$\frac{1}{q} \sum_i l_i^2 - \lambda \frac{1}{q} \sum_i l_i - 2\mu \frac{1}{q} \sum_i e_i l_i = 0$$

Using the λ from (4.12-5) and the μ from (4.12-6), we have

$$\frac{1}{q} \sum_i l_i^2 - \left(\frac{1}{q} \sum_i l_i \right)^2 - \frac{\left(\frac{1}{q} \sum_i e_i l_i \right)^2}{\frac{1}{q} \sum_i e_i^2} = 0$$

Using (4.12-3) this takes the form

$$\left(\frac{1}{q} \sum_i e_i l_i \right)^2 = \left[\frac{1}{q} \sum_i l_i^2 - \left(\frac{1}{q} \sum_i l_i \right)^2 \right] \sigma^2 \qquad (4.12\text{-}7)$$

$$= [\text{variance of } (l_i)][\text{variance of } (e_i)]$$

These are the extreme (Chebyshev) values possible for a fixed σ^2. The equation shows that the more variable the l_i, the more harm (or good) the errors in the estimates of the p_i can cause in the average of the symbol length.

That errors e_i can make no change in the average length can be seen from the following example. For $q \geq 3$, let, for some e,

$$
\begin{aligned}
e_1 &= (l_2 - l_3)e \\
e_2 &= (l_3 - l_1)e \\
e_3 &= (l_1 - l_2)e \\
e_i &= 0 \qquad (i > 3)
\end{aligned}
\tag{4.12-8}
$$

Clearly,

$$
\frac{1}{q} \sum e_i = 0
$$

To find the corresponding σ^2 we have, from equation (4.12-3),

$$
[(l_2 - l_3)^2 + (l_3 - l_1)^2 + (l_1 - l_2)^2]e^2 = \sigma^2
$$

Now consider the average code-length change,

$$
\begin{aligned}
l_1 e_1 + l_2 e_2 + l_3 e_3 + 0 &= (l_1 l_2 - l_1 l_3 + l_2 l_3 - l_2 l_1 + l_3 l_1 - l_3 l_2)e \\
&= 0
\end{aligned}
$$

Hence these changes e_i (4.12-8) do not change the average code length.

From this we conclude that Huffman coding is fairly robust; small changes in the probabilities do not seriously degrade the system. But we have *not* answered the question of how much a redesign using the new probabilities could have improved matters.

4.13   USE OF HUFFMAN CODES

The design of a Huffman code is highly recursive and therefore is easy to program on a computer. The finite automata scheme (tree) of decoding mentioned in Section 4.2 provides a method for decoding Huffman codes using a single r-way branch per received code symbol of radix r. The method is simple and rapid and each received symbol is examined *only once*.

The encoding of a Huffman code is, for reasonably sized source alphabets, a simple table lookup. If we have a lot of information to put into long-term backup storage in a computer, for example, and if the source code has symbols whose probabilities vary greatly, then it may well be worth encoding the information into an appropriate Huffman code to save long-term storage. As we have seen, it depends on the variability of the probabilities p_i.

Programs have been written to *automatically* scan a text, design a code, compress the text, and store the text along with the decoding algorithm. The program counts the frequencies of the source symbols and adds one special symbol called "end of text" of frequency 1. This special symbol is used to end the decoding. Such programs have been known to reduce the storage of data to less than half the original amount.

Exercise

4.13-1   Discuss writing a computer program to find a Huffman code from the p_i.

4.14   HAMMING–HUFFMAN CODING

How can we combine the source compression of Huffman encoding with the noise protection of Hamming encoding? So far as is now known, you encode in a Huffman code and take the output stream, break it up into blocks, and encode it into a suitable noise-protecting Hamming code. For decoding you reverse the process: decode Hamming, then Huffman.

A reasonable problem is to ask if a single encoding process can do a better job. It is left to the reader to try. We note that in the decoding, tree nodes near a terminal must not be used by other branches of the tree. One such variable-length error-detecting code is

Encodings	Errors
$s_1 = 000$	001
$s_2 = 0110$	010
	100
$s_3 = 1010$	0111
$s_4 = 1100$	1011
$s_5 = 1111$	1101
	1110

Exercises

4.14-1   Draw the decoding tree and verify that the code "works."

4.14-2   Discuss the use of a decoding tree for Hamming codes rather than the computing methods of Chapter 3.

4.14-3   For the comma code $s_1 = 0$, $s_2 = 10$, $s_3 = 11$, show that an error in 1 bit can be propagated arbitrarily far. [*Hint:* Consider $s_1(s_3)^n s_2$.]

5

Miscellaneous Codes

5.1 INTRODUCTION

There are many different codes for the many different situations that arise in practice, and we can study only a few of the more important ones.

We shall first look at *Markov processes*, which enable us to handle some of the larger probability structures that arise typically in languages, larger than the simple frequency of occurrence that is used by the Huffman code.

We will then examine *predictive coding*, which is very general and takes advantage of *any* structure you know about which can help you predict the next symbol accurately. The better your ability to predict the next symbol, the shorter the final message you have to use. Nothing is said about how you predict, only that you have written a program that incorporates all the structure of the message you are going to use. This is a very general method of code compression. Thus, as we said we would, we have gone to very general methods and have skipped the many special codes for special cases. However, it is hoped that the reader, when faced with a special case, and having seen the codes we have given, will be able to invent their own method of suitably encoding messages.

We then discuss the remarkable idea of *random encoding*, both for its practical value and for its theoretical use in proving the main result of information theory. The particular method we examine, called "hash coding," is widely used in computer software but has applications to other situations.

Finally, we will look at *Gray codes*, used to go reliably from analog-to-digital representations and back. Since this occurs so often in practice (because nature provides us basically with analog signals), it is a part of the education of computer science students and others who have to deal with "real" signals.

For more material, see Ref. [J].

5.2 WHAT IS A MARKOV PROCESS?

Up to this point we have used only the probabilities of occurrence of the source alphabet $s_1, s_2, \ldots, s_q$. Familiarity with natural languages shows that there is often much more structure in a language. Thus, as we noted before, in English the letter Q is almost always followed by the letter U; the probability of seeing the letter U depends very much on the letter that came before it. In probability theory the notation

$$p(U \mid Q)$$

means "the probability of seeing U given that ($\mid$) you have just seen the letter Q." In general, in the notation of a jth-order Markov process

$$p(s_i \mid s_{i_1}, s_{i_2}, \ldots, s_{i_j})$$

is the *conditional probability* of seeing s_i given that you have just seen all the letters $s_{i_1}, s_{i_2}, \ldots, s_{i_j}$, in that order. *Note* that the sequence of symbols is

$$s_{i_1}, s_{i_2}, \ldots, s_{i_j}, s_i$$

This is clearly a situation that arises in practice—the previous part of the message can often greatly influence the probabilities for the next symbol that you will see from the source.

In computer language a *zero memory source* uses each source symbol independently of what has preceded it. A *j-memory source* uses the previous j symbols, and this idea corresponds exactly to a jth-order Markov process.

We consider the system as being in some *state*. For a one-memory source there are q states, one for each symbol s_i of the source alphabet. The standard weather prediction that "tomorrow will be like today" is an example of a one-memory predictor. For a two-memory source there are q^2 states, one state for each pair of source symbols. The linear trend predictor

$$y_{n+1} = 2y_n - y_{n-1}$$

is a two-memory source; the next value y_{n+1} is estimated from the two previous symbols, y_n and y_{n-1}. In general, for a j-memory source there are q^j states in the Markov process.

As an example of a simple one-memory source, suppose that we have an alphabet of three symbols, a, b, and c. Let the probability that an a is followed by any of the three letters be each $\frac{1}{3}$. Let the probability that the letter b is followed by another b be $\frac{1}{2}$, and either of the other two letters, a or c, be $\frac{1}{4}$. Finally, let the probability that the letter c is followed by a c be $\frac{1}{2}$, and either of the other two, a, or b, be $\frac{1}{4}$. We have

$$p(a\,|\,a) = \tfrac{1}{3} \qquad p(b\,|\,a) = \tfrac{1}{3} \qquad p(c\,|\,a) = \tfrac{1}{3}$$

$$p(a\,|\,b) = \tfrac{1}{4} \qquad p(b\,|\,b) = \tfrac{1}{2} \qquad p(c\,|\,b) = \tfrac{1}{4}$$

$$p(a\,|\,c) = \tfrac{1}{4} \qquad p(b\,|\,c) = \tfrac{1}{4} \qquad p(c\,|\,c) = \tfrac{1}{2}$$

It is conventional to use a *transition graph* to illustrate such a Markov process. There are, of course, three states in this case (Figure 5.2-1), labeled a, b, and c and indicated by the circles. Each directed line is a transition from one state to another state, whose probability is indicated by the number alongside the line. For example, $p(a\,|\,b)$ is the directed line from b to a and has the probability of transition of $\frac{1}{4}$. In this example each state has three lines "out" and three lines "in."

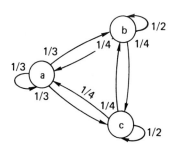

FIGURE 5.2-1   TRANSITION GRAPH

We may assign a concrete interpretation to this diagram. Let a mean "fair weather," b mean "rain," and c mean "snow." Given that today is fair, it is equally likely that tomorrow it will be any of the three states fair, rain, or snow. But if today is either rain or snow it is a 50–50 chance that it will be the same tomorrow, and only one in four that it will be either of the other two.

We may write the graph in matrix form as follows, where the label of the current state is given by the letter on the left of the matrix and the next state after the transition is given above the matrix. The matrix entry is the *transition probability*. We have

$$
\begin{array}{c}
 \quad a \uparrow \ b \quad\ c \\
\begin{array}{c} a \\ \longrightarrow \ b \\ c \end{array}
\begin{pmatrix}
\frac{1}{3} & \frac{1}{3} & \frac{1}{3} \\
\frac{1}{4} & \frac{1}{2} & \frac{1}{4} \\
\frac{1}{4} & \frac{1}{4} & \frac{1}{2}
\end{pmatrix}
\end{array}
\tag{5.2-1}
$$

In a transition matrix the sum of the elements in any row must total exactly 1, since the current state must go somewhere.

Now suppose that instead of having a definite state today, we have a probability distribution for today's state (p_a, p_b, p_c), where, of course, $p_a + p_b + p_c = 1$. It can be that one $p_i = 1$ and the other two are 0, which means that we have a definite state today. If we multiply this row vector on the right by the transition matrix (5.2-1), we get the probability of tomorrow's weather:

$$
(p_a, p_b, p_c)\begin{pmatrix}
\frac{1}{3} & \frac{1}{3} & \frac{1}{3} \\
\frac{1}{4} & \frac{1}{2} & \frac{1}{4} \\
\frac{1}{4} & \frac{1}{4} & \frac{1}{2}
\end{pmatrix}
$$

$$
= [\tfrac{1}{3}p_a + \tfrac{1}{4}p_b + \tfrac{1}{4}p_c, \tfrac{1}{3}p_a + \tfrac{1}{2}p_b + \tfrac{1}{4}p_c, \tfrac{1}{3}p_a + \tfrac{1}{4}p_b + \tfrac{1}{2}p_c]
$$

To find the probabilities 2 days ahead, we multiply on the right again by the transition matrix (5.2-1). Because of the associativity of matrix (and vector) multiplication, this is the same as first multiplying the matrix by itself to get the square of the matrix, and then multiplying the original distribution on the right by this. We get, for the square of the transition matrix,

$$
\begin{pmatrix}
\frac{1}{3} & \frac{1}{3} & \frac{1}{3} \\
\frac{1}{4} & \frac{1}{2} & \frac{1}{4} \\
\frac{1}{4} & \frac{1}{4} & \frac{1}{2}
\end{pmatrix}
\begin{pmatrix}
\frac{1}{3} & \frac{1}{3} & \frac{1}{3} \\
\frac{1}{4} & \frac{1}{2} & \frac{1}{4} \\
\frac{1}{4} & \frac{1}{4} & \frac{1}{2}
\end{pmatrix}
=
\begin{pmatrix}
\frac{10}{36} & \frac{13}{36} & \frac{13}{36} \\
\frac{13}{48} & \frac{19}{48} & \frac{16}{48} \\
\frac{13}{48} & \frac{16}{48} & \frac{19}{48}
\end{pmatrix}
$$

Writing this matrix in the form

$$
\frac{1}{144}\begin{pmatrix}
40 & 52 & 52 \\
39 & 57 & 48 \\
39 & 48 & 57
\end{pmatrix}
\tag{5.2-2}
$$

we see immediately that the entries in the square of the transition matrix are less variable than were those of the original, (5.2-1). If we square this matrix (5.2-2), we get the matrix for predicting 4 days ahead. For this particular original transition matrix it is not hard to prove that the successive powers converge to a limiting matrix.

Do the successive transition matrices preserve the property that the sum of any row is exactly 1? To prove that they do, we have from the two general matrices P and P' the entries for the next one, P'':

$$p''_{i,j} = \sum_k p_{i,k} p'_{k,j}$$

where by hypotheses the row sums for both matrices are

$$\sum_k p_{i,k} = 1 \quad \text{and} \quad \sum_j p'_{k,j} = 1$$

We compute, therefore,

$$\sum_j p''_{i,j} = \sum_j \left(\sum_k p_{i,k} p'_{k,j} \right) = \sum_k \sum_j p_{i,k} p'_{k,j} = \sum_k p_{i,k} = 1$$

as required.

For the limiting matrix, what is the probability distribution of the states $a, b,$ and c? Clearly, we must have a distribution that does not change its probabilities when going to the next day; that is, we must have, for our particular matrix, (5.2-1),

$$(p_a, p_b, p_c) \begin{pmatrix} \frac{1}{3} & \frac{1}{3} & \frac{1}{3} \\ \frac{1}{4} & \frac{1}{2} & \frac{1}{4} \\ \frac{1}{4} & \frac{1}{4} & \frac{1}{2} \end{pmatrix} = (p_a, p_b, p_c)$$

This is equivalent to the three equations

$$\tfrac{1}{3}p_a + \tfrac{1}{4}p_b + \tfrac{1}{4}p_c = p_a$$
$$\tfrac{1}{3}p_a + \tfrac{1}{2}p_b + \tfrac{1}{4}p_c = p_b$$
$$\tfrac{1}{3}p_a + \tfrac{1}{4}p_b + \tfrac{1}{2}p_c = p_c$$

or

$$-\tfrac{2}{3}p_a + \tfrac{1}{4}p_b + \tfrac{1}{4}p_c = 0$$
$$\tfrac{1}{3}p_a - \tfrac{1}{2}p_b + \tfrac{1}{4}p_c = 0$$
$$\tfrac{1}{3}p_a + \tfrac{1}{4}p_b - \tfrac{1}{2}p_c = 0$$

Only two of these three equations are independent, so we solve the top two with the side condition,

$$p_a + p_b + p_c = 1$$

After some algebra we get for the *equilibrium solution*

$$p_a = \tfrac{3}{11} \qquad p_b = p_c = \tfrac{4}{11} \tag{5.2-3}$$

Thus, regardless of what state distribution we start with, for this transition matrix (5.2-1) we get the same equilibrium state distribution $(\tfrac{3}{11}, \tfrac{4}{11}, \tfrac{4}{11})$.

Exercises

5.2-1   Compute the fourth and eighth powers of the transition matrix (5.2-1) and compare the variabilities of all four matrices.

5.2-2   Using the square of the transition matrix (5.2-2), compute the equilibrium-state distribution.

5.3   ERGODIC MARKOV PROCESSES

The Markov process described above is called **ergodic**—from any state we can get to any other state, and in time the system settles down to a limiting distribution independent of the initial state. This does not mean that for the matrix above the weather in time becomes a mixture of fair, rain, and snow, but only that in the long run *our expectation* settles down to a probability mixture of the states. The long-term probabilities are independent of today's weather.

There are many other types of Markov processes. For example, Figure 5.3-1 shows a nonergodic graph. We see that once we leave state a, we will never get back there. Depending on which path we first take, we may go to the single ending state d, or end up going around three states g, h, and i. We do not expect that this kind of graph will be a good model of an information source, so we will set this type aside.

Even if we do end up in a set of states for which we can get from any one to any other, it does not mean that the probabilities settle down to a single number. Consider, for example, a checkerboard with the transitions being up or down, or left or right, but not diagonal. If we start on a red square, we will find that after an even number of transitions we are on a red

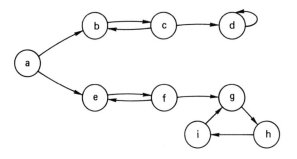

FIGURE 5.3-1   NONERGODIC GRAPH

square, but for an odd number of transitions we are on a black square. Thus there is an alternation of probabilities for each color of the current square. The theory of all possible Markov processes is therefore messy in principle, but the Markov processes we care about for information systems are ergodic and do not have these peculiarities. In the long run the message symbols settle down to fixed probabilities, although as noted above, not to a mixture of actual symbols but to a probability distribution. It is easy, for example, to understand the words "terminal state" and the words "a set of terminal states." And it is easy to see that if the terminal set is not all the states of the system, then the system is not ergodic in the sense that we can get from any one to any other. Furthermore, we must avoid any alternation of states. For any information source that we may have to encode we expect to have an ergodic source, although it is not completely impossible that other systems could occur. The complications, if they do arise, are not difficult to work out. We shall assume in the future that all our systems are ergodic.

Exercise

5.3-1   If the symbols are 0 and 1, draw a one-, two-, and a three-memory Markov diagram.

5.4   EFFICIENT CODING OF AN ERGODIC MARKOV PROCESS

It should be immediately evident that we can use the Markov structure of the source to improve the encoding of the source. For each state in the Markov system we can use the appropriate Huffman code obtained from the corresponding transition probabilities for leaving that state. Depending on how variable the probabilities are for each state, the encoding will gain a lot or not. However, as we increase the order of the Markov process, we tend to gain less and less while the number of states approaches infinity rapidly.

Let us do this Huffman encoding for the weather matrix of Section 5.2. For state a (today) we get (tomorrow) the binary encoding

$$a = 1 \qquad p_a = \tfrac{1}{3}$$
$$b = 00 \qquad p_b = \tfrac{1}{3} \qquad L_a = \tfrac{5}{3} = 1.6667\ldots$$
$$c = 01 \qquad p_c = \tfrac{1}{3}$$

For state b,

$$a = 10 \qquad p_a = \tfrac{1}{4}$$
$$b = 0 \qquad p_b = \tfrac{1}{2} \qquad L_b = \tfrac{3}{2} = 1.5$$
$$c = 11 \qquad p_c = \tfrac{1}{4}$$

For state c,

$$a = 10 \qquad p_a = \tfrac{1}{4}$$
$$b = 11 \qquad p_b = \tfrac{1}{4} \qquad L_c = \tfrac{3}{2} = 1.5$$
$$c = 0 \qquad p_c = \tfrac{1}{2}$$

At equilibrium we get [using the equilibrium probabilities (5.2-3)] the average code length

$$L_M = \tfrac{3}{11}L_a + \tfrac{4}{11}L_b + \tfrac{4}{11}L_c = \tfrac{17}{11} = 1.5454\ldots$$

On the other hand, let us code the average frequencies of the letters a, b, and c. The probabilities are clearly the equilibrium probabilities (5.2-3)

$$p_a = \tfrac{3}{11} \qquad p_b = \tfrac{4}{11} \qquad p_c = \tfrac{4}{11}$$

The code is

$$a = 01$$
$$b = 00$$
$$c = 1$$

We get, therefore,

$$L = \tfrac{3}{11}(2) + \tfrac{4}{11}(2) + \tfrac{4}{11}(1) = \tfrac{18}{11}$$

Thus the average code length L_M for the individual state encoding is less than the encoding L of the average frequencies

$$L_M = \tfrac{17}{11} < \tfrac{18}{11} = L$$

As we expect, the Markov-state system shortens the average code length.

Exercise

5.4-1 If the fair weather a has probabilities $p(a|a) = \tfrac{3}{4}$, $p(b|a) = p(c|a) = \tfrac{1}{8}$ and the others are the same as in this section, then show that $L_M = \tfrac{11}{8} < \tfrac{12}{8} = L$.

5.5 EXTENSIONS OF A MARKOV PROCESS

We have already (Section 4.2) defined an extension of a source. For example, the octal code is the third extension of the binary code. In a sense, an extension is simply a concatenation of the source symbols into longer symbols. We need to examine the extension of a Markov process.

Definition. If S is an mth-order Markov information source with alphabet $s_1, s_2, \ldots, s_q$, and if its transition probabilities from one of the q^m states to the next is given by the

$$p(s_i | s_{j_1}, s_{j_2}, \ldots, s_{j_m}) \tag{5.5-1}$$

then the nth extension of this source is labeled $S^n = T$ with q^n symbols t_1, $t_2, \ldots, t_{q^n}$. Each t is a sequence of n symbols from the alphabet of S. The system S^n is a kth-order Markov process where k is the first integer greater than or equal to m/n. Since each t_i corresponds to some sequence of n of the s_j, the conditional probabilities of T,

$$p(t_i | t_{j_1}, t_{j_2}, \ldots, t_{j_k}) \tag{5.5-2}$$

can be obtained from the original transitional probabilities of S by predicting one s_i at a time while looking back at m earlier symbols. Rewriting (5.5-2) we have for $(kn \geq m)$ and repeated applications of (5.5-1),

$$p(s_{i_1}, s_{i_2}, \ldots, s_{i_n} | s_{j_1}, s_{j_2}, \ldots, s_{j_m})$$
$$= p(s_{i_1} | s_{j_1}, s_{j_2}, \ldots, s_{j_m})p(s_{i_2} | s_{j_2}, s_{j_3}, \ldots, s_{j_m}, s_{i_1})$$
$$\cdot \ldots p(s_{i_n} | s_{i_{n-m}}, s_{i_{n-m+1}}, \ldots, s_{i_{n-1}})$$

This product assumes that $n > m$; if not, the last term would be

$$p(s_{i_n} | s_{j_n}, s_{j_{n+1}}, \ldots, s_{i_{n-1}})$$

Later we will need the results of this section.

5.6   PREDICTIVE RUN ENCODING

We have just shown how to use the transition probability structure of the messages to reduce the length of the encoded messages; the simple frequencies of the separate input symbols can be used to design a Huffman code, and the Markov process can handle the larger correlations. Besides these, there are many other possible structures of the input messages that could be used to shorten the encoded message, but they are far too numerous to investigate in detail in this text. Instead, we examine the general case; we *assume* that you have either a program, or else some hard-wired equipment, that can recognize the patterns to be used to predict the next symbol. For simplicity we assume a binary source. Using this program we will then encode the input stream of binary messages into a corresponding binary stream which has relatively long runs of 0's separated by comparatively few 1's. The better your ability to predict the next symbol, the longer will be the runs of 0's. A second stage of encoding, and where the code compression occurs, will send a stream of numbers, each number giving the length of the corresponding run of 0's, and the receiver will be able to reconstruct the original message using equipment almost exactly like the encoder.

5.7   THE PREDICTIVE ENCODER

Whatever the pattern of the input message that you can recognize and use to predict the next symbol, we assume that you have written a program to do this. You are merely required to predict the next symbol in the input stream. Your predictor can be a fixed one, or it can be "adaptive" in the sense that it can gather statistics about how well it does, and from them make modifications to itself. It can be linear or nonlinear—nothing is being said about how you do the predicting.

It is necessary to emphasize the generality of the program you are supposed to supply for your particular application. The method we are going to discuss makes the single assumption that the program predicts the next input symbol correctly most of the time. The better the predictions are, the more the input message is finally compressed.

As shown in Figure 5.7-1, there is a source S of input symbols s_i. In part (a) there is a predicting program in the square box labeled P which predicts from the stream of symbols s_i (for $i < n$) the next predicted symbol p_n. Assuming that both input and output are using the binary system of 0's and 1's, we *logically add* the two current symbols, input s_n and predicted p_n, to get the error e_n of the nth prediction. The output symbol e_n is a 0 whenever the prediction p_n is the same as the input symbol s_n, and a 1 when the prediction is wrong. The predictor P also gets the error messages e_n and is therefore in a position to correct itself and to know exactly the past message stream up to the next prediction.

As noted, if the predictor is fairly good, there will be a stream of 0's with an occasional 1 here and there. A random predictor would have half 0's and half 1's. Even a poor predictor would have many more 0's than 1's.

5.8 THE DECODER

At the receiving end (Figure 5.7-1c) there is a *decoder*, which is essentially the same as the predictor. Assuming that the box labeled P is identically the same as the box in the encoder, then if the two start out in the same state it follows that each will make the same predictions. When a 1 comes to the decoder in Figure 5.7-1c, it logically adds this error to its prediction and thus the correct output emerges. Again, the error message e_n is supplied to the predictor. The slight difference between the form of the information at the two ends requires only slight modification to the equipment; thus the two ends of the signaling system are essentially the same.

We need to model the situation in mathematical symbols so that we can evaluate how good it is. Let p be the probability of the predictor P being right for each symbol. (Note the reversal of the role of p; it is now the probability of being right.) We assume that the probability is a constant since otherwise there is a known structure which you should have incorporated into the predictor. For the same reason we *assume* that each prediction error is independent of the others. Your formula may, of course, be recursive; it is the

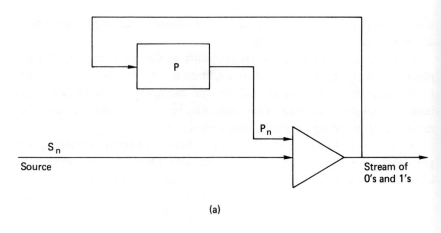

(a)

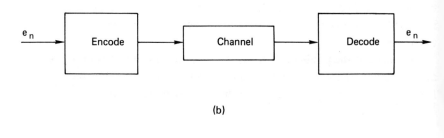

(b)

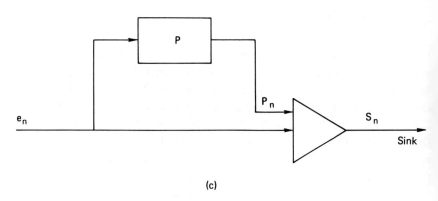

(c)

FIGURE 5.7-1   PREDICTIVE ENCODING

errors we are assuming are independent. Let $1 - p = q$ be the probability of guessing wrong. Naturally, we assume that $p \geq \frac{1}{2}$, since otherwise we would simply reverse the symbols p and q by complementing the predicted 0's and 1's and have a suitable p.

These probabilities are not to be confused with the errors in the equipment; they are associated with the predictor P. Because of the assumptions above about the predictor the output stream of 0's and 1's has a fixed probability of error and adjacent positions are independent. The errors are "white noise" (Section 2.4). A large p means a good encoder; a p near $\frac{1}{2}$ means that you are doing hardly better than guessing.

5.9 RUN LENGTHS

The probability $p(n)$ of a run of exactly n 0's is (since each run of 0's ends with a 1)

$$p(n) = p^n q \qquad (n = 0, 1, \ldots)$$

Summed over all lengths n, we have

$$\sum_{n=0} p^n q = q \sum_{n=0} p^n = \frac{q}{1-p} = \frac{q}{q} = 1$$

as it should be.

Suppose for the moment that we decide to send a k-digit binary number to represent a run length. For a reason we will soon see we can do this only for run lengths 0 to $2^k - 2$. At the receiving end the receiver copies down the indicated number of 0's and follows this by a 1. If the sent number is 0, we simply copy down a 1. For the binary number $(2^k - 1)$ the receiver copies down $(2^k - 1)$ 0's and does *not* copy down a 1. If the next number sent is 0, then of course a 1 is copied, and for any other number that number of 0's is copied followed by the 1. Thus we can send any length of a run of 0's we need to by sending a sufficient number of k-digit binary numbers.

We shall not attempt to use a Huffman coding system. In the original case we have a potentially infinite input alphabet, since in principle any run length could occur; after "blocking it" into runs at most k digits, we could, if we wished, use Huffman encoding.

Returning to the proposed method, what is the *expected* number of digits sent? To find out, we need to sum the probabilities of occurrence times the number sent in each case. Thus we construct the table

Length of Run	*Number of Digits Sent*
$0 \leq n \leq (2^k - 1) - 1$	k digits
$(2^k - 1) \leq n \leq 2(2^k - 1) - 1$	$2k$ digits
$2(2^k - 1) \leq n \leq 3(2^k - 1) - 1$	$3k$ digits

etc.

and the expected length is (setting $2^k - 1 = m$ and $p(n)$ as the probability of a run of exactly n 0's)

$$[p(0) + p(1) + \ldots + p(m - 1)]k$$
$$+ [p(m) + p(m + 1) + \ldots + p(2m - 1)]2k$$
$$+ [p(2m) + p(2m + 1) + \ldots + p(3m - 1)]3k$$
$$+ \ldots$$

Since

$$p(n) = p^n q$$

we get

$$q[1 + p + \ldots + p^{m-1}]k$$
$$+ qp^m[1 + p + \ldots + p^{m-1}]2k$$
$$+ qp^{2m}[1 + p + \ldots + p^{m-1}]3k$$
$$+ \ldots$$

Summing the terms in brackets, we arrange the expression in the form

$$q\left[\frac{1 - p^m}{q}\right][1 + 2p^m + 3p^{2m} + \ldots]k$$

TABLE 5.9-1   Table of $\dfrac{k}{1 - p^{2^k - 1}}$

					p			
k	0.5	0.6	0.7	0.8	0.9	0.95	0.98	0.99
1	2.00	2.50	3.33	5.00	10.0	20.0	50.0	100
2	2.29	2.55	3.04	4.10	7.38	14.0	34.0	67.3
3			3.27	3.80	5.75	9.94	22.7	44.2
4				4.15	5.04	7.45	15.3	28.6
5					5.20	6.28	10.7	18.7
6						6.25	8.33	12.8
7						7.01	7.58	9.71
8							8.05	8.67
9								9.05
10								

This sum is, in turn,

$$q\left[\frac{1 - p^m}{q}\right]\left[\frac{1}{(1 - p^m)^2}\right]k = \frac{k}{1 - p^m}$$

We need a short table (Table 5.9-1) of the function

$$\frac{k}{1 - p^{2^{k-1}}}$$

so that for a given $p \geq \frac{1}{2}$ we can pick the best k, Table 5.9-2.

TABLE 5.9-2   Table of Efficiency of Encoding

p	Optimum k	Expected Number of Digits	Expected Length of Runs	Compression Ratio
.5	1	2.00	2.00	1
.6	1	2.50	2.50	1
.7	2	3.04	3.33	0.91
.8	3	3.80	5.00	0.76
.9	4	5.04	10.00	0.50
.95	6	6.25	20.00	0.31
.98	7	7.58	50.00	0.16
.99	8	8.67	100.00	0.087

The expected length of runs is

$$\sum_{k=1}^{\infty} kp^k q = q\frac{1}{(1 - p)^2} = \frac{1}{1 - p}$$

From these tables we see that the efficiency of the run encoding depends on the choice of k, and for optimal design this in turn depends on p. Evidently, it is easy to select an appropriate k when p is given.

Exercise

5.9-1   Discuss the use of Huffman encoding of the run of zeros.

5.10   SUMMARY OF PREDICTIVE ENCODING

Because of the generality of this scheme of message compression, it is necessary to emphasize both that it does not do everything and that its efficiency depends completely on the predictor that is supplied. The better the predictor, the longer the runs of 0's and hence the compression at the second stage of encoding. The generality of the predictor is unlimited in theory, although in practice it must be simple enough so that it can keep up with the stream of the input alphabet. All it has to do is predict the next symbol in the input stream. How it does its job is not a part of the theory. If the encoding is to run in real time, then there are buffer-size problems, but on a computer problem this is not a vital point.

5.11 WHAT IS HASHING?

Hashing is a method of reducing the redundancy of an ensemble of m messages that have been selected from a much larger ensemble of M possible messages. It is, however, a reduction in a particular sense only.

To make matters specific, consider the ensemble of names of people, the names of variables in a FORTRAN program, or any other rich source of names. In any particular application, payroll, FORTRAN compilation, or other processing of the names, we expect to have only a very small sample of the ensemble of possible names. Suppose, to be definite, that we expect 500 names. We will assign 10 bits ($2^{10} = 1024$, which is more than twice 500). For each name we will take the first 10 bits, do a logical addition of the next 10 bits, the next 10, and continue to the end of the name (padding out the last 10 with 0's if necessary). This process generates a unique "hash" sum from a given name, but of course two different names could generate the same hash sum.

Given this original name, we place a pointer to the original name in a hash table at the computed 10-bit hash number location (perhaps with a constant added). As a result we have a table of pointers back to the original names, but the table allows direct location of an item by simply going indirectly via the hash table to the calculated location rather than by a search through the table of names to find the required name.

What is the probability of two different names leading to the same hash sum? If the hashed names were random, and that is what we are trying to do by the logical addition of each 10 bits, then there are approximately $\frac{1}{2}$ times 500^2 possible *collisions*. Like the famous birthday problem where 23 different people gives a probability of more than half of at least one duplicate birth date, the probability of at least one collision is very high. Yet the probability of any one name having a collision with any other name is less than $\frac{1}{2}$, since we have more than twice as many name locations in the table as there are names. Thus the typical name when hashed (encoded) into the 10 bits has less than half a chance of having a collision with any other name; still some collision in the full 500 names is highly probable. We must, therefore, allow for them.

5.12   HANDLING COLLISIONS

How shall we handle collisions? A simple method is to go to the calculated (hashed) place; if this is empty, we make the entry, but if it has an occupant, then we look down the table and insert the new entry in the first empty location that follows. This means that when we look for an entry at some later time we have to look not only at the computed place, but if the pointer there does not point back to the correct name, then we must continue looking at the consecutive nonempty places and checking if their pointers give the name until we come to either a match or else a blank. In the later case we know that there is no entry corresponding to the original name. If we want to make a new entry, as we would in a FORTRAN compilation, then we enter it in the empty location. In this way we can construct a table of hashed names.

Of course, if we knew all the names in advance, we could find a particular encoding that would avoid collisions. But if we either have to handle a growing table of names, or else do not want to spend the time to find a special encoding, then this approach, through what can be called "random encoding," is useful.

5.13   REMOVALS FROM THE TABLE

In some problems it may occasionally be necessary to remove a name from the file of names. This would not happen in a FORTRAN compilation, but it does happen in some applications. How can we do this? Evidently, we compute the address of the name's pointer and if it is there (or in some following location), we remove it. If there is an occupied cell following the removed one, then we must look to see if when it was entered it had been moved down, and if so we must move it back up. Indeed, we must examine *all* the successive entries until we come to a blank, to see how each should be placed. This is done most simply by constructing a pseudo file of names from the following adjacent pointers, and simply reentering them. In this fashion we can keep a file of computed names up to date.

5.14 SUMMARY OF HASHING

We see that given a collection of names that may individually be represented by very long (or possibly only occasionally very long) strings of characters, we have compressed them into a length that is slightly longer than minimum. The use of more than minimal redundancy decreases the frequency of collisions and the attendant waste of computer time, and it is an engineering decision as to how many more than the minimal number of bits to use. In our example we used one extra bit and had half the cells of our table empty. The use of two extra bits would greatly decrease the number of collisions, but would double the space of the table in storage.

We see that the random encoding is based on the number of entries expected but not on their detailed structure, and this allows the use of a greatly compressed table which can be used in a direct lookup fashion rather than a searching fashion. We have substituted computing power (the hashing algorithm) for searching, since we go directly to the computed address, and with at most some local fiddling around we find the entry, if the entry exists.

This random encoding is based on the idea that the hashing algorithm we used gives random encodings. Certainly, two names that differ by a single letter will still be separated. It will only be by chance that two fairly different names will collide. The hashing algorithm we used is a very simple one, and there is an extensive theory for how to design a hashing algorithm for various kinds of data, (Ref. [K]). The one we used is clearly fairly effective, but probably could be improved upon. We will not go into this point further.

We are exploiting the fact that random encoding produces a degree of uniformity from an unknown but structured source—it tends to spread out bunchings.

The main results we want to emphasize are two. First, this is a useful method of encoding data for some purposes; it reduces the redundancy without actually using the redundant structure of the messages (names). Second, this is an example of random encoding, a concept that we will need in Chapter 10.

5.15 THE PURPOSE OF THE GRAY CODE

Another important code is the Gray code. It is designed to meet a common need which is best described in terms of a particular application although it has wider uses. Suppose that we have a rotating analog wheel (see Figure 5.15-1) and have a number of brushes rubbing the wheel, each

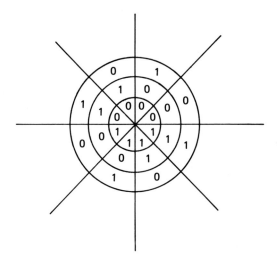

FIGURE 5.15-1   EIGHT-SECTOR BINARY WHEEL

on its own track. In order to record how far the wheel has rotated, the tracks are divided into sectors. For the typical binary system the number of sectors would be a power of 2, thus giving rise to a binary number of n digits. There are, of course, n racks, one for each digit (the figure has three racks).

If we use direct binary coding of the sectors, then when the wheel moved from, say the binary number 011 to the next binary number 100, each of the three brushes would find that its value changed. Suppose that we tried to read at the moment of changing sectors. We could expect any number to emerge from this attempt to read.

The Gray code is a method of encoding for which successive numbers change by only one position all around the wheel. Thus the attempt to read when the brushes are between two sectors can give only one of these two numbers.

5.16   DETAILS OF A GRAY CODE

We have just effectively defined a Gray code, but the definition does not give a unique code. In practice we use one simple version, usually known as *the Gray code.*

The definition of the Gray code is made inductively. For a one-digit code we have the two states, labeled as 0 and 1 (see Figure 5.16-1). Notice that in going around the circle we have also the transition from the 1 to the 0 that

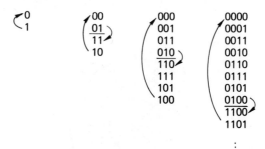

FIGURE 5.16-1 GRAY CODES

occurs in going from the bottom of the column to the top. Imagine these as a column. Below these two we write the symbols in reverse order, and attach to the first two a leading digit 0 and to the last two a leading digit 1. Examination shows that as we pass from the original set to the new set, we change only the leading digit from a 0 to a 1, the other digits being a copy. All the rest of the new symbols also change by one place only because they are the same as the original except in reverse order. The transition from the last to the first is a change in only the first (attached) digit. In the figure we show the process of going from one to two digits, from two to three digits, and part of going from three to four digits.

Exercise

5.16-1   Show that for a four-binary-digit code, there can be different codes with the basic property of changing only one digit in going to the next sector.

5.17   DECODING THE GRAY CODE

The numbers that come from the coding wheel of an analog device are typically in the Gray code, and we usually need them in the binary code if we are to process them in a computer. Reading from left to right we take all the 0's as being correct and also take the first 1. But the next position should be complemented. If this position is a zero, we continue complementing, but if it is a 1, we complement it and stop complementing until we pass another 1. Thus the number of earlier 1's we met controls whether we complement the next digit or not. We complement on an odd number of earlier 1's and do not complement on an even number of 1's. This simple rule, together with the general simplicity, makes the particular code the favorite solution to this problem of having only one digit change between successive numbers. The state diagram is easy to prepare.

Exercise

5.17-1   Make a state diagram for decoding the Gray code.

5.18   OTHER CODES

A topic of some interest is that of resynchronizing a decoding system if either a single symbol is lost or is added to the stream of digits coming into the receiver. In a Huffman code we could be in some trouble, but usually fairly soon the receiver will resynchronize. But how long it will take on the average is not a simple question, although it has been investigated in some studies. Evidently, in any particular case a Monte Carlo simulation of a code with errors can be run, and from the simulation suitable conclusions can be made. Within a computer these synchronization errors are not likely to occur—only a changed digit is likely.

One way of avoiding resynchronization problems is to use a parallel channel. Another way when using serial transmission is to embed the message in a longer block with synchronization pulses at both ends. This, of course, wastes capacity, but it does catch spurious pulses.

With the current low cost of accurate crystal clocks it is common practice to use clock pulses either from a single clock, or by keeping several clocks in synchronization, so that both the sender and the receiver have the same timing pulses.

The topic is not of enough general interest to do more than point out the problem and the obvious solutions.

Many other methods of code compression can be found in Ref. [DG].

6

Entropy and Shannon's First Theorem

6.1 INTRODUCTION

Up to this point we have been concerned with coding theory; now we begin information theory. Coding theory answers the questions of (1) how to design codes for white noise (mainly), and (2) how to compress the message when the probabilities (structure) of the messages are known.

We now need a general method for describing the structure of the source. To do this we need the concept of *entropy*. While entropy was used long ago in many physical situations, and the concept in information theory bears a strong resemblance to the classical definition, we shall study entropy on its own merits in this particular field and not get involved in the various suggestive analogies. For us, entropy is simply a function of a probability distribution p_i. For some analogies, see Refs. [Ga and Gu].

Information theory combines noise protection and efficiency of channel use into a single theory. However, the simple model of channel noise (white noise) is sometimes unrealistic, and we will occasionally treat more general patterns of errors. This leads to the important concept of *channel capacity*, which is taken up in Chapter 8.

The result we are headed for is Shannon's main theorem in Chapter 10, which gives a relationship between the channel capacity C (to be defined more accurately later) and the maximum rate of signaling possible. We will prove the remarkable theorem that we can come arbitrarily close to the maximum rate of signaling and also achieve an arbitrarily low rate of error. Unfortunately, the proof is not constructive, so that while information theory sets the bounds on what can be done, it does not tell us how to achieve them. Yet, as we said in Section 1.2, the theory is very useful.

In this chapter we prove a very special case of the main theorem, namely the *noiseless coding theorem*, where we ignore the problem of noise. When this theorem and its proof are understood, then the proof of the main theorem will appear a bit clearer—once a lot of preliminary results are gotten over in Chapter 9.

6.2 INFORMATION

Suppose that we have the source alphabet of q symbols $s_1, s_2, \ldots, s_q$, each with its probability $p(s_1) = p_1, p(s_2) = p_2, \ldots, p(s_q) = p_q$. When we receive one of these symbols, how much information do we get? For example, if $p_1 = 1$ (and of course all the other $p_i = 0$), then there is no "surprise," no information, since we know what the message must be. On the other hand, if the probabilities are all very different, then when a symbol with a low probability comes we would feel more surprised, get more information, than when a symbol with a higher probability came. Thus information is somewhat inversely related to the probability of occurrence.

We also feel that *surprise is additive*—the information from two different *independent* symbols is the sum of the information from each separately. Since the probabilities of two independent choices are multiplied together to get the probability of the compound event, it is natural to define the amount of information as

$$I(s_i) = \log_2 \frac{1}{p_i}$$

As a result, we have

$$I(s_1) + I(s_2) = \log_2 \frac{1}{p_1 p_2} = I(s_1, s_2)$$

This clearly exhibits the two probabilities as a product and the amount of information as a sum. Thus this definition fits many of our ideas about what information must be.

The words "uncertainty," "surprise," and "information" are related. Before the event (experiment, reception of a message symbol, etc.) there is the amount of uncertainty; when the event happens there is the amount of surprise; and after the event there is the gain in the amount of information. All these amounts are the same.

This is an engineering definition based on probabilities and is not a definition based on the meaning of the symbols to the human receiver. The confusion at this point has been very great for outsiders who glance at information theory; they fail to grasp that this is a highly technical definition that captures *only part* of the richness of the usual idea of information.

To see how far this definition differs from "common sense" consider the question: "What book contains the most information?" We, of course, have to standardize the question by stating the book, page, and type-font sizes, as well as the variety (alphabet) of type fonts to be used. Once this is done, the answer is clearly: "The book with the most information is the one with the type chosen completely and uniformly at random!" Each new symbol will come as a complete surprise. (See Section 6.4 for the justification for this statement.)

What base of the log system shall we use? It is simply a matter of convention, since any set of logs is proportional to any other set. This follows directly from the fundamental relationship

$$\log_a x = \frac{\log_b x}{\log_b a} = (\log_a b) \log_b x$$

It is convenient to use the base 2 logs; the resulting unit of information is called a *bit* (binary digit). If we use base e, as we must whenever we get into the calculus, then the unit of information is called a *nat*. Finally, sometimes the base 10 is used and the unit is called a *Hartley*, after R. V. L. Hartley, who first proposed the use of the logarithmic measure of information

We are using the word "bit" in two different ways, both as a digit in the number base 2, and as a unit of information. They are not the same, and we shall be careful to say "bit of information" when we mean that definition and there could be confusion.

It is easy to convert from one base to another since

$$\log_{10} 2 = 0.30103 \ldots \qquad \log_2 10 = 3.32193 \ldots$$

$$\log_{10} e = 0.43429 \ldots \qquad \log_e 10 = 2.30259 \ldots$$

$$\log_e 2 = 0.69315 \ldots \qquad \log_2 e = 1.44270 \ldots$$

6.3 ENTROPY

If we get $I(s_i)$ units of information when we receive the symbol s_i, how much do we get on the average? The answer is that since p_i is the probability of getting the information $I(s_i)$, then on the average we get for each symbol s_i,

$$p_i I(s_i) = p_i \log_2 \left(\frac{1}{p_i}\right)$$

From this it follows that on the average, over the whole alphabet of symbols s_i, we will get

$$\sum_{i=1}^{q} p_i \log_2 \left(\frac{1}{p_i}\right)$$

Following custom, we label this important quantity (for radix r)

$$\boxed{H_r(S) = \sum_{i=1}^{q} p_i \log_r \left(\frac{1}{p_i}\right)} \qquad (6.3\text{-}1)$$

and call it the *entropy* of the signaling system S having symbols s_i and probabilities p_i. Of course,

$$H_r(S) = H_2(S) \log_r 2$$

This is the entropy function for a distribution *when all that is considered are the probabilities p_i of the symbols s_i*. In Section 6.10 we will consider the entropy of a Markov process.

It is important to realize that a remark such as "Consider the entropy of the source" can have no meaning unless a model of the source is included. Again using random numbers as an example, we have formulas for generating *pseudo-random* numbers. Suppose that we had a table of such numbers. If we do not recognize that they are pseudo-random numbers, then we would probably compute the entropy based on the frequencies of occurrence of the individual numbers. Since pseudo-random number generators do a good job of simulating random numbers, we would also find that each new number came as a complete surprise to us. But if we knew the structure of the formula used to generate the table, we would, after a few numbers, be able to predict perfectly the next number—there would be no surprise. Our estimate of the entropy of the source of the symbols depends, therefore, on the model we adopt for it.

The entropy function (6.3-1) involves only the distribution of the probabilities—it is a function of a probability distribution p_i and does not involve the s_i. For example, if the probabilities are 0.4, 0.3, 0.2, and 0.1, then from the table of Appendix B, column 3, we have

p	$p \, log \, \dfrac{1}{p}$
0.4	0.52877
0.3	0.52109
0.2	0.46439
0.1	0.33219
Sum	1.84644

The entropy of this distribution is therefore 1.84644 (approximately). Although we should write the entropy function $H(p)$ as a function of p, we will continue to refer to the alphabet S and write $H(S)$, although occasionally we will write $H(p)$, when there are only two events.

The function of $p \log_2 (1/p)$ is graphed in Figure 6.3-1. From

$$\frac{d}{dp}\left(p \log_2 \frac{1}{p}\right) = \frac{d}{dp}\left(p \log_e \frac{1}{p}\right) \log_2 e$$

$$= \log_2 \frac{1}{p} - \log_2 e$$

We see both the infinite slope at $p = 0$ and that the maximum occurs at $p = 1/e$.

We also need the property

$$\lim_{x \to 0} (x \log_e x) = 0$$

To prove this, we write it as

$$\lim_{x \to 0} \left(\frac{\log_e x}{1/x}\right)$$

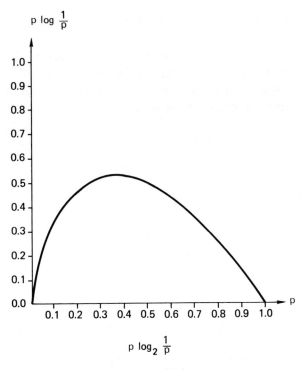

$$p \log \frac{1}{p}$$

$$p \log_2 \frac{1}{p}$$

FIGURE 6.3-1

and apply l'Hospital's rule by differentiating both numerator and denominator separately:

$$\lim_{x \to 0} \left(\frac{1/x}{-1/x^2} \right) = \lim_{x \to 0} (-x) = 0$$

As another example of the entropy of a distribution, consider the source alphabet $S = \{s_1, s_2, s_3, s_4\}$, where $p_1 = \frac{1}{2}$, $p_2 = \frac{1}{4}$, $p_3 = \frac{1}{8}$, and $p_4 = \frac{1}{8}$. With $r = 2$ we have the entropy

$$H_2(S) = \frac{1}{2} \log_2 2 + \frac{1}{4} \log_2 4 + \frac{1}{8} \log_2 8 + \frac{1}{8} \log_2 8$$

$$= (\tfrac{1}{2})1 + (\tfrac{1}{4})2 + (\tfrac{1}{8})3 + (\tfrac{1}{8})3$$

$$= 1\tfrac{3}{4} \text{ bits of information}$$

As one application of the idea of entropy, consider the toss of a coin when both sides are considered to be equally likely.

$$I(s_i) = \log_2 \left(\tfrac{1}{2}\right)^{-1} = \log_2 2 = 1$$

$$H_2(S) = \tfrac{1}{2}I(s_1) + \tfrac{1}{2}I(s_2) = 1$$

The distribution consisting of just two events is very common. If p is the probability of the first symbol (event), then the entropy function is

$$H_2(p) = p \log_2 \left(\frac{1}{p}\right) + (1-p) \log_2 \left(\frac{1}{1-p}\right)$$

and is tabulated in the last column of the table in Appendix B. The graph of this function is given Figure 6.3-2. Note that at $p = 0$ and $p = 1$ it has a vertical tangent, since

$$\frac{d}{dp}\left[p \log_2 \left(\frac{1}{p}\right) + (1-p) \log_2 \left(\frac{1}{1-p}\right)\right]$$

$$= \left[\log_e \left(\frac{1}{p}\right) - 1 - \log_e \left(\frac{1}{1-p}\right) + 1\right] \log_2 e$$

$$= \log_2 \left(\frac{1}{p}\right) - \log_2 \left(\frac{1}{1-p}\right)$$

Similarly, for the roll of a well-balanced die (singular of dice),

$$I(s_i) = \log_2(\tfrac{1}{6})^{-1} = \log_2 6$$

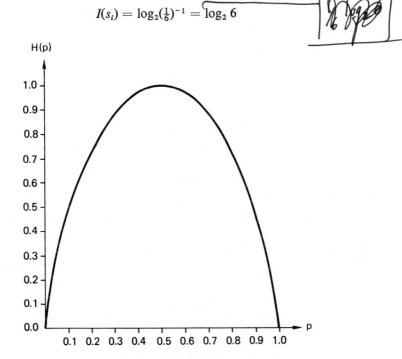

FIGURE 6.3-2   ENTROPY FUNCTION FOR TWO PROBABILITIES

and the entropy is

$$H(S) = 6[\tfrac{1}{6}I(s_i)] = \log_2 6$$
$$= 2.5849 \ldots \text{ bits of information}$$

As we see from this example, whenever all the probabilities are equal, the average over the alphabet is the same as the information for any one event.

The entropy function of a distribution summarizes one aspect of a distribution much as the *average* in statistics summarizes a distribution. The entropy has properties of both the arithmetic mean (the average) and the geometric mean.

Exercises

6.3-1   How many bits of information do we get from one draw of a card from a deck of 52 cards?

6.3-2   For $p_1 = \tfrac{1}{3}, p_2 = \tfrac{1}{4}, p_3 = \tfrac{1}{6}, p_4 = \tfrac{1}{9}, p_5 = \tfrac{1}{12}, p_6 = \tfrac{1}{18}$, compute the entropy.

Answer. $\tfrac{8}{9} + \tfrac{11}{12} \log 3 \simeq 2.34177$

6.4   MATHEMATICAL PROPERTIES OF THE ENTROPY FUNCTION

The entropy function measures the amount of uncertainty, surprise, or information we get from the outcome of some situation, say the reception of a message or the outcome of some experiment. It is therefore an important function of the probabilities of the individual events that can occur. Thus in designing an experiment we usually wish to maximize the amount of information we expect to get; we wish to maximize the entropy function. To do this we need to at least partially control the probabilities of the individual outcomes of the experiment; we need to "design the experiment" suitably. The maximum entropy is increasingly used as a criterion in many situations. Therefore, the entropy function is worth some study for its own sake, independent of the particular applications we will make of it.

The entropy function has a number of mathematical properties that are very useful, and we examine them before getting deeper into the theory. A first property of the $\log_e x$ function can be seen from Figure 6.4-1.

Fitting the tangent line at the point $(1, 0)$, we find that the slope is

$$\frac{d(\log_e x)}{dx}\bigg|_{x=1} = 1$$

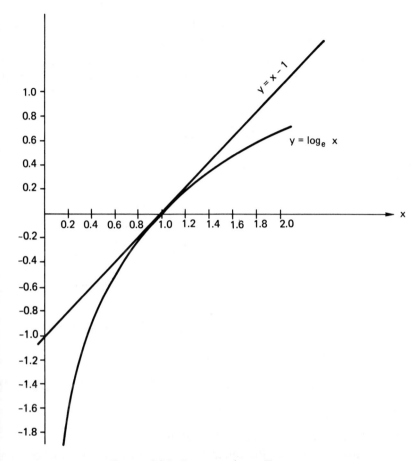

FIGURE 6.4-1   BOUND ON $\log_e x$ FUNCTION

so that the tangent line is

$$y - 0 = 1(x - 1)$$

or

$$y = x - 1$$

Thus we have for all x greater than zero the useful inequality

$$\boxed{\log_e x \leq x - 1} \qquad (6.4\text{-}1)$$

The equality holds *only* at the point $x = 1$.

The second result we need is the fundamental relationship between two probability distributions. Let the first probability distribution be x_i, with (of course) $\sum x_i = 1$, and the second probability distribution be y_i, correspondingly with $\sum y_i = 1$. Consider, now, the expression involving both distributions,

$$\sum_{i=1}^{q} x_i \log_2 \left(\frac{y_i}{x_i}\right) = \frac{1}{\log_e 2} \sum_{i=1}^{q} x_i \log_e \left(\frac{y_i}{x_i}\right)$$

Using the previous relation (6.4-1), we get

$$\frac{1}{\log_e 2} \sum_i x_i \log_e \left(\frac{y_i}{x_i}\right) \leq \frac{1}{\log_e 2} \sum_i x_i \left(\frac{y_i}{x_i} - 1\right)$$

$$\leq \frac{1}{\log_e 2} \sum_i (y_i - x_i)$$

$$\leq \frac{1}{\log_e 2} \left(\sum_i y_i - \sum_i x_i\right) = 0$$

Converting back to logs base 2, we have the *fundamental inequality*

$$\boxed{\sum_{i=1}^{q} x_i \log_2 \left(\frac{y_i}{x_i}\right) \leq 0} \qquad (6.4\text{-}2)$$

Note that the equality holds *only* when *all* the $x_i = y_i$.

It is natural to ask for the conditions on a probability distribution that lead to the maximum entropy (the minimum clearly occurs when one $p_i = 1$ and all the others $= 0$). We have

$$H_2(S) = \sum_i p_i \log_2 \frac{1}{p_i} \qquad \text{with } \sum_i p_i = 1$$

We begin by considering the quantity

$$H_2(S) - \log_2 q = \sum_{i=1}^{q} p_i \log_2 \left(\frac{1}{p_i}\right) - \log_2 q \sum_{i=1}^{q} p_i$$

$$= \sum_{i=1}^{q} p_i \log_2 \frac{1}{q p_i}$$

$$= \log_2 e \sum_{i=1}^{q} p_i \log_e \frac{1}{q p_i}$$

We apply our first inequality (6.4-1), to get

$$H_2(S) - \log_2 q \le \log_2 e \sum_{i=1}^{q} p_i \left(\frac{1}{qp_i} - 1 \right)$$

$$\le \log_2 e \left(\sum_{i=1}^{q} \frac{1}{q} - \sum_{i=1}^{q} p_i \right)$$

$$\le \log_2 e \, (1 - 1) = 0$$

Therefore,

$$\boxed{H_2(S) \le \log_2 q} \qquad (6.4\text{-}3)$$

For equality in (6.4-3) we must have all the $p_i = 1/q$.

For an alternative derivation of this important result, we use the Lagrange multipliers and consider the function

$$f(p_1, p_2, \ldots, p_q) = \frac{1}{\log_e 2} \sum_i p_i \log_e \left(\frac{1}{p_i} \right) + \lambda \left(\sum_i p_i - 1 \right)$$

$$\frac{\partial f}{\partial p_j} = \frac{1}{\log_e 2} \left[\log_e \left(\frac{1}{p_j} \right) - 1 \right] + \lambda = 0 \qquad (j = 1, 2, \ldots, q)$$

Since everything in this equation is a constant, it follows that each p_j is the same constant. If all the p_j are equal, each has the value $1/q$, where, as usual, the distribution has q members. Thus the maximum entropy is

$$H_2(S) = \log_2 q$$

For any other distribution than the equally likely distribution, the entropy is less than $\log_2 q$.

A simple, familiar application of this principle is given by the standard grading system of A, B, C, D, and F. Setting aside F as having special properties, namely that the student must take the course again, *if* we want to communicate the maximum amount of information with the grading system, then we should use all the other grades equally often. Of course, we may want to especially distinguish the very best, and give comparatively few A's. This is, however, giving a different meaning to information than the one we have defined. The common habit in graduate schools of giving only A's and B's is a plain waste of signaling capacity. The extreme of one probability being

1 and all the others therefore being 0 is the case of a constant signal. There is no information transmitted. "The constant complainer is soon ignored."

6.5   ENTROPY AND CODING

We now prove a fundamental relationship between the average code length L and the entropy $H(S)$. Given *any instantaneous code* it has some definite code word lengths l_i represented in some radix r. From the Kraft inequality (4.5-1), we have

$$K = \sum_{i=1}^{q} \frac{1}{r^{l_i}} \leq 1 \qquad (6.5\text{-}1)$$

We now define the numbers Q_i:

$$Q_i = \frac{r^{-l_i}}{K} \qquad (6.5\text{-}2)$$

where, of course,

$$\sum_{i=1}^{q} Q_i = 1$$

The Q_i may be regarded as a probability distribution. Therefore, we can use the fundamental inequality (6.4-2),

$$\sum_{i=1}^{q} p_i \log_2 \left(\frac{Q_i}{p_i} \right) \leq 0$$

Upon expanding the log term into a sum of logs, we notice that one term leads to the entropy function,

$$H_2(S) = \sum_{i=1}^{q} p_i \log_2 \left(\frac{1}{p_i} \right) \leq \sum_{i=1}^{q} p_i \log_2 \left(\frac{1}{Q_i} \right)$$

Using (6.5-2) in the right-hand side, we obtain

$$\leq \sum_{i=1}^{q} p_i \left(\log_2 K - \log_2 r^{-l_i} \right)$$

$$\leq \log_2 K + \sum_{i=1}^{q} p_i l_i \log_2 r$$

By the Kraft inequality $K \le 1$, so $\log_2 K \le 0$. Dropping this term can only strengthen the inequality. We have, therefore,

$$H_2(S) \le \sum_{i=1}^{q} (p_i l_i) \log_2 r = L \log_2 r$$

or

$$\boxed{H_r(S) \le L} \tag{6.5-3}$$

where L is the average code word length,

$$L = \sum_{i=1}^{q} p_i l_i \tag{6.5-4}$$

This is the fundamental result we need; the entropy supplies a lower bound on the average code length L for any instantaneous decodable system. By the McMillan inequality of Section 4.7, it also applies to any uniquely decodable system.

For efficient binary codes $K = 1$ and we have $\log_2 K = 0$. Therefore, the inequality occurs (in the binary case) only when

$$p_i \ne Q_i = 2^{-l_i}$$

6.6   SHANNON–FANO CODING

In Section 6.5 we assumed that the code word lengths l_i were given. Suppose, as is more likely, that the probabilities p_i are given. Huffman coding gives the lengths, but that method makes each length depend on the *whole* set of probabilities.

Shannon–Fano coding is less efficient than is Huffman coding, but has the advantage that you can go directly from the probability p_i to the code word length l_i. Given the source symbols $s_1, s_2, \dots, s_q$ and their corresponding probabilities $p_1, p_2, \dots, p_q$, then for each p_i there is an integer l_i such that

$$\log_r \left(\frac{1}{p_i}\right) \le l_i < \log_r \left(\frac{1}{p_i}\right) + 1 \tag{6.6-1}$$

Removing the logs we get

$$\frac{1}{p_i} \le r^{l_i} < \frac{r}{p_i}$$

Take the reciprocal of each term. We obtain

$$p_i \geq \frac{1}{r^{l_i}} > \frac{p_i}{r}$$

Since $\sum p_i = 1$, when we sum this inequality, we get

$$1 \geq \sum_{i=1}^{q} \left(\frac{1}{r^{l_i}}\right) > \frac{1}{r} \tag{6.6-2}$$

which gives the Kraft inequality. Therefore, there is an instantaneous decodable code having these lengths.

To get the entropy of the distribution of p_i we multiply equation (6.6-1) by p_i and sum:

$$H_r(S) = \sum_{i=1}^{q} p_i \log_r \left(\frac{1}{p_i}\right) \leq \sum_{i=1}^{q} p_i l_i \leq H_r(S) + 1$$

In terms of the average length L of the code (6.5-4), we have

$$\boxed{H_r(S) \leq L < H_r(S) + 1} \tag{6.6-3}$$

Thus for Shannon–Fano coding we again have the entropy as a lower bound on the average length of the code. It is also part of the upper bound. It is not as easy to directly find an upper bound for Huffman coding (Chapter 4), but since Huffman coding is optimal, it is at least as good as Shannon–Fano.

How do we find the actual code symbols? We simply assign them in order. For example, from the probabilities

$$p_1 = p_2 = \tfrac{1}{4} \qquad p_3 = p_4 = p_5 = p_6 = \tfrac{1}{8}$$

we get the Shannon–Fano lengths,

$$l_1 = l_2 = 2 \qquad l_3 = l_4 = l_5 = l_6 = 3$$

We then assign

$$\begin{aligned}
s_1 &= 00 & s_3 &= 100 \\
s_2 &= 01 & s_4 &= 101 \\
& & s_5 &= 110 \\
& & s_6 &= 111
\end{aligned}$$

We are assured by the Kraft inequality, which we showed Shannon–Fano coding obeys, that there are always enough symbols to assign for an instantaneous code. Our orderly assignment leads readily to the decoding tree.

This shows that we can do fairly well even with Shannon–Fano coding, but it is interesting to see how the left-hand inequality arises. First, if each probability p_i were exactly equal to the reciprocal of a power of the radix r, we would have equality for this assignment of code word lengths—the average word length would be exactly the entropy. To get the code words we simply assign $r$ary numbers in increasing sequence and of the required lengths.

6.7   HOW BAD IS SHANNON–FANO CODING?

Since Huffman coding is optimal, and we have temporarily descended to the less-than-optimal (at times) Shannon–Fano coding, it is reasonable to ask "How bad is Shannon–Fano coding?" Consider the following examples.

For a source alphabet s_1, s_2 with probabilities

$$p_1 = 1 - \frac{1}{2^k} \qquad p_2 = \frac{1}{2^k} \qquad (k \geq 2)$$

we get

$$\log_2 \left(\frac{1}{p_1} \right) \leq \log_2 2 = 1$$

Thus $l_1 = 1$. But for l_2, we have

$$\log_2 \left(\frac{1}{p_2} \right) = \log_2 2^k = k = l_2$$

Hence where the Huffman encoding gives both code words one binary digit, Shannon–Fano has s_1, a one-bit word, and s_2, a k-bit word.

Before getting too worried about this inefficiency, let us compute the average word length. Clearly, Huffman has

$$L_H = 1$$

For Shannon–Fano, we have

$$L_{SF} = 1\left(1 - \frac{1}{2^k}\right) + k\left(\frac{1}{2^k}\right)$$

$$= 1 + \frac{k-1}{2^k}$$

We have the table

k	$1 + \dfrac{k-1}{2^k}$
2	$1 + \frac{1}{4}\ = 1.25$
3	$1 + \frac{1}{4}\ = 1.25$
4	$1 + \frac{3}{16} = 1.1875$
5	$1 + \frac{1}{8}\ = 1.125$
6	$1 + \frac{5}{64} = 1.078125$
	etc.

As another example of the possible loss of efficiency, suppose that a the code symbols have the same probability, $1/q$. Shannon–Fano would have

$$\log_2 q \leq 1 < \log_2 q + 1$$

If q is not a power of 2, then Huffman would shorten some of the symbol but Shannon–Fano would not.

The loss in the average code length for using Shannon–Fano is not great and we shall later see it does not matter in the theory; only in practice doe Huffman dominate Shannon–Fano coding.

6.8   EXTENSIONS OF A CODE

We introduced the idea of entropy in a simple situation, namely *inde pendent* symbols s_i with fixed probabilities p_i of occurring. We need to develo the idea of entropy for both the extensions (Section 4.2) and the Marko processes (Sections 5.2 to 5.5) we studied earlier. This we do in Sections 6. and 6.10.

The loss in Shannon–Fano coding compared to Huffman, when measure by the entropy function, occurs when the reciprocals of the probabilities ar not exact powers of the radix r. If we encoded not one symbol at a time, bu made up a code for blocks of n symbols of the source code at a time, then w could hope to get a better approximation to the lower bound $H_r(S)$.

But more important, as we earlier noted (Section 4.10), the probabilite of the extension are more variable than the original probabilities; so w expect that the larger the extension, the more we will find that both Huffma and Shannon–Fano encoding are efficient. We first review the concept of the extension of a code.

Definition. The nth extension of a source alphabet $s_1, s_2, \ldots, s_q$ has symbols of the form $s_{i_1} s_{i_2} \ldots s_{i_n}$ having the probabilities $Q_i = p_{i_1} p_{i_2} \ldots p_{i_n}$. Each block of the n original symbols now becomes a single symbol t_i with probability Q_i. We label this alphabet $S^n = T$. We saw this definition in Sections 4.2 and 5.5, so it is not a new idea.

The entropy of this new system is easily calculated as follows:

$$H_r(S^n) = H_r(T) = \sum_{i=1}^{q^n} Q_i \log_r \left(\frac{1}{Q_i} \right)$$

$$= \sum_{i=1}^{q^n} Q_i \log_r \left(\frac{1}{p_{i_1} p_{i_2} \ldots p_{i_n}} \right)$$

Expand the log term as a sum of logs. We get

$$= \sum_{i=1}^{q^n} Q_i \sum_{k=1}^{n} \log_r \left(\frac{1}{p_{i_k}} \right)$$

$$= \sum_{k=1}^{n} \sum_{i=1}^{q^n} p_{i_1} p_{i_2} \ldots p_{i_n} \log_r \left(\frac{1}{p_{i_k}} \right)$$

For a typical single term that occurs in the summation over k, we have

$$\sum_{i=1}^{q^n} p_{i_1} p_{i_2} \ldots p_{i_n} \log_r \left(\frac{1}{p_{i_k}} \right) = \sum_{i_1=1}^{q} \sum_{i_2=1}^{q} \ldots \sum_{i_n=1}^{q} p_{i_1} p_{i_2} \ldots p_{i_n} \log_r \left(\frac{1}{p_{i_k}} \right)$$

For each summation *not* involving i_k the sum is 1 (since the sum of the probabilities must be 1). That leaves only the summation over i_k. But

$$\sum_{i_k=1}^{q} p_{i_k} \log_r \left(\frac{1}{p_{i_k}} \right) = H_r(S)$$

Hence the sum of all the terms, since they all have the same form, is

$$\boxed{H_r(T) = H_r(S^n) = n H_r(S)} \qquad (6.8\text{-}1)$$

The entropy of the nth extension of an alphabet is n times the entropy of the original alphabet. But note also that it has q^n symbols.

We can now apply the result (6.6-3) to the extension T. We have (where L_n is the average code length of the nth extension)

$$H_r(S^n) \leq L_n < H_r(S^n) + 1$$

Apply (6.8-1) and divide by n:

$$H_r(S) \leq \frac{L_n}{n} < H_r(S) + \frac{1}{n} \qquad (6.8\text{-}2)$$

Since the extension has n symbols s_{i_k} in each t_i, it follows that a better measure is $L = L_n/n$. Thus for a sufficiently large nth extension of the code, we can bring the average code word length L as close as we please to the entropy $H_r(S)$. This is Shannon's *noiseless coding theorem*: *The nth extension of a code satisfies* (6.8-2).

6.9   EXAMPLES OF EXTENSIONS

Suppose that the source alphabet is s_1, s_2 with $p_1 = \frac{2}{3}, p_2 = \frac{1}{3}$. The entropy is

$$
\begin{aligned}
H_2(S) &= \tfrac{2}{3} \log_2 \tfrac{3}{2} + \tfrac{1}{3} \log_2 3 \\
&= \log_2 3 - \tfrac{2}{3} = 1.5849\ldots - 0.6666\ldots \\
&= 0.9182958\ldots
\end{aligned}
$$

Huffman coding gives

$$s_1 = 0 \qquad s_2 = 1$$

so the average length of the code is 1. Shannon–Fano would give

$$l_1 = 1 \qquad l_2 = 2$$

and the average length is

$$(\tfrac{2}{3})1 + (\tfrac{1}{3})2 = \tfrac{4}{3} = 1 + \tfrac{1}{3}$$

In Section 4.10 we gave the average Huffman code lengths for several extensions. For Shannon–Fano we get, for the second extension,

$$\log_2 \tfrac{9}{4} \leq l_1 \qquad l_1 = 2$$

$$\log_2 \tfrac{9}{2} \leq l_2 \qquad l_2 = 3$$

$$\log_2 \tfrac{9}{2} \leq l_3 \qquad l_3 = 3$$

$$\log_2 \tfrac{9}{1} \leq l_4 \qquad l_4 = 4$$

The average code length is

$$L_{SF} = (\tfrac{4}{9})2 + (\tfrac{2}{9})(3)(2) + (\tfrac{1}{9})4$$

$$= \frac{8 + 12 + 4}{9} = \frac{24}{9} = 2.666\ldots$$

It happens that for this case we can compute the extensions for Shannon–Fano coding. In the nth extension there will be

Number of Terms	Probability
$C(n, 0)$	$2^n/3^n$
$C(n, 1)$	$2^{n-1}/3^n$
$\cdot$	$\cdot$
$\cdot$	$\cdot$
$\cdot$	$\cdot$
$C(n, i)$	$2^{n-i}/3^n$
$\cdot$	$\cdot$
$\cdot$	$\cdot$
$C(n, n)$	$1/3^n$

To find the corresponding l_i, we have

$$\log_2\left(\frac{1}{p_i}\right) = \log_2\left(\frac{3^n}{2^{n-i}}\right) = n\log_2 3 - (n - i) \qquad (6.9\text{-}1)$$

$$= n(\log_2 3 - 1) + i \leq l_i \qquad (i = 1, 2, \ldots, n)$$

Let

$$A_n = \text{first integer} \geq n(\log_2 3 - 1) \qquad (6.9\text{-}2)$$

Then the average code word length is

$$L_{\text{SF}}(n) = \frac{1}{3^n} \sum_{i=0}^{n} C(n, i) 2^{n-i} (A_n + i)$$

$$= \frac{1}{3^n} \left[A_n \sum_{i=0}^{n} C(n, i) 2^{n-i} + \sum_{i=0}^{n} [n - (n - i)] C(n, i) 2^{n-i} \right]$$

But we know the binomial expansion of $(1 + x)^n$ by definition can be written in either form,

$$(1 + x)^n = \sum_{i=0}^{n} C(n, i) x^i = \sum_{i=0}^{n} C(n, i) x^{n-i} \tag{6.9-3}$$

Differentiating this second form and then multiplying by x, we have

$$n(1 + x)^{n-1} x = \sum_{i=0}^{n} C(n, i)(n - i) x^{n-i} \tag{6.9-4}$$

Putting $x = 2$ in (6.9-3) and (6.9-4), we get

$$3^n = \sum_{i=0}^{n} C(n, i) 2^{n-i}$$

and

$$\left(\frac{2n}{3}\right) 3^n = \sum_{i=0}^{n} C(n, i)(n - i) 2^{n-i}$$

We have, therefore,

$$L_{\text{SF}}(n) = \frac{1}{3^n} \left(A_n 3^n + n3^n - \frac{2n}{3} 3^n \right)$$

$$= A_n + \frac{n}{3}$$

where, from (6.9-2),

$$A_n \geq n(\log_2 3 - 1) = n(0.5849625 \ldots)$$

We compute a short table of A_n and include in the last column of the table the results for Huffman coding:

n	n(log_2 3 - 1)	A_n	$L_{SF}(n)/n$	$L_H(n)/n$
1	0.5849...	1	1.33333...	1.00000
2	1.1699...	2	1.33333...	0.94444...
3	1.7549...	2	1.00000...	0.93827...
4	2.3398...	3	1.08333...	0.93827...
5	2.9248...	3	0.93333...	0.92263...
6	3.5098...	4	1.00000...	
7	4.0947...	5	1.04762...	
8	4.6797...	5	0.95833...	
9	5.2646...	6	1.00000...	
10	5.8496...	6	0.93333...	

From (6.5-3) the lower bound is $H(S) = 0.91829$ .... Shannon–Fano coding approaches the entropy irregularly, but according to the earlier result (Section 6.8), it does approach it finally.

Summarizing our discussion up to this point:

1. From equation (6.5-3), for any instantaneous code the Kraft inequality shows that

$$H_2(S) \leq L \log_2 r$$

2. Equation (6.6-3) shows that

$$H_2(S) \leq L_{SF} \log_2 r < H_2(S) + \log_2 r$$

3. In Section 4.10, since Huffman coding is optimal,

$$L_H \log_2 r \leq L_{SF} \log_2 r$$

4. In equation (6.8-2) the nth extension satisfies

$$H_2(S) \leq \frac{L \log_2 r}{n} \leq H_2(S) + \frac{\log_2 r}{n}$$

Assembling all this we get for the nth extension,

$$H_2(S) \leq \frac{L_H(n) \log_2 r}{n} \leq \frac{L_{SF}(n) \log_2 r}{n} < H_2(S) + \frac{\log_2 r}{n}$$

where $L_H(n)$ is the average code length for the nth extension for Huffman and $L_{SF}(n)$ is for Shannon–Fano. The table bears this out experimentally. This running inequality shows clearly why in Section 6.7 we are justified in saying that the theoretical loss in going to Shannon–Fano coding instead of the optimal Huffman coding was not serious *for large n*. For small n the practical loss may be significant.

6.10   ENTROPY OF A MARKOV PROCESS

In Section 5.2 we introduced the idea of a Markov process to enable us to represent certain types of structure in the input stream of data. In particular, it handles correlations between successive symbols. We now examine the entropy of a Markov process.

Given that we have already seen the previous m symbols,

$$s_{i_1}, s_{i_2}, \ldots, s_{i_m}$$

what is the probability that the next symbol will be s_i? In mathematical symbols this conditional probability is written

$$p(s_i \mid s_{i_1}, s_{i_2}, \ldots, s_{i_m})$$

Note again that the sequence of the symbols is

$$s_{i_1}, s_{i_2}, \ldots, s_{i_m}, s_i$$

For the zeroth-order Markov process the probabilities depend only on the symbol s_i, and are written in the earlier notation as p_i. For the first-order Markov source we have the digraph frequencies of pairs of symbols of the alphabet.

Using our "surprise" definition for the amount of information we get when we receive a symbol s_i, we define the information as

$$I(s_i \mid s_{i_1}, s_{i_2}, \ldots, s_{i_m}) = \log_2 \left[\frac{1}{p(s_i \mid s_{i_1}, s_{i_2}, \ldots, s_{i_m})} \right]$$

given that we have already seen (are in the state)

$$s_{i_1}, s_{i_2}, \ldots, s_{i_m}$$

The *conditional entropy* over the alphabet S of symbols s_i is naturally given by the expression

$$H(S \,|\, s_{i_1}, s_{i_2}, \ldots, s_{i_m}) = \sum_S p(s_i \,|\, s_{i_1}, s_{i_2}, \ldots, s_{i_m}) \log_2 \left[\frac{1}{p(s_i \,|\, s_{i_1}, s_{i_2}, \ldots, s_{i_m})} \right]$$

This is the conditional entropy of the source alphabet S *given* that we have the sequence of symbols

$$s_{i_1}, s_{i_2}, \ldots, s_{i_m}$$

We next consider the larger system and allow for the probability of the states of the Markov process occurring. Let

$$p(s_{i_1}, s_{i_2}, \ldots, s_{i_m})$$

be the probability of being in the state

$$s_{i_1}, s_{i_2}, \ldots, s_{i_m}$$

Then it is natural to define the entropy of the Markov system as the probabilities of being in a state times the conditional entropies of the states, that is, by the expression

$$H(S) = \sum_{S^m} p(s_{i_1}, s_{i_2}, \ldots, s_{i_m}) H(S \,|\, s_{i_1}, s_{i_2}, \ldots, s_{i_m})$$

Using our earlier definition of the conditional entropy, we get

$$H(S) = \sum_{S^m} \sum_S p(s_{i_1}, s_{i_2}, \ldots s_{i_m}) p(s_i \,|\, s_{i_1}, s_{i_2}, \ldots, s_{i_m}) \log_2 \left[\frac{1}{p(s_i \,|\, s_{i_1}, s_{i_2}, \ldots, s_{i_m})} \right]$$

But since

$$p(s_{i_1}, s_{i_2}, \ldots, s_{i_m}) p(s_i \,|\, s_{i_1}, s_{i_2}, \ldots, s_{i_m}) = p(s_{i_1}, s_{i_2}, \ldots, s_{i_m} s_i)$$

we have the entropy of the Markov process as

$$H(S) = \sum_{S^{m+1}} p(s_{i_1}, s_{i_2}, \ldots, s_{i_m}, s_i) \log_2 \left[\frac{1}{p(s_i \,|\, s_{i_1}, s_{i_2}, \ldots, s_{i_m})} \right]$$

6.11 AN EXAMPLE OF A MARKOV PROCESS

As an example, consider the Markov process (in a binary alphabet) shown in Figure 6.11-1. In symbols the second-order Markov process is defined by

$$p(0 \mid 0, 0) = 0.8 = p(1 \mid 1, 1)$$
$$p(1 \mid 0, 0) = 0.2 = p(0 \mid 1, 1)$$
$$p(0 \mid 0, 1) = 0.5 = p(1 \mid 1, 0)$$
$$p(1 \mid 0, 1) = 0.5 = p(0 \mid 1, 0)$$

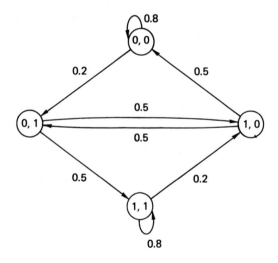

FIGURE 6.11-1 MARKOV PROCESS

What are the probabilities of being in the particular states 0,0; 0,1; 1,0; and 1,1? Using the obvious symmetry, we see that

$$p(0, 0) = p(1, 1) \quad \text{and} \quad p(0, 1) = p(1, 0)$$

Therefore, we must have the equations

$$p(0, 0) = 0.5p(0, 1) + 0.8p(0, 0)$$
$$p(0, 1) = 0.2p(0, 0) + 0.5p(0, 1)$$

These equations both come to the same form:

$$0.2p(0, 0) - 0.5p(0, 1) = 0 \tag{6.11-1}$$

Since we must be some place, we also have

$$p(0, 0) + p(0, 1) + p(1, 0) + p(1, 1) = 1$$

or

$$2p(0, 0) + 2p(0, 1) = 1 \qquad (6.11\text{-}2)$$

The solution of (6.11-1) and (6.11-2) is

$$p(0, 0) = \tfrac{5}{14} = p(1, 1)$$
$$p(0, 1) = \tfrac{2}{14} = p(1, 0)$$

These are the *equilibrium probabilities* of the ergodic process.

In the general case, these equilibrium probabilities can be computed in principle, but in practice they are often hard to find. Continuing with the example, we now have the table for the equilibrium state

s_{i_1}, s_{i_2}, s_i	$p(s_i \mid s_{i_1}, s_{i_2})$	$p(s_{i_1}, s_{i_2})$	$p(s_{i_1}, s_{i_2}, s_i)$
0 0 0	0.8	$\tfrac{5}{14}$	$\tfrac{4}{14}$
0 0 1	0.2	$\tfrac{5}{14}$	$\tfrac{1}{14}$
0 1 0	0.5	$\tfrac{2}{14}$	$\tfrac{1}{14}$
0 1 1	0.5	$\tfrac{2}{14}$	$\tfrac{1}{14}$
1 0 0	0.5	$\tfrac{2}{14}$	$\tfrac{1}{14}$
1 0 1	0.5	$\tfrac{2}{14}$	$\tfrac{1}{14}$
1 1 0	0.2	$\tfrac{5}{14}$	$\tfrac{1}{14}$
1 1 1	0.8	$\tfrac{5}{14}$	$\tfrac{4}{14}$

From the table we can now compute

$$H(S) = \sum_{2^3} p(s_{i_1}, s_{i_2}, s_i) \log_2 \left[\frac{1}{p(s_i \mid s_{i_1}, s_{i_2})} \right]$$

$$= 2\left[\frac{4}{14} \log_2 \left(\frac{1}{0.8} \right) \right] + 2\left[\frac{1}{14} \log_2 \left(\frac{1}{0.2} \right) \right] + 4\left[\frac{1}{14} \log_2 \left(\frac{1}{0.5} \right) \right]$$

$$= \frac{4}{7}(\log_2 10 - 3) + \frac{1}{7}(\log_2 10 - 1) + \frac{2}{7}(\log_2 2)$$

$$= 0.801377 \ldots \text{ bits per binary digit}$$

6.12 THE ADJOINT SYSTEM

To find the entropy of the Markov source, we need to find the stationary probabilities of being in each state of the Markov process. But as noted before, they are often very hard to find. Therefore, we need some method of bounding the entropy. This method, which we will now develop, is based on the concept of an adjoint system.

How can we find a bound on the entropy of a Markov process? We will use a first-order Markov process for simplicity; nothing except the notation differs for the nth-order system.

Since we have found that the fundamental inequality for two distributions is our basic tool, we write it down for the distributions we know, namely $p(s_i)$, $p(s_j)$, and $p(s_j, s_i)$. The symbol $p(s_j, s_i)$ is the probability of the pair of symbols, and is also $p(s_i, s_j)$. We have, already,

$$\sum_j p(s_j, s_i) = p(s_i) = p_i$$

and

$$\sum_i p(s_j, s_i) = p(s_j) = p_j \qquad .$$

Thus we start with, using (6.4-2),

$$\sum_{S^2} p(s_j, s_i) \log_2 \left[\frac{p(s_i)p(s_j)}{p(s_j, s_i)} \right] \leq 0$$

The equality occurs only when for all i and j we have the equalities $p(s_j, s_i) = p(s_i)p(s_j)$. We now use the conditional probability expression

$$p(s_j, s_i) = p(s_i \mid s_j)p(s_j)$$

to get

$$\sum_{S^2} p(s_j, s_i) \log_2 \left[\frac{p(s_i)}{p(s_i \mid s_j)} \right] \leq 0$$

or expanding the log term and transposing, we get

$$\sum_{S^2} p(s_j, s_i) \log_2 \left[\frac{1}{p(s_i \mid s_j)} \right] \leq \sum_i \sum_j p(s_j, s_i) \log_2 \left[\frac{1}{p(s_i)} \right]$$

Therefore, again using the conditional probability,

$$\sum_j p(s_j) \sum_i p(s_i \mid s_j) \log_2 \left[\frac{1}{p(s_i \mid s_j)}\right] \leq \sum_i p(s_i) \log_2 \left[\frac{1}{p(s_i)}\right]$$

$$\leq H(\bar{S})$$

where $H(\bar{S})$ is the entropy of the original symbols, which we will call the *adjoint system*. We can therefore write

$$\sum_j p(s_j) H(S \mid s_j) \leq H(\bar{S})$$

and the entropy of the Markov process is bounded by the entropy of the adjoint system, which is the zero memory source with probabilities of the source alphabet $p(s_i) = p_i$.

The equality holds only if $p(s_j, s_i) = p_j p_i$. Thus we have proved the result that the constraints can only lower the entropy.

The entropy of an extension of a Markov process is easily found from our earlier entropy calculations of a Markov source and of an extension. Again we consider, for the sake of simple notation, only a first-order Markov chain. We have

$$H(S^n) = \sum_{S^n} \sum_{S^n} p(t_j, t_i) \log_2 \left[\frac{1}{p(t_i \mid t_j)}\right]$$

$$= \sum_{S^{2n}} p(t_j, t_i) \log_2 \left[\frac{1}{p(t_i \mid t_j)}\right]$$

But it is a first order process, hence

$$p(t_j \mid t_i) = p(s_{i_1}, s_{i_2}, \dots, s_{i_n} \mid s_{j_n})$$

We now apply the original conditional probabilities *repeatedly* to get

$$p(t_j, t_i) = p(s_{i_1} \mid s_{j_n}) p(s_{i_2} \mid s_{i_1}) \dots p(s_{i_n} \mid s_{i_{n-1}})$$

$$H(S^n) = \sum_{S^n} p(t_j, t_i) \log_2 \left[\frac{1}{p(s_i \mid s_j)}\right] + \dots$$

$$+ \sum_{S^{2n}} p(t_j, t_i) \log_2 \left[\frac{1}{p(s_{i_n} \mid s_{i_{n-1}})}\right]$$

Each term may be reduced by summing over all the symbols not in the log term

$$\sum_{S^{2n}} p(t_j, t_i) \log_2 \left[\frac{1}{p(s_{i_1} | s_{i_2})} \right] = \sum_{S^2} p(s_j, s_i) \log_2 \left[\frac{1}{p(s_i | s_j)} \right]$$
$$= H(\bar{S})$$

Therefore,

$$H(S^n) = nH(\bar{S})$$

as we expect.

6.13 SUMMARY

We have introduced the concept of entropy and have applied it to various sources of information to obtain bounds on what can be done by suitable encoding of the source. Entropy, which measures uncertainty, surprise, and information, is clearly the natural mathematical tool to use in such situations. In practice, entropy has uses far beyond this limited area of application, but we cannot go into them here.

Shannon's *noiseless* coding theorem shows that by using a suitably large extension of the source, the average length of the encoded message can be brought as close to the entropy of the source as desired. We demonstrated this both for a simple source and for the more complicated Markov source. However, we have not done it for all possible types of sources. The noiseless theorem is a forerunner of Shannon's main result that even in the presence of noise (errors), we can find a suitable encoding system. This we will prove in Chapter 10.

7

The Channel
and Mutual Information

7.1 INTRODUCTION

Let us review where we are. We are concerned with sending information either from here to there (transmission), or from now to then (storage). As shown in Figure 7.1-1, we start with a source of information (symbols) on the left and encode it in some fashion such as discussed in Chapters 2 through 5. It is then sent through a channel. In actual practice the channel is noisy, in the sense that the output is not always the same as the input. Next, the message is decoded, and finally the decoded message is sent on to its destination.

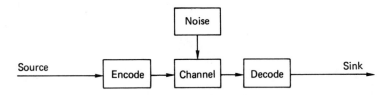

FIGURE 7.1-1 SIGNALING MODEL

It is time to look more closely at the channel. We will use as the major tool the concept of entropy developed in Chapter 6. How much information actually gets through the channel? How shall we measure the *mutual information* of the two ends of the system? How shall we define the *capacity* of the channel? These are the questions we examine in this and the next chapter.

Furthermore, we must learn to look at the system from the receiving end, where the decisions are to be made, instead of looking at the front end and following what happens to the signal as it goes through the system.

7.2 THE INFORMATION CHANNEL

An information channel is a statistical model of the medium through which the signal passes (or in which it is stored). In practice there are physical limitations on the fidelity with which the transmission can occur. We need to formalize this idea in order to compute how much information goes through a given channel.

Figure 7.2-1 illustrates what we mean by a channel. A channel is described by a set of conditional probabilities $P(b_j \mid a_i)$, which are the probabilities that an input a_i from an alphabet of q letters will appear as some b_j from an alphabet of s letters. We use a capital P for the channel probabilities. The sizes of q and s of the alphabets need not be the same. For example, in an error-correcting code, the alphabet of possible received symbols is much larger than is the alphabet of sent symbols; thus $s \geq q$. On the other hand, a channel may always emit the same symbol when either of two different input symbols are sent, so $s \leq q$.

In this model the channel is completely described by the matrix of conditional probabilities

$$(P_{i,j}) = \big(P(b_j \mid a_i)\big)$$

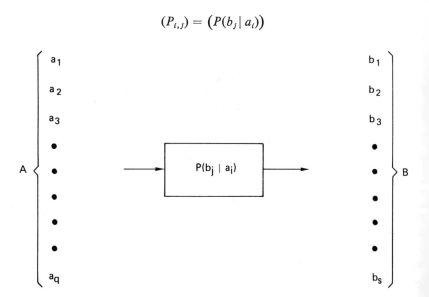

FIGURE 7.2-1 CHANNEL

Note the customary reversal of the subscripts. A row contains all the probabilities that a particular input symbol a_i becomes the output symbol b_j. This matrix appears in Figure 7.2-1.

The channel transition matrix has the following properties:

1. The ith row corresponds to the ith input symbol, a_i.
2. The jth column corresponds to the jth output symbol, b_j.
3. The sum of the elements in a row is always 1; that is,

$$\sum_{j=1}^{s} P_{i,j} = \sum_{j=1}^{s} P(b_j \mid a_i) = 1$$

This merely means that for each input a_i we are certain that something will come out, and that the $P(b_j \mid a_i)$ give the distribution of these probabilities.

4. If $p(a_i)$ is the probability of the input symbol a_i of occurring, then

$$\sum_{i=1}^{q} \sum_{j=1}^{s} P(b_j \mid a_i) p(a_i) = 1$$

This means that when something is put into the system, then certainly something comes out.

The probabilities $P_{i,j}$ characterize the channel completely. We are, of course, supposing that the channel is *stationary*, meaning that the probabilities do not change with time, and for the moment we are supposing that the errors that do occur are independent of each other.

7.3   THE CHANNEL RELATIONSHIPS

In the transmission system the input symbols are selected with probabilities $p(a_i)$ and consequently the received symbols b_j will have some corresponding probabilities of occurring $p(b_j)$. (This notation is clear, although it does not satisfy the strict canons of mathematics.) The two sets of probabilities $p(a_i)$ and $p(b_j)$ are related by the following channel equations:

$$
\begin{aligned}
p(a_1)P_{1,1} + p(a_2)P_{2,1} + \ldots + p(a_q)P_{q,1} &= p(b_1) \\
p(a_1)P_{1,2} + p(a_2)P_{2,2} + \ldots + p(a_q)P_{q,2} &= p(b_2) \\
&\ \ \vdots \\
p(a_1)P_{1,s} + p(a_2)P_{2,s} + \ldots + p(a_q)P_{q,s} &= p(b_s)
\end{aligned}
\tag{7.3-1}
$$

or in compressed notation,

$$\sum_{i=1}^{q} p(a_i)P(b_j \mid a_i) = p(b_j) \qquad (j = 1, 2, \dots, s)$$

We write the probability of a pair of symbols a_i and b_j occurring as $P(a_i, b_j)$. This has the same meaning as $P(b_j, a_i)$. We can write this probability in two ways, either as

$$P(a_i, b_j) = p(a_i)P(b_j \mid a_i)$$

or else as

$$P(a_i, b_j) = p(b_j)P(a_i \mid b_j)$$

Equating these two forms of the same thing, we get

$$P(a_i \mid b_j) = \frac{P(b_j \mid a_i)p(a_i)}{p(b_j)} \qquad (7.3\text{-}2)$$

This is known as *Bayes' theorem* on conditional probabilities. It is clearly symmetric in the two sets of symbols. The $P(b_j \mid a_i)$ are known as the *forward conditional probabilities*, since they start at the front with the a_i given and express the probabilities of occurrence of the b_j. The $P(a_i \mid b_j)$ are correspondingly known as the *backward conditional probabilities*; given the output, what symbol probably caused it?

In the Bayes' formula (7.3-2) we may use the channel relationships (7.3-1) for the $p(b_j)$ and put them in the denominator to get the equivalent expression,

$$P(a_i \mid b_j) = \frac{P(b_j \mid a_i)p(a_i)}{\sum_{i=1}^{q} P(b_j \mid a_i)p(a_i)} \qquad (7.3\text{-}3)$$

Summing this over all the a_i clearly gives

$$\sum_{i=1}^{q} P(a_i \mid b_j) = 1$$

which means, given output b_j, some a_i was certainly put into the channel.

7.4 THE EXAMPLE OF THE BINARY SYMMETRIC CHANNEL

A binary channel is probably the single most useful model of a channel. It has two input symbols, 0 and 1, and two output symbols, 0 and 1. Figure 7.4-1 illustrates this channel. The binary channel is said to be *symmetric* if

$$P_{0,0} = P_{1,1} \qquad P_{1,0} = P_{0,1}$$

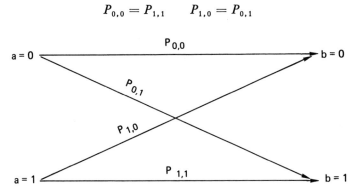

FIGURE 7.4-1   BINARY SYMMETRIC CHANNEL

Let the probabilities of the input symbols be (lowercase letters)

$$p(a = 0) = p$$
$$p(a = 1) = 1 - p$$

Next, let the binary symmetric channel probabilities be (uppercase letters)

$$P_{0,0} = P_{1,1} = P$$
$$P_{0,1} = P_{1,0} = Q$$

The channel matrix is therefore

$$\begin{pmatrix} P & Q \\ Q & P \end{pmatrix}$$

The channel relationships (7.3-1) become

$$pP + (1 - p)Q = p(b = 0)$$
$$pQ + (1 - p)P = p(b = 1)$$
$$(7.4\text{-}1)$$

133

Note that these equations can be simply checked by computing their sum:

$$p(b = 0) + p(b = 1) = p(P + Q) + (1 - p)(P + Q)$$
$$= (p + 1 - p)(P + Q) = (1)(1) = 1$$

Given that we know what symbol we received, what are the probabilities for the various symbols that might have been sent?

We first compute the two denominators for equation (7.3-3):

$$\sum_{i=1}^{2} P(b_1 \mid a_i)p(a_i) = Pp + Q(1 - p)$$

$$\sum_{i=1}^{2} P(b_2 \mid a_i)p(a_i) = Qp + P(1 - p)$$

We then have

$$P(a = 0 \mid b = 0) = \frac{Pp}{Pp + Q(1 - p)}$$

$$P(a = 1 \mid b = 0) = \frac{Q(1 - p)}{Pp + Q(1 - p)}$$

$$P(a = 0 \mid b = 1) = \frac{Qp}{Qp + P(1 - p)}$$

$$P(a = 1 \mid b = 1) = \frac{P(1 - p)}{Qp + P(1 - p)}$$

which involve the choice of the probabilities of the source.

In the special case of equally likely input symbols ($p = \frac{1}{2}$) we have the very simple equations

$$P(a = 0 \mid b = 0) = P = P(a = 1 \mid b = 1)$$
$$P(a = 1 \mid b = 0) = Q = P(a = 0 \mid b = 1)$$

As an example of a peculiar channel, suppose that $P = \frac{9}{10}$ and $Q = \frac{1}{10}$ for the binary symmetric channel probabilities. But suppose also that the probability of the input $a = 0$ is sent is $\frac{19}{20} = p$ and $a = 1$ is sent is $\frac{1}{20} = (1 - p)$. We then have

$$P(a = 0 \mid b = 0) = \frac{171}{172}$$
$$P(a = 1 \mid b = 0) = \frac{1}{172}$$
$$P(a = 0 \mid b = 1) = \frac{19}{28}$$
$$P(a = 1 \mid b = 1) = \frac{9}{28}$$

Thus if we receive a $b = 0$, almost certainly an $a = 0$ was sent. But if a $b = 1$ is received, it is still a $\frac{19}{28} > \frac{2}{3}$ probability that $a = 0$ was sent. Therefore, regardless of what symbol is received, we must assume that an $a = 0$ was sent!

This situation arises whenever both

$$P(a = 0 \,|\, b = 0) > P(a = 1 \,|\, b = 0)$$
$$P(a = 0 \,|\, b = 1) > P(a = 1 \,|\, b = 1)$$

From the earlier equations for the binary symmetric channel these conditions are

$$Pp > Q(1 - p)$$
$$Qp > P(1 - p)$$

or both

$$p > Q$$
$$p > P$$

In words, this says that the bias in the choice of input symbols is greater than the bias of the channel. In short, clearly channels can be misused.

7.5   SYSTEM ENTROPIES

In Chapter 6 we developed the concept of the entropy of an information source, which we now label A. It measures the average amount of information per symbol of the source or, equivalently, the uncertainty associated with the source. $H(A) = 0$ when the source is certain and $H(A)$ is maximum when all the a_i are equally likely. We have the definition of the entropy as

$$H_r(A) = \sum_{i=1}^{q} p(a_i) \log_r \left[\frac{1}{p(a_i)} \right] \tag{7.5-1}$$

As noted, the entropy function has the following properties:

1. $H_r(A) \geq 0$.
2. $H_r(A) \leq \log_r q$, where q is the number of input symbols.
3. $H_r(A) = \log_r q$, when all the source symbols are equally likely.

The rest of this chapter is simply the systematic use of the entropy function applied to various aspects of the model of the signaling system.

Clearly corresponding to (7.5-1), the entropy of the *received* symbols should be defined by

$$H_r(B) = \sum_{j=1}^{s} p(b_j) \log_r \left[\frac{1}{p(b_j)} \right] \tag{7.5-2}$$

This quantity measures the uncertainty of the output symbols and has the same properties as the entropy of the source, since all the properties were derived from the form of the entropy function.

Similar expressions for the conditional entropy may be derived as follows. We naturally have for the *conditional entropy*, given a particular b_j,

$$H_r(A \mid b_j) = \sum_{i=1}^{q} P(a_i \mid b_j) \log_r \left[\frac{1}{P(a_i \mid b_j)} \right] \tag{7.5-3}$$

If we average (7.5-3) over all the b_j, using of course the appropriate probabilities $p(b_j)$ as weights, we get

$$H_r(A \mid B) = \sum_{j=1}^{s} p(b_j) H(A \mid b_j)$$

$$= \sum_{j=1}^{s} \sum_{i=1}^{q} p(b_j) P(a_i \mid b_j) \log_r \left[\frac{1}{P(a_i \mid b_j)} \right] \tag{7.5-4}$$

$$= \sum_{j=1}^{s} \sum_{i=1}^{q} P(a_i, b_j) \log_r \left[\frac{1}{P(a_i \mid b_j)} \right]$$

Doing exactly the same thing *except* that we view it from the sending end, corresponding to (7.5-3), we get the conditional entropy having sent a_i:

$$H_r(B \mid a_i) = \sum_{j=1}^{s} P(b_j \mid a_i) \log_r \left[\frac{1}{P(b_j \mid a_i)} \right] \tag{7.5-5}$$

Similar to (7.5-4), averaging this time over the input alphabet, we get the corresponding conditional entropy,

$$H_r(B \mid A) = \sum_{i=1}^{q} \sum_{j=1}^{s} P(a_i, b_j) \log_r \left[\frac{1}{P(b_j \mid a_i)} \right] \tag{7.5-6}$$

We now connect two ends of the channel together. To measure the uncertainty of the joint event for both source and receiver, we define *the joint entropy* in a similar way:

$$H_r(A, B) = \sum_{i=1}^{q} \sum_{j=1}^{s} P(a_i, b_j) \log_r \left[\frac{1}{P(a_i, b_j)} \right] \tag{7.5-7}$$

First we examine the joint entropy for the special case when A and B are *statistically independent* for all i and j (meaning that what comes out does *not* depend on what goes in). The independence condition is expressed by the equation

$$P(a_i, b_j) = p(a_i)p(b_j)$$

The joint entropy therefore becomes

$$H_r(A, B) = \sum_{i=1}^{q} \sum_{j=1}^{s} p(a_i)p(b_j) \left\{ \log_r \left[\frac{1}{p(a_i)} \right] + \log_r \left[\frac{1}{p(b_j)} \right] \right\}$$

Since

$$\sum_{i=1}^{q} p(a_i) = 1 \quad \text{and} \quad \sum_{j=1}^{s} p(b_j) = 1$$

we get (for independent input and output)

$$H_r(A, B) = H_r(A) + H_r(B) \tag{7.5-8}$$

Normally, the output of a channel depends at least partly on the input (otherwise, why are we using it?). In this case we can write

$$P(a_i, b_j) = p(a_i)P(b_j \mid a_i)$$

and the joint entropy is

$$H_r(A, B) = \sum_{i=1}^{q} \sum_{j=1}^{s} P(a_i, b_j) \log_r \left[\frac{1}{p(a_i)} \right]$$

$$+ \sum_{i=1}^{q} \sum_{j=1}^{s} P(a_i, b_j) \log_r \left[\frac{1}{P(b_j \mid a_i)} \right]$$

But

$$\sum_{j} P(a_i, b_j) = p(a_i)$$

Therefore,

$$H_r(A, B) = \sum_{i=1}^{q} p(a_i) \log_r \left[\frac{1}{p(a_i)} \right] + \sum_{i=1}^{q} \sum_{j=1}^{s} P(a_i, b_j) \log_r \left[\frac{1}{P(b_j \mid a_i)} \right] \quad (7.5\text{-}9)$$

$$= H_r(A) + H_r(B \mid A)$$

The joint entropy is the sum of the source entropy and the conditional entropy given A.

The conditional entropy $H_r(B \mid A)$ represents the information loss in the channel in going from input to output. It is how much must be added to the source entropy to get the joint entropy. $H_r(B \mid A)$ is called *the equivocation*. It is also called the *noise entropy* of the channel.

Since A and B play symmetric roles, we clearly have the expression corresponding to (7.5-9),

$$H_r(A, B) = H_r(B) + H_r(A \mid B) \quad (7.5\text{-}10)$$

In summary, in this section we have defined various entropies: $H(B)$ by (7.5-2), $H(A, B)$ by (7.5-7), $H(A \mid B)$ by (7.5-4), $H(B \mid A)$ by (7.5-6), $H(A \mid b_j)$ by (7.5-3), and $H(B \mid a_i)$ by (7.5-5). Each is derived by using the appropriate probability distribution.

7.6   MUTUAL INFORMATION

Consider again the transmission system of Figure 7.2-1. The input symbols are the a_i and the output are the b_j, and the channel is defined by the conditional probabilities $P_{i,j}$.

Prior to reception the probability of the input symbol a_i was $p(a_i)$. This is the *a priori probability* of a_i. After reception of b_j, the probability that the input symbol was a_i becomes $P(a_i \mid b_j)$, the conditional probability that we sent a_i given that we received b_j. This is an *a posteriori probability* of a_i. The change in the probability measures how much the receiver learned from the reception of the b_j. In the ideal channel with no noise, the a posteriori probability is 1, since we are certain from the received b_j exactly what was sent. In practical systems there are finite nonzero probabilities that errors will occur and the receiver cannot be absolutely sure what was sent. The difference between the information uncertainty before (the a priori probabilities) and after reception of a b_j (the a posteriori probabilities) measures the gain in information due to the reception of the b_j. This information is called the *mutual information* and is naturally defined as

$$I(a_i; b_j) = \log_r\left[\frac{1}{p(a_i)}\right] - \log_r\left[\frac{1}{P(a_i|b_j)}\right] = \log_r\left[\frac{P(a_i|b_j)}{p(a_i)}\right] \quad (7.6\text{-}1)$$

If the two probabilities $p(a_i)$ and $P(a_i|b_j)$ are the same, then we have gained no information and the mutual information is zero. No information has been transmitted. It is only when we have learned something new about the probabilities of the a_i from the received b_j that the mutual information can be positive.

Multiply numerator and denominator of the log term of (7.6-1) by $p(b_j)$. Since

$$P(a_i|b_j)p(b_j) = P(a_i, b_j) = P(b_j|a_i)p(a_i)$$

we have

$$I(a_i; b_j) = \log_r\left[\frac{P(a_i, b_j)}{p(a_i)p(b_j)}\right] = I(b_j; a_i) \quad (7.6\text{-}2)$$

The mutual information $I(a_i; b_j)$ has the following properties:

1. From the symmetry of the a_i and b_j, the definition gives

$$I(a_i; b_j) = \log_r\left[\frac{P(a_i|b_j)}{p(a_i)}\right]$$

$$I(b_j; a_i) = \log_r\left[\frac{P(b_j|a_i)}{p(b_j)}\right]$$

and

$$I(a_i; b_j) = I(b_j; a_i)$$

2. We also have

$$I(a_i; b_j) \leq I(a_i) \quad (7.6\text{-}3)$$

This follows from the definition

$$I(a_i) = \log_r\left[\frac{1}{p(a_i)}\right]$$

and

$$I(a_i; b_j) = \log_r P(a_i | b_j) + I(a_i)$$

The maximum for the probability $P(a_i | b_j)$ is 1, and the maximum for the log is therefore 0:

$$I(a_i; b_j) \leq I(a_i)$$

3. If a_i and b_j are independent, that is, if

$$P(a_i | b_j) = p(a_i)$$

or what is the same thing, if

$$P(a_i, b_j) = p(a_i)p(b_j)$$

then

$$I(a_i; b_j) = 0 \qquad (7.6\text{-}4)$$

Because of the inevitable noise the behavior of a channel can be understood only on the average. We therefore begin by averaging the mutual information over the alphabets using the appropriate probabilities of the symbols occuring:

$$I(A; b_j) = \sum_i P(a_i | b_j)I(a_i; b_j)$$
$$= \sum_i P(a_i | b_j) \log_r \left[\frac{P(a_i | b_j)}{p(a_i)}\right] \qquad (7.6\text{-}5)$$

Similarly,

$$I(a_i; B) = \sum_j P(b_j | a_i) \log_r \left[\frac{P(b_j | a_i)}{p(b_j)}\right] \qquad (7.6\text{-}6)$$

Finally, we get

$$I(A; B) = \sum_{i=1} p(a_i)I(a_i; B)$$
$$= \sum_i \sum_j P(a_i, b_j) \log_r \left[\frac{P(a_i, b_j)}{p(a_i)p(b_j)}\right] \qquad (7.6\text{-}7)$$
$$= I(B; A)$$

by symmetry. The first two, (7.6-5) and (7.6-6), are called the *conditional mutual information*. $I(A; b_j)$ measures the information gain provided by the reception of b_j. $I(a_i; B)$ is the information gain about the alphabet B given that a_i was sent.

The third, $I(A; B)$, which is symmetric in the two alphabets, provides a measure of the information gain of the whole system and does not depend on the individual input and output symbols but only on their frequencies; it is called *the system mutual information*. The system mutual information has the properties:

1. $I(A; B) \geq 0$ (from fundamental inequality, Section 6.4).
2. $I(A; B) = 0$ if and only if A and B are independent.
3. $I(A; B) = I(B; A)$ (from symmetry).

We can relate these various entropies to each other by the following algebraic manipulations:

$$I(A; B) = \sum_{i=1}^{q} \sum_{j=1}^{s} P(a_i, b_j) \log \left[\frac{P(a_i, b_j)}{p(a_i)p(b_j)} \right]$$

$$= \sum_{i=1}^{q} \sum_{j=1}^{s} P(a_i, b_j) \left[\log P(a_i, b_j) - \log p(a_i) - \log p(b_j) \right]$$

$$= - \sum_{i} \sum_{j} P(a_i, b_j) \log \left[\frac{1}{P(a_i, b_j)} \right]$$

$$+ \sum_{i} p(a_i) \log \left[\frac{1}{p(a_i)} \right] + \sum_{j} p(b_j) \log \left[\frac{1}{p(b_j)} \right]$$

$$= H(A) + H(B) - H(A, B) \geq 0$$

Using the results in the previous section (7.5-9) and (7.5-10), namely

$$H(A, B) = H(A) + H(B \mid A)$$

$$= H(B) + H(A \mid B)$$

we get the two results

$$I(A; B) = H(A) - H(A \mid B) \geq 0$$

$$= H(B) - H(B \mid A) \geq 0$$

$$(7.6\text{-}8)$$

Therefore,

$$0 \le H(A|B) \le H(A)$$
$$0 \le H(B|A) \le H(B)$$

(7.6-9)

and

$$H(A, B) \le H(A) + H(B)$$

(7.6-10)

Equation (7.6-10) shows that the joint entropy is maximum when the two alphabets are independent.

As examples of relationships, the average mutual information is

$$I(A; B) = \begin{cases} H(A) + H(B) - H(A, B) \\ H(A) - H(A|B) \\ H(B) - H(B|A) \end{cases}$$

The equivocation is

$$H(A|B) = H(A) - I(A; B)$$
$$H(B|A) = H(B) - I(A; B)$$

The joint entropy is

$$H(A, B) = \begin{cases} H(A) + H(B) - I(A; B) \\ H(A) + H(B|A) \\ H(B) + H(A|B) \end{cases}$$

7.7   SHANNON'S THEOREM FOR MULTIALPHABET SIGNALING

We have indicated that in a Markov process it would be advantageous to use different alphabets in different states. We now ask: "What is the most efficient method of encoding a source?" Never mind that it is not practical, what is the best possible? Given that we have received some b_j, how best could the a_i have been encoded? The answer is in a variable-length Huffman code which depends on the $P(a_i|b_j)$. This code will, of course, vary from b_j to b_j. Using the more convenient, but slightly less efficient, Shannon–Fano coding for the jth code based on having received b_j we pick for the various

a_i the lengths $l_{i,j}$ as defined by the usual condition (for all i and fixed j)

$$\log_r \left[\frac{1}{P(a_i | b_j)} \right] \le l_{i,j} < \log_r \left[\frac{1}{P(a_i | b_j)} \right] + 1 \qquad (7.7\text{-}1)$$

or

$$P(a_i | b_j) \ge \frac{1}{r^{l_{i,j}}} \ge \frac{1}{r} P(a_i | b_j)$$

Since

$$\sum_{i=1}^{q} P(a_i | b_j) = 1$$

we have met the Kraft inequality for the jth code, and there exists an instantaneous code *for each* j. Let the codes have lengths $l_{i,j}$ as shown:

Input Symbol	Code 1	Code 2	...	Code s
a_1	$l_{1,1}$	$l_{1,2}$		$l_{1,s}$
a_2	$l_{2,1}$	$l_{2,2}$		$l_{2,s}$
.	.	.		.
.	.	.		.
a_q	$l_{q,1}$	$l_{q,2}$		$l_{q,s}$

Multiply equation (7.7-1) by $P(a_i | b_j)$ and sum over all i. We have (Shannon's first theorem for code j)

$$H(A | b_j) \le \sum_{i=1}^{q} P(a_i | b_j) l_{i,j} = L_j < H(A | b_j) + 1$$

where L_j is the average length of the jth code. This code is to be used only when b_j is received.

Since $p(b_j)$ is the probability of getting b_j, we will have, on the average,

$$H(A | B) = \sum_{j=1} p(b_j) H(A | b_j) \le \sum_{i=1} \sum_{j=1} p(b_j) P(a_i | b_j) l_{i,j} = L$$

where L is the average length, and again

$$H(A | B) \le L < H(A | B) + 1$$

It is messy notation to go to extensions. It is clear, however, what happens: the entropies are simply n times as large. Thus we get, as before, for the nth extension,

$$H(A\,|\,B) \leq \frac{L(n)}{n} < H(A\,|\,B) + \frac{1}{n}$$

By increasing n sufficiently, we can get the average code length as close as we please to the conditional entropy $H(A\,|\,B)$. Thus we have extended Shannon's noiseless coding theorem to a family of instantaneous (uniquely decodable) codes.

8

Channel Capacity

8.1 DEFINITION OF CHANNEL CAPACITY

Given the conditional probabilities $P(b_j | a_i) = P_{i,j}$ which define a channel, what is the maximum amount of information we can send through the channel? This is the main question attacked in this chapter.

The mutual information connects the two ends of the channel together. It is defined by equation (7.6-8),

$$I(A; B) = H(A) - H(A | B)$$

where the entropy $H(A)$ is the uncertainty of the source *before* the reception of B, and $H(A | B)$ is the uncertainty *after* the reception of B. Thus $I(A; B)$ is the change in the information. An alternative expression for $I(A; B)$ is equation (7.6-7)

$$I(A; B) = \sum_{A,B} P(a, b) \log_r \left(\frac{P(a, b)}{p(a)p(b)} \right)$$

where we have dropped subscripts and adopted an obvious summation convention.

This formula involves the input symbol frequencies $p(a)$. We saw in the example of a binary symmetric channel (Section 7.4) how a poor match of the $p(a)$ to the channel can ruin a channel. Indeed, we know that if the probability of one symbol is $p(a) = 1$, then all the others must be zero and the constant signal contains no information. How can we best choose the $p(a)$ to get the most through the channel, and what is that amount?

We postpone the problem of choosing the $p(a)$ by using a standard mathematical trick; we simply define the *channel capacity* as the maximum over all possible assignments of the $p(a)$,

$$C = \max_{p(a)} I(A;B) \tag{8.1-1}$$

This makes the channel capacity depend only on the $P(a, b)$ and temporarily evades the difficulty of finding the suitable $p(a)$. The probabilities $p(b)$ are determined from both the $p(a)$ and the $P_{i,j}$ via the channel equations (7.3-1). By this definition there is no question of ever having a higher mutual information than the channel capacity C, since by definition C is the maximum.

8.2 THE UNIFORM CHANNEL

From equation (7.6-8) we have the mutual information

$$I(A;B) = H_r(B) - H_r(B \mid A)$$

From equation (7.5-6) this is

$$I(A;B) = H_r(B) - \sum_A \sum_B P(a, b) \log_r \left[\frac{1}{P(b \mid a)} \right]$$

$$= H_r(B) - \sum_A p(a) \sum_B P(b \mid a) \log_r \left[\frac{1}{P(b \mid a)} \right]$$

In a highly symmetric code, such as a parity error-detecting code, a perfect error-correcting code, and many others, each symbol is equivalent, in a sense, to any other symbol in the code—the differences in the probabilities for errors in the various symbols are inessential. For example, we can convert any symbol into the $0, 0, \ldots, 0$ symbol (in the binary system) by the trivial process of complementing each position which has a 1 in it. If the channel has white noise, and this is what most of the codes were designed to handle, then the entries in any row of the channel matrix, for the cases above, are merely a permutation (rearrangement) of those in the first row. Each symbol has the same set of transition probabilities as any other symbol.

Under the condition that each row is a permutation of the first row, it follows that the sums

$$\sum_B P(b\,|\,a) \log_r \left[\frac{1}{P(b\,|\,a)} \right] = W \tag{8.2-1}$$

are independent of a. No matter which symbol a you pick, this *average will be the same*. We can, therefore, sum over all the symbols of the alphabet B and get for each a,

$$I(A\,;B) = H_r(B) - W \sum_A p(a) = H_r(B) - W \tag{8.2-2}$$

Thus we see the need for the following definition.

Definition. A *uniform channel has a matrix*

$$\begin{pmatrix} P_{11} & P_{12} \ldots P_{1s} \\ P_{21} & P_{22} \ldots P_{2s} \\ \cdot & \cdot & \cdot \\ \cdot & \cdot & \cdot \\ \cdot & \cdot & \cdot \\ P_{q1} & P_{q2} \ldots P_{qs} \end{pmatrix}$$

such that each row is a permutation of the first row.

Suppose that we think of our channel as an *extension of the binary symmetric channel*. Each alphabet symbol is a block of n bits and each bit is subject to the same independent probability of success P (and failure Q). This definition makes the error-detecting and perfect error-correcting codes have symmetric channels.

As a trivial example, consider the noiseless channel where each input symbol a goes into exactly one output symbol b; that is, for each given a, one $P(b\,|\,a) = 1$ and all other $P(b\,|\,a) = 0$ for that a. Each term, therefore, is

$$P(b\,|\,a) \log_r \left[\frac{1}{P(b\,|\,a)} \right] = 0$$

Hence $W = 0$ and

$$I(A\,;B) = H_r(B) = H_r(A)$$

as we expect.

8.3   UNIFORM INPUT

Given a uniform channel, clearly the sensible way to use it is to use uniform $p(a)$ for the input alphabet symbols. We have the formula (8.2-2)

$$I(A; B) = H_2(B) - W \tag{8.3-1}$$

Suppose that we apply this formula to an n-bit single error-detecting binary code. The number of input symbols q is $q = 2^{n-1}$, since (due to the parity check) only half of the possible sequences of n binary digits are possible inputs. Because of the errors that are possible, any binary sequence could come out. We have the following situation (where P = probability of no error):

Number of Cases	Type	Probability
1	No errors	P^n
n	One error	$P^{n-1}Q$
$\dfrac{n(n-1)}{2}$	Two errors	$P^{n-2}Q^2$
.	.	.
.	.	.
.	.	.
$C(n, k)$	k errors	$P^{n-k}Q^k$

But

$$W = \sum_B P(b\,|\,a) \log_2 \left[\frac{1}{P(b\,|\,a)} \right]$$

Grouping together the number of cases having the same probability, we have

$$= \sum_{k=0}^{n} C(n, k) P^{n-k} Q^k \log_2 \left[\frac{1}{P^{n-k}Q^k} \right] \tag{8.3-2}$$

Expand the product in the log term into two log terms:

$$(n - k) \log_2 \left(\frac{1}{P} \right) + k \log_2 \left(\frac{1}{Q} \right) \tag{8.3-3}$$

From the first term we get for the sum (8.3-2),

$$\log_2\left(\frac{1}{P}\right)\sum_{k=0}^{n-1}\frac{n!}{k!(n-1-k)!}\frac{n-k}{n-k}P^{n-k}Q^k$$

$$= P\log_2\left(\frac{1}{P}\right)\sum_{k=0}^{n-1}\frac{n(n-1)!}{k!(n-1-k)!}P^{n-1-k}Q^k$$

$$= nP\log_2\left(\frac{1}{P}\right)(P+Q)^{n-1} = nP\log_2\left(\frac{1}{P}\right)$$

From the second term of (8.3-3) we get for the sum (8.3-2), correspondingly,

$$nQ\log_2\left(\frac{1}{Q}\right)$$

Together they give

$$n\left[P\log_2\left(\frac{1}{P}\right) + Q\log_2\left(\frac{1}{Q}\right)\right] = nH_2(P)$$

where we have used the natural notation

$$H_2(P) = P\log_2\left(\frac{1}{P}\right) + Q\log_2\left(\frac{1}{Q}\right) \tag{8.3-4}$$

The mutual information (8.3-1) now becomes

$$I(A;B) = H_2(B) - nH_2(P) \tag{8.3-5}$$

8.4   ERROR-CORRECTING CODES

In Section 1.3 we observed that sometimes the encoding process was broken up into two stages, one to suitably match the source of information, the second to match the channel. We may, if we wish, combine this second stage of encoding with the definition of the channel and call it part of the channel. Indeed, sometimes it is arranged so that as far as the user is concerned, it appears as if it were the channel. Let us examine what this channel looks like.

For a perfect error-correcting code of n bits and probability P of being correct for each single bit in the white noise channel, then for the channel errors $P_{i,j}$ the user sees the following table. Remember that in this channel a single error is correctly corrected, and a double error is wrongly corrected into a triple error.

Occurrence of	Actual Probability
No errors	$P^n + nQP^{n-1}$
1 error	0
2 errors	0
3 or more errors	$1 -$ (no error)

Thus the channel errors have a peculiar structure in terms of the original causes of errors. However, we may still apply the methods of the previous section to this uniform channel.

When the error correction is either in hardware or is *automatically* included in the software, the user sees the above. It also indicates what was earlier observed: in practice, for a variable probability source, we are likely to use a Huffman code to match the source, and then apply some error-correcting code to blocks of this encoding. More and more often computers are being built with error detection and/or correction in the hardware. Whether you wish to regard this as a single process of encoding or two processes or whether you wish to regard the second stage of encoding as belonging to the channel itself is a matter of preference on your part. How to handle the situation should be clear.

Exercises

8.4-1   Apply this section to the 7-bit single-error-correcting code.
8.4-2   Extend this section to a minimum distance of four codes.

8.5 THE CAPACITY OF A BINARY SYMMETRIC CHANNEL

If P is the probability of correct transmission, then the channel matrix for a binary symmetric channel (Section 7.4)

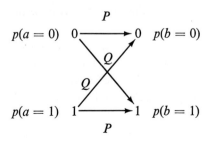

is given as

$$\begin{pmatrix} P & Q \\ Q & P \end{pmatrix}$$

Let p = probability of choosing $a = 0$. Then $1 - p$ = probability of choosing $a = 1$ and the mutual information for this uniform channel is equation (8.2-2). Using $\log_2$ and temporarily dropping the subscript 2 on the entropy function H,

$$I(A; B) = H(B) - W$$

where, from (8.2-1),

$$W = \sum_B P(b \mid a) \log \left(\frac{1}{P(b \mid a)} \right)$$

$$= P \log \left(\frac{1}{P} \right) + Q \log \left(\frac{1}{Q} \right)$$

$$= H(P)$$

using (8.3-4). Therefore,

$$I(A; B) = H(B) - H(P) \tag{8.5-1}$$

To find $H(B)$ we note that [equation (7.4-1)]

$$p(b = 0) = pP + (1 - p)Q$$
$$p(b = 1) = pQ + (1 - p)P$$

It is easy to see that

$$p(b = 0) + p(b = 1) = 1$$

For convenience we set

$$p(b = 0) = pP + (1 - p)Q = x \tag{8.5-2}$$

Hence

$$p(b = 1) = 1 - x$$

and using the notation of (8.3-4),

$$I(A; B) = x \log \left(\frac{1}{x} \right) + (1 - x) \log \left(\frac{1}{1 - x} \right) - H(P) = H(x) - H(P)$$

To get the channel capacity C we ask: "What choice of the symbol probability p maximizes the mutual information $I(A; B)$?" Since we are working with the variable x, this is the same as asking what maximizes

$$H(x) = x \log \left(\frac{1}{x}\right) + (1 - x) \log \left(\frac{1}{1 - x}\right)$$

From Section 6.4 the maximum occurs for $x = \frac{1}{2}$, and

$$H(\tfrac{1}{2}) = \tfrac{1}{2} \log 2 + \tfrac{1}{2} \log 2 = \log 2 = 1$$

The capacity of the channel is therefore

$$C = \max_A I(A; B) = 1 - H(P) \tag{8.5-3}$$

We can find the value of p from (8.5-2) as follows:

$$x = \tfrac{1}{2} = pP + (1 - p)Q$$
$$\tfrac{1}{2} = pP + (1 - p)(1 - P)$$
$$= pP + 1 - p - P + pP$$

Transposing and rearranging, we get

$$(1 - 2P)p = \frac{1 - 2P}{2}$$

Since the channel probability $P \neq \frac{1}{2}$ (else no information is sent) it follows, on dividing by $1 - 2P \neq 0$, that the symbol probability

$$p = \tfrac{1}{2}$$

which is what we would expect from the symmetry.

Thus we have shown that the binary symmetric channel has the capacity

$$\boxed{C = 1 - H_2(P)} \tag{8.5-4}$$

which occurs when the two input symbols are chosen with equal frequency.

8.6 THE CONDITIONAL MUTUAL INFORMATION

How can we find the symbol probabilities $p(a)$ to meet the channel capacity in more general cases? This section gives one very useful result that helps answer this question in many situations.

Returning to the general channel, we can write

$$I(A;B) = \sum_A p(a) \sum_B P(b|a) \log \left(\frac{P(b|a)}{p(b)} \right)$$
$$= \sum_A p(a) I(a;B)$$

where we have written the *conditional mutual information* as

$$I(a;B) = \sum_B P(b|a) \log \left(\frac{P(b|a)}{p(b)} \right)$$

In general, $I(a;B)$ depends on a, but we have the theorem: *When the input symbols are picked to meet the channel capacity C, then*

$$I(a;B) = C$$

for every a [assuming that $p(a) \neq 0$].

To prove this, we assume the contrary, that some symbol, say a_1, is operating above capacity. Then, since the average is C, there must be some symbol, say a_2, that is operating below C. Thus we assume that

$$I(a_1;B) > C$$
$$I(a_2;B) < C$$

For an infinitesimal change that increases $p(a_1)$ and decreases $p(a_2)$ by the same amount (to keep the total probability equal to 1), the direct rate of change in $I(A;B)$ is the difference

$$\frac{\partial I(A;B)}{\partial p(a_1)} - \frac{\partial I(A;B)}{\partial p(a_2)}$$

But the change in the $p(a)$ induces a change through the channel equations in the $p(b)$. The rate of change in each $p(b)$ is given by

$$P(b|a_1) - P(b|a_2)$$

From the expression for the mutual information,

$$I(A;B) = \sum_A p(a) \sum_B P(b \mid a) \log \left[\frac{P(b \mid a)}{p(b)} \right]$$

we have, therefore, the instantaneous rate of change in $I(A;B)$ as

$$\sum_B P(b \mid a_1) \log \left[\frac{P(b \mid a_1)}{p(b)} \right] - \sum_B P(b \mid a_2) \log \left[\frac{P(b \mid a_2)}{p(b)} \right]$$

$$+ \sum_A p(a) \left\{ - \sum_B P(b \mid a) \left[\frac{1}{p(b)} \right] [P(b \mid a_1) - P(b \mid a_2)] \right\}$$

$$= I(a_1;B) - I(a_2;B) - \sum_B \sum_A p(a) \left[\frac{P(b \mid a)}{p(b)} \right] [P(b \mid a_1) - P(b \mid a_2)]$$

$$= I(a_1;B) - I(a_2;B) - \sum_B [P(b \mid a_1) - P(b \mid a_2)]$$

$$= I(a_1;B) - I(a_2;B) - (1 - 1) = I(a_1;B) - I(a_2;B) > 0$$

Since we were operating at channel capacity and it is the maximum that can occur, and since the change has an instantaneous rate that is positive, we see that if our hypothesis were true, we could get above the maximum by a suitably small change in $p(a_1)$ and $p(a_2)$. We conclude, therefore, that the hypothesis that any symbol operates above the channel capacity must be wrong; every symbol in the source alphabet operates at capacity when the whole alphabet operates at channel capacity.

We can often use this result in particular situations to help us find the individual $p(a)$'s that meet channel capacity—we can find them one at a time.

9

Some Mathematical Preliminaries

9.1 INTRODUCTION

Some people believe that a theorem is proved when a logically correct proof is given; but some people believe that a theorem is proved *only* when the student sees why it is inevitably true. The author tends to belong to this second school of thought. Therefore, we make a digression at this point to prove, rather than assume, a number of results that are needed to understand the proof of Shannon's main result. The subjects are presented in sufficient detail so that a general appreciation of them is obtained, not just a mere acquaintance with the result. Thus more than the minimum material is occasionally presented.

The two main ideas are n-dimensional space and the law of large numbers. The two mathematical details are approximations for $n!$ and for a certain sum of binomial coefficients. We have already seen how n-dimensional space is useful for representing code symbols. Since we are going to use large extensions of codes to get near the entropy, and hence the channel capacity, the dimension of the space of the proof will be very high indeed.

The law of large numbers is needed to handle the fact that when we are near ideal signaling rates, the number of errors in a code word is very high. The manner in which the probable number of errors is distributed is central to the proof of Shannon's main result.

We also will need to bound the tail of a binomial distribution to show that it does not contribute very much. For this we need the famous Stirling approximation to n! This approximation is often used but rarely presented in a simple manner.

9.2 THE GAMMA FUNCTION $\Gamma(n)$

We begin with the study of a certain definite integral as a function of a parameter n. Consider the integral

$$\Gamma(n) = \int_0^\infty e^{-x} x^{n-1} \, dx \tag{9.2-1}$$

The exponent $n - 1$ is conventional. For $n > 1$ we can integrate by parts to get

$$\Gamma(n) = x^{n-1} \frac{e^{-x}}{-1} \Big|_0^\infty + (n-1) \int_0^\infty e^{-x} x^{n-2} \, dx$$

or

$$\Gamma(n) = (n-1)\Gamma(n-1)$$

For $n = 1$ we have

$$\Gamma(1) = \int_0^\infty e^{-x} \, dx = -e^{-x} \Big|_0^\infty = 1$$

and it follows that for integer n,

$$\Gamma(2) = 1$$
$$\Gamma(3) = 2!$$
$$\Gamma(4) = 3!$$
$$\vdots$$
$$\Gamma(n) = (n-1)! \qquad (n = 1, 2, \ldots)$$

The gamma function provides the natural generalization for the factorial function, since the integral also exists for noninteger n.

We consider next the gamma function for argument $\tfrac{1}{2}$. We have

$$\Gamma(\tfrac{1}{2}) = \int_0^\infty e^{-x} x^{-1/2} \, dx$$

The substitution $x = t^2$ rationalizes the integrand and gives

$$\Gamma(\tfrac{1}{2}) = \int_0^\infty e^{-t^2} \frac{2t}{t}\, dt = 2 \int_0^\infty e^{-t^2}\, dt$$

Since the integrand is an even function, we can write this as

$$\Gamma(\tfrac{1}{2}) = \int_{-\infty}^\infty e^{-t^2}\, dt$$

This is often called the *error integral.*

Consider, now, the product

$$\Gamma(\tfrac{1}{2})\Gamma(\tfrac{1}{2}) = \int_{-\infty}^\infty e^{-x^2}\, dx \int_{-\infty}^\infty e^{-y^2}\, dy$$

We transform (formally) to polar coordinates

$$[\Gamma(\tfrac{1}{2})]^2 = \int_0^{2\pi} \int_0^\infty e^{-r^2} r\, dr\, d\theta$$

$$= 2\pi \frac{e^{-r^2}}{-2}\Big|_0^\infty = \pi$$

Therefore,

$$\Gamma(\tfrac{1}{2}) = \sqrt{\pi}$$

To justify the formal change to polar coordinate, suppose that we consider finite limits

$$I(L) = \int_{-L}^L e^{-x^2}\, dx \int_{-L}^L e^{-y^2}\, dy$$

We have, from Figure 9.2-1,

$$\int_0^{2\pi} \int_0^L e^{-r^2} r\, dr\, d\theta \le I(L) \le \int_0^{2\pi} \int_0^{L\sqrt{2}} e^{-r^2} r\, dr\, d\theta$$

or

$$\pi(1 - e^{-L^2}) \le I(L) \le \pi(1 - e^{-2L^2})$$

As $L \longrightarrow \infty$ we get

$$\pi \le I(\infty) = \Gamma^2(\tfrac{1}{2}) \le \pi$$

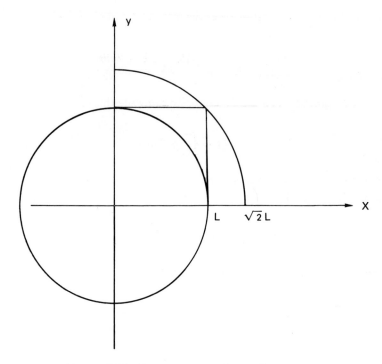

FIGURE 9.2-1 RECTANGULAR-TO-POLAR COORDINATES

Thus the transformation from rectangular to polar coordinates is justified and we believe that $\Gamma(\tfrac{1}{2}) = \sqrt{\pi}$.

9.3 THE STIRLING APPROXIMATION TO $n!$

The Stirling approximation to $n!$ is

$$n! \simeq n^n e^{-n} \sqrt{2\pi n} \qquad (9.3\text{-}1)$$

It is widely used but is seldom completely presented. We need it, so we shall derive it.

The quantity $n!$ is a product, and products are hard to approximate. This suggests approximating the log of $n!$:

$$\log n! = \sum_{k=1}^{n} \log k$$

(all logs in this section are $\log_e$). The summation, in turn, suggests the integral (which we do by integration by parts)

$$\int_1^n \log x \, dx = (x \log x - x)\Big|_1^n = n \log n - n + 1 \qquad (9.3\text{-}2)$$

If we use the trapezoid rule to approximate the integral (see Figure 9.3-1) we will underapproximate. Therefore,

$$\int_1^n \log x \, dx \geq \tfrac{1}{2} \log 1 + \log 2 + \log 3 + \ldots + \log (n-1) + \tfrac{1}{2} \log n$$

$$\geq \log n! - \tfrac{1}{2} \log n$$

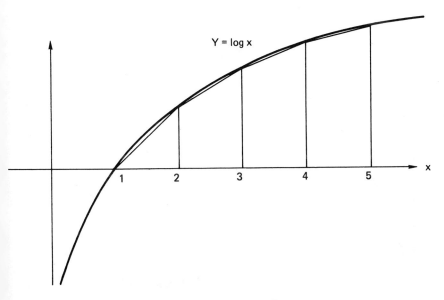

$Y = \log x$

FIGURE 9.3-1   TRAPEZOID RULE

We have, using (9.3-2) and transposing one term,

$$n \log n - n + \tfrac{1}{2} \log n + 1 \geq \log n!$$

Taking antilogs (which due to the positive growth and monotonicity of the log function preserves the inequality direction), we get, term by term,

$$n^n e^{-n} \sqrt{n} \, e \geq n! \qquad (9.3\text{-}3)$$

To overapproximate the integral we use the midpoint integration formula and note (Figure 9.3-2) that if the midpoint line segment is tilted until it is tangent to the curve, then the area under the line segment is not changed. For the first half-interval, $1 \leq x \leq \frac{3}{2}$, we use the tangent line at $x = 1$ to get a bounding triangle of area $\frac{1}{8}$. For the last half-interval we use the maximum, $\log n$, and get a bounding area $\frac{1}{2} \log n$. We have, therefore,

$$\int_1^n \log x \, dx \leq \tfrac{1}{8} + \log 2 + \log 3 + \ldots + \log (n-1) + \tfrac{1}{2} \log n$$

$$\leq \log n! + \tfrac{1}{8} - \tfrac{1}{2} \log n$$

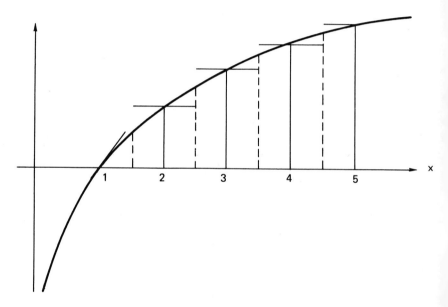

FIGURE 9.3-2 MIDPOINT FORMULA

Again use (9.3-2) and rearrange, to get

$$n \log n - n + 1 - \tfrac{1}{8} + \tfrac{1}{2} \log n \leq \log n!$$

Take antilogs,

$$n^n e^{-n} \sqrt{n} \; e^{7/8} \leq n! \tag{9.3-4}$$

The coefficient C of the approximation

$$n! = n^n e^{-n} \sqrt{n} \; C \tag{9.3-5}$$

lies, from (9.3-3) and (9.3-4), between

$$e^{7/8} \leq C \leq e$$

or, in numbers,

$$2.39887 \ldots \leq C \leq 2.71828 \ldots \tag{9.3-6}$$

Since the midpoint formula has approximately $1/2$ the error of the trapezoid rule, and the errors of the two formulas have opposite signs, a better guess at C is the weighted average

$$\frac{2e^{7/8} + e}{3} = 2.50534 \ldots = C \tag{9.3-7}$$

It will turn out that the value for C (for infinite n) is

$$\sqrt{2\pi} = 2.50663 \ldots$$

If we want to get this coefficient C exactly (for infinite n) we use a trick and consider the integral

$$I_k = \int_0^{\pi/2} \cos^k x \, dx \qquad (k \geq 0)$$

A trigonometric substitution gives $(k \geq 2)$

$$I_k = \int_0^{\pi/2} \cos^{k-2} x \, (1 - \sin^2 x) \, dx$$

$$= I_{k-2} + \int_0^{\pi/2} \cos^{k-2} x \, (-\sin x) \sin x \, dx$$

Integration by parts gives

$$I_k = I_{k-2} + \frac{\cos^{k-1} x}{k-1} \sin x \bigg|_0^{\pi/2} - \frac{1}{k-1} \int_0^{\pi/2} \cos^{k-1} x \cos x \, dx$$

$$= I_{k-2} - \left(\frac{1}{k-1}\right) I_k$$

Solving for I_k we have the recurrence relation for the integral,

$$I_k = \left(\frac{k-1}{k}\right) I_{k-2} \qquad (k \geq 2) \tag{9.3-8}$$

It is easy to show that

$$I_1 = 1$$

$$I_0 = \frac{\pi}{2}$$

We next note that since $\cos x \leq 1$ for all x in the interval,

$$I_{2k-1} > I_{2k} > I_{2k+1}$$

Divide through by I_{2k-1}:

$$1 > \frac{I_{2k}}{I_{2k-1}} > \frac{I_{2k+1}}{I_{2k-1}}$$

Substitute from (9.3-8) for the integrals to get

$$1 > 2k \left[\frac{2k-1}{2k} \frac{2k-3}{2k-2} \cdots \frac{3}{2} \right]^2 \frac{\pi}{2} > \frac{2k}{2k+1}$$

We can make the numerator in the square bracket equal to $(2k)!$ by multiplying both numerator and denominator by the denominator. We also use the fact that

$$2k(2k-2)(2k-4)\ldots 2 = 2^k k!$$

to get

$$1 > \pi k \left[\frac{(2k)!}{2^k(k!)2^k(k!)} \right]^2 > \frac{2k}{2k+1}$$

We now take the positive square root of each term:

$$1 > \sqrt{\pi k} \left[\frac{(2k)!}{(k!)^2 2^{2k}} \right] > \sqrt{1 - \frac{1}{2k+1}}$$

Finally, we substitute the approximation (9.3-5),

$$n! = n^n e^{-n} \sqrt{n} \, C$$

into this for each factorial to get

$$1 > \sqrt{\pi k} \left[\frac{(2k)^{2k} e^{-2k} \sqrt{2k} \, C}{2^{2k} k^k e^{-k} \sqrt{k} \, C k^k e^{-k} \sqrt{k} \, C} \right] > \sqrt{1 - \frac{1}{2k+1}}$$

Practically everything cancels and we have

$$1 > \frac{\sqrt{2\pi}}{C} > \sqrt{1 - \frac{1}{2k+1}}$$

Therefore, for large k,

$$C \longrightarrow \sqrt{2\pi}$$

Thus we have the Stirling approximation. As Table 9.7-1 shows, the ratio of Stirling's approximation to the true value is remarkably good even for small values.

TABLE 9.7-1   Stirling Approximation

n	Stirling	True	Stirling/True
1	0.92214	1	0.92214
2	1.91900	2	0.95950
3	5.83621	6	0.97270
4	23.50618	24	0.97942
5	118.01916	120	0.98349
6	710.07818	720	0.98622
7	4,980.3958	5,040	0.98817
8	39,902.395	40,320	0.98964
9	359,536.87	362,880	0.99079
10	3,598,695.6	3,628,800	0.99170

The table shows that the approximation was designed to be *relatively* exact for $n = \infty$, but the difference does *not* approach zero.

9.4   A BINOMIAL BOUND

The other mathematical result we need is the number of vertices in the unit cube of Section 3.6 that are in a sphere of radius λn. Thus we need a bound on a sum of binomial coefficients

$$1 + C(n, 1) + C(n, 2) + \ldots + C(n, \lambda n) \qquad (9.4\text{-}1)$$

where $0 < \lambda < \frac{1}{2}$. (We suppose that λn is an integer).

Since $\lambda < \frac{1}{2}$, the terms are all monotonically growing in size, and the largest is therefore the last one,

$$C(n, \lambda n) = \frac{n!}{(\lambda n)!(n - \lambda n)!} \tag{9.4-2}$$

We apply Stirling's approximation to each factorial to get

$$C(n, \lambda n) \simeq \frac{n^n e^{-n}\sqrt{2\pi n}}{(\lambda n)^{\lambda n} e^{-\lambda n}\sqrt{2\pi \lambda n}(n - \lambda n)^{n - \lambda n} e^{-(n - \lambda n)}\sqrt{2\pi(n - \lambda n)}}$$

Regrouping terms, we get

$$C(n, \lambda n) \simeq \left[\frac{n^n}{n^{\lambda n}n^{n - \lambda n}}\right]\left[\frac{1}{\lambda^{\lambda n}(1 - \lambda)^{(1 - \lambda)n}}\right]\left[\frac{e^{-n}}{e^{-\lambda n}e^{-(n - \lambda n)}}\right]$$

$$\times \left[\frac{\sqrt{2\pi}\sqrt{n}}{\sqrt{2\pi}\sqrt{\lambda}\sqrt{n}\sqrt{2\pi}\sqrt{(1 - \lambda)n}}\right]$$

The first and third sets of brackets are each exactly 1 and the other two become

$$C(n, \lambda n) \simeq \left[\frac{1}{\lambda^{\lambda}(1 - \lambda)^{1 - \lambda}}\right]^n\left[\frac{1}{2\pi\lambda(1 - \lambda)n}\right]^{1/2} \tag{9.4-3}$$

The log to the base 2 of the denominator of the term in the first set of brackets is

$$\log[\lambda^{\lambda}(1 - \lambda)^{1 - \lambda}] = \lambda \log \lambda + (1 - \lambda) \log(1 - \lambda) = -H(\lambda)$$

hence the first set of brackets of (9.4-3) is

$$2^{nH(\lambda)} \tag{9.4-4}$$

The second set of brackets is a constant times $n^{-(1/2)}$.

We now write the original series (9.4-1) in the reverse direction;

$$C(n, \lambda n) + C(n, \lambda n - 1) + \ldots + C(n, 1) + 1$$

and we bound the sum by a geometric progression. To get the "rate" of the geometric progression, note that in going from term to term in the *usual way*, each binomial coefficient is found from the preceding one by multiplying by (term by term)

$$\frac{n}{1}, \frac{n - 1}{2}, \frac{n - 2}{3}, \ldots, \frac{n - \lambda n + 1}{\lambda n}$$

If we start from our maximum term $C(n, \lambda n)$ and go *down*, we have the multipliers which are the reciprocals of the previous numbers and are in the reverse order

$$\frac{\lambda n}{n - \lambda n + 1}, \cdots, \frac{3}{n - 2}, \frac{2}{n - 1}, \frac{1}{n}$$

We need to bound these. An upper bound of these numbers is

$$\frac{\lambda}{1 - \lambda}$$

so an upper bound on the sum of the binomial coefficient terms is the largest term times

$$\sum_{m=0}^{\infty} \left(\frac{\lambda}{1 - \lambda}\right)^m = \frac{1}{1 - \left(\frac{\lambda}{1 - \lambda}\right)} = \frac{1 - \lambda}{1 - 2\lambda} \qquad (9.4\text{-}5)$$

Assembling everything of (9.4-1), we have [use (9.4-4) and (9.4-5)]

$$\sum_{k=0}^{\lambda n} C(n, k) \leq 2^{nH(\lambda)} \left[\frac{1}{2\pi\lambda(1 - \lambda)}\right]^{1/2} \frac{1 - \lambda}{1 - 2\lambda}\left(\frac{1}{n}\right)^{1/2}$$

For all n such that (remember that $\lambda < \frac{1}{2}$)

$$n \geq \frac{1 - \lambda}{2\pi\lambda(1 - 2\lambda)^2}$$

the product of the last three terms is less than 1; hence for sufficiently large n,

$$\sum_{k=0}^{\lambda n} C(n, k) \leq 2^{nH(\lambda)} \qquad (9.4\text{-}6)$$

where $H(\lambda)$ is the entropy function of λ. This is our needed inequality.

9.5   N-DIMENSIONAL EUCLIDEAN SPACE

N-dimensional space merely means that we have n independent variables $x_1, x_2, \ldots, x_n$. Euclidean space means that we use the Pythagorean distance

$$x_1^2 + x_2^2 + \ldots + x_n^2 = r^2 \qquad (9.5\text{-}1)$$

and we can define a *sphere of radius r* by this expression.

A little reflection on classical Euclidean geometry will suffice to see why the volume of an n-dimensional sphere depends on the radius r as r^n. We have the formula for the volume,

$$V_n(r) = C_n r^n \tag{9.5-2}$$

where C_n is some constant depending on n. For example,

$$C_2 = \pi \quad \text{and} \quad C_3 = \frac{4\pi}{3} \quad \text{(note that } C_1 = 2)$$

To find the values of C_n we use the same trick as in Section 9.2 of multiplying the gamma integral by itself and then going to polar coordinates (which worked so well). Let us consider the product of n of the integrals. We have [using (9.5-1)]

$$[\Gamma(\tfrac{1}{2})]^n = \pi^{n/2} = \int_{-\infty}^{\infty} \int_{-\infty}^{\infty} \cdots \int_{-\infty}^{\infty} e^{-r^2} \, dx_1 \, dx_2 \ldots dx_n$$

$$= \int_0^{\infty} e^{-r^2} \frac{dV_n(r)}{dr} \, dr$$

This last takes a moment's thinking about the shell of thickness Δr, and comparing this with our result in two dimensions,

$$\int_0^{\infty} e^{-r^2} \frac{d(\pi r^2)}{dr} \, dr = 2\pi \int_0^{\infty} e^{-r^2} r \, dr$$

as we really did in Section 9.2 (although it was disguised somewhat by the conventional method).

We have, therefore, using (9.5-2),

$$\pi^{n/2} = C_n \int_0^{\infty} e^{-r^2} n r^{n-1} \, dr$$

Set $r^2 = t$. Then $dr = \tfrac{1}{2} t^{-1/2} \, dt$, and

$$\pi^{n/2} = \frac{nC_n}{2} \int_0^{\infty} e^{-t} \frac{t^{(n-1)/2} \, dt}{t^{1/2}}$$

$$= \frac{nC_n}{2} \int_0^{\infty} e^{-t} t^{(n/2-1)} \, dt$$

$$= \frac{nC_n}{2} \Gamma(n/2) = C_n \Gamma(n/2 + 1)$$

Therefore,

$$C_n = \frac{\pi^{n/2}}{\Gamma(n/2 + 1)}$$

It is easy to show that

$$C_n = \frac{2\pi}{n} C_{n-2}$$

and we can compute the table (of the volume of a unit sphere in n dimensions)

n	C_n		C_n
1	2	$=$	$2.00000\ldots$
2	π	$=$	$3.14159\ldots$
3	$4\pi/3$	$=$	$4.18879\ldots$
4	$\pi^2/2$	$=$	$4.93480\ldots$
5	$8\pi^2/15$	$=$	$5.26379\ldots$
6	$\pi^3/6$	$=$	$5.16771\ldots$
7	$16\pi^3/105$	$=$	$4.72477\ldots$
8	$\pi^4/24$	$=$	$4.05871\ldots$
.	.		.
.	.		.
.	.		.
$2k$	$\pi^k/k!$	$=$	$\longrightarrow 0$

From the table we see that the volume of the unit sphere, or equivalently the coefficient for r^n, comes to a maximum at $n = 5$ and falls off rather rapidly toward zero as n approaches infinity.

For $n = 2k$, the volume of an n-dimensional sphere of radius r is

$$\left(\frac{\pi^k}{k!}\right)r^{2k} = \frac{(\pi r^2)^k}{k!}$$

From this we see that once

$$k > \pi r^2$$

then increasing k (or equivalently n) will *decrease* the volume. Indeed, given any radius, no matter how large, the dimension of the space n can be increased until the volume of the sphere is arbitrarily small. [For odd-dimensional spaces, we have, from the original definition of $\Gamma(n)$, equation (9.2-1), that

$$V_n(r) = C_n r^n = \frac{\pi^{n/2} r^n}{\Gamma(n/2 + 1)}$$

will change smoothly with increasing n.]

We now consider the *fraction* of the volume of an n-dimensional sphere that is within a distance ϵ of the surface (ϵ is used here as any small positive number). We have

$$\frac{\text{shell}}{\text{volume}} = \frac{C_n r^n - C_n (r - \epsilon)^n}{C_n r^n} = 1 - \left(1 - \frac{\epsilon}{r}\right)^n$$

which approaches 1 as n gets large. Thus for a high-dimensional space, almost all the volume of a sphere is arbitrarily close to the surface. Indeed, no matter how thin a shell you wish to use and how close you wish to get to 1 (say 99.44%), it is possible to find an n_0 such that for all greater n, the two conditions are met. There simply is not much volume inside a high-dimensional sphere; almost all of it is "on the surface."

Exercise

9.5-1   Show for any family of convex similar figures that "almost all the volume is on the surface."

9.6   A PARADOX

The results of this section are not needed but are included to show how unreliable one's intuition is about spheres in n-dimensional Euclidean space.

Suppose, as shown in Figure 9.6-1, that we have a 4 × 4 square centered about the origin (0, 0) and have four unit circles in each of the four corners. Now consider the radius of the circle about the origin that is tangent on the inside to the four circles. It has a radius

$$r_2 = \sqrt{(1 - 0)^2 + (1 - 0)^2} - 1 = \sqrt{2} - 1 = 0.414\ldots$$

Next consider the same situation in three dimensions. We have a 4 × 4 × 4 cube with eight unit spheres in the corners. The inner sphere has the radius

$$r_3 = \sqrt{3} - 1 = 0.732\ldots$$

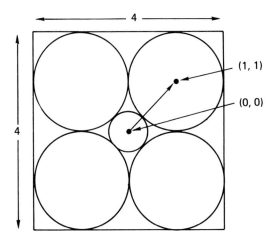

FIGURE 9.6-1   A PARADOX

Finally, consider the similar situation in n dimensions. We have a $4 \times 4 \times \ldots \times 4$ cube with 2^n unit spheres in the corners, each one touching all its n neighboring spheres. The spheres are packed in properly. The distance from the origin to the center of a sphere is given by the expression

$$\sqrt{(1 - 0)^2 + (1 - 0)^2 + \ldots + (1 - 0)^2} = \sqrt{n}$$

Again subtracting the radius of the corner unit sphere, we get the radius of the inner sphere in n dimensions as

$$r_n = \sqrt{n} - 1 \qquad (9.6\text{-}1)$$

When $n = 10$, this is

$$r_{10} = \sqrt{10} - 1 = 3.16 \ldots - 1 = 2.16 \ldots > 2$$

and the inner sphere reaches outside the cube! Does this seem impossible? The spheres are convex surfaces to be sure, the distance is surely the correct Euclidean distance, the radius of the corner sphere is surely 1—so there is no escape from the conclusion. Contrary to any normal intuition, the inner sphere for $n \geq 10$ reaches outside the cube.

To compound the paradox further, consider the volume of this inner sphere *relative* to the whole cube as a function of n. We have, for the special case of n an even number $n = 2k$, and using (9.6-1),

$$\text{ratio} = \frac{\text{volume of sphere}}{\text{volume of whole cube}} = C_n \frac{(\sqrt{n} - 1)^n}{4^n}$$

$$= C_{2k} \frac{(\sqrt{2k} - 1)^{2k}}{4^{2k}}$$

$$= \frac{\pi^k (\sqrt{2})^{2k}}{k!} \frac{(\sqrt{k})^{2k}}{4^{2k}} \left[\left(1 - \frac{1}{\sqrt{2k}} \right)^{\sqrt{2k}} \right]^{\sqrt{2k}}$$

$$= \frac{\pi^k 2^k k^k}{4^{2k} k!} \left[\left(1 - \frac{1}{\sqrt{2k}} \right)^{\sqrt{2k}} \right]^{\sqrt{2k}}$$

(9.6-2)

Using Stirling's approximation (9.3-1) for $k!$,

$$k! \simeq k^k e^{-k} \sqrt{2\pi k}$$

and the result from the calculus,

$$\lim_{x \to \infty} \left(1 - \frac{1}{x} \right)^x = e^{-1}$$

We get for (9.6-2),

$$\text{ratio} \simeq \frac{\pi^k 2^k k^k}{4^{2k} k^k e^{-k} \sqrt{2\pi k}} e^{-\sqrt{2k}}$$

$$\simeq \left(\frac{\pi e}{8} \right)^k \frac{e^{-\sqrt{2k}}}{\sqrt{2\pi k}}$$

(9.6-3)

But

$$\frac{\pi e}{8} = 1.06747 \ldots$$

Taking $\log_e$ of both sides, we get, as k approaches infinity, $\log_e$ (ratio) $= (0.065288 \ldots)k - \sqrt{2k} - \frac{1}{2} \log_e k - \frac{1}{2} \log_e 2\pi \to \infty$ Therefore, we see that the factor

$$\left(\frac{\pi e}{8} \right)^k$$

will go to infinity faster than the other two factors in the product (9.6-3),

$$e^{-\sqrt{2k}} \quad \text{and} \quad \frac{1}{\sqrt{2\pi k}}$$

can decrease it.

We conclude that the volume of the *inner* sphere becomes arbitrarily larger than the volume of the cube which contains all the $2^{2k} = 2^n$ unit spheres in the corners.

The case of the odd dimension $n = 2k - 1$ does not change matters; it only makes the details more messy.

Exercise

9.6-1   Show that for sufficient large n, the line from the origin to the point $(1, 1, \ldots, 1)$ is "almost perpendicular" to all the coordinate axes. (*Hint:* $\cos \theta = 1/\sqrt{n}$.)

9.7   CHEBYSHEV'S INEQUALITY AND THE VARIANCE

If a random variable X is discrete, the mean square is given by the expectation

$$E\{X^2\} = \sum_{i=-\infty}^{\infty} x_i^2 p(x_i)$$

and if the variable is continuous, it is given by

$$E\{X^2\} = \int_{-\infty}^{\infty} x^2 p(x)\, dx$$

For any $\epsilon > 0$, since the integrand is positive, we have

$$\int_{-\infty}^{\infty} x^2 p(x)\, dx \geq \int_{|x| \geq \epsilon} x^2 p(x)\, dx$$

and this can be written as

$$E\{X^2\} \geq \int_{|x| \geq \epsilon} x^2 p(x)\, dx \geq \epsilon^2 \int_{|x| \geq \epsilon} p(x)\, dx$$

It follows therefore that

$$E(X^2) \geq \epsilon^2 \operatorname{Prob}\{|X| \geq \epsilon\}$$

or

$$\operatorname{Prob}\{|X| \geq \epsilon\} \leq \frac{E\{X^2\}}{\epsilon^2} \tag{9.7-1}$$

This is the famous *Chebyshev inequality* (expressed either in continuous or discrete notation).

The *variance*, or dispersion, of a random variable X, labeled $V\{X\}$, is the mean square measured about the mean value

$$E\{X\} = a$$

Thus the variance of a random variable X is

$$
\begin{aligned}
V\{X\} &= E\{(X - a)^2\} \\
&= E\{X^2\} - 2aE\{X\} + E\{a^2\} \\
&= E\{X^2\} - 2a^2 + a^2 \\
&= E\{X^2\} - a^2 = \sigma^2
\end{aligned}
$$

Clearly, since $E\{1\} = 1$, the variance has the property that for any constant

$$V\{c\} = 0$$

We also have

$$V\{cX\} = c^2 V\{X\}$$

If X_1 and X_2 are *independent* random variables, then if we write

$$
\begin{aligned}
E\{X_1\} &= a_1 \qquad V\{X_1\} = \sigma_1^2 \\
E\{X_2\} &= a_2 \qquad V\{X_2\} = \sigma_2^2
\end{aligned}
$$

we find that

$$E\{(X_1 - a_1)(X_2 - a_2)\} = E\{(X_1 - a_1)\}E\{(X_2 - a_2)\} = 0$$

The variance of a sum of two independent random variables X_1 and X_2 is

$$
\begin{aligned}
V\{X_1 + X_2\} &= E\{(X_1 + X_2 - a_1 - a_2)^2\} \\
&= E\{(X_1 - a_1)^2\} + 2E\{(X_1 - a_1)(X_2 - a_2)\} \\
&\quad + E\{(X_2 - a_2)^2\} \\
&= V\{X_1\} + V\{X_2\} = \sigma_1^2 + \sigma_2^2
\end{aligned}
\tag{9.7-2}
$$

It follows by induction that the variance of a sum of any number of independent random variables is the sum of their variances.

Exercises

9.7-1   Carry out the proof of the Chebyshev inequality for the discrete variable case.

9.7-2   The entropy is the expected value of $\log 1/p_i$. Examine the corresponding formula for the variance.

$$\textit{Answer.} \quad \sum p_i \log^2 (1/p_i) - H^2$$

9.8   THE LAW OF LARGE NUMBERS

If we make a large number of *Bernoulli trials* (meaning that success or failure is a random variable X with values 1 or 0, respectively, and each trial is independent of all other trials), then we can ask for the number of successes *relative* to the total number of trials, and hope that this ratio will approach the probability of a single trial. This is simply hoping that the frequency of successes in a long run of trials will approach the probability of a success for a single trial. To get the formalism going, we consider the random variable X_i, which is 1 if the ith trial is successful and 0 if it is not. What will the average be? We set up the expression for the expectation of the average

$$E\left\{\frac{1}{n}(X_1 + X_2 + \ldots + X_n)\right\} = \frac{1}{n} \sum_i E\{X_i\} = a$$

where a is the expected value of a single trial.

We next look at the variance of the average

$$V\left\{\left(\frac{1}{n} \sum X_i\right)\right\} = E\left\{\frac{1}{n^2}[\sum (X_i - a)]^2\right\}$$

$$= \frac{1}{n^2} E\{\sum (X_i - a)^2\}$$

by (9.7-2), since the cross products drop out. But these are identical trials, hence:

$$V\left\{\frac{1}{n} \sum X_i\right\} = \frac{1}{n^2} \sum V\{X_i\}$$

$$= \frac{1}{n} V\{X_i\} = \frac{\sigma^2}{n}$$

We now apply Chebyshev's inequality (9.7-1),

$$\text{Prob}\left\{\left|\frac{1}{n}\sum(X_i - a)\right| > \epsilon\right\} \leq \frac{1}{\epsilon^2}E\left\{\frac{1}{n^2}[\sum(X_i - a)]^2\right\}$$
$$\leq \frac{\sigma^2}{n\epsilon^2}$$

(9.8-1)

Reversing things we can write this as

$$\text{Prob}\left\{\left|\frac{1}{n}\sum(X_i - a)\right| < \epsilon\right\} \geq 1 - \frac{\sigma^2}{n\epsilon^2}$$

Theorem: *Weak law of large numbers.* If $X_1, X_2, \ldots, X_n$ are n independent identically distributed random variables with mean a and variance σ^2, then given any $\epsilon > 0$ and $\delta > 0$, however small, there is an integer n_0 such that for all $n > n_0$,

$$a - \epsilon \leq \frac{1}{n}\{X_1 + X_2 + \ldots + X_n\} \leq a + \epsilon$$

(9.8-2)

with probability greater than $1 - \delta$. The theorem states that the average can be brought, *probably*, as close as you please to the expected value a.

The proof follows whenever we pick n_0 such that [from (9.8-1)]

$$\frac{\sigma^2}{n_0\epsilon^2} < \delta$$

or

$$n_0 > \frac{\sigma^2}{\delta\epsilon^2}$$

Since this theorem is widely misunderstood, we pause to comment on it. In the first place, since they are Bernoulli trials, that means that the trials are independent—the trials have no memory of what has happened in the past. Therefore, the very concept that the law of large numbers means that in time any run of bad luck will later be "compensated for" must be false. What happens is that any fluctuation from the average will be "swamped" (probably) in the long run, not that there will be compensation.

Furthermore, it does not mean that the sum comes close to the expected value, which is, of course, np. For example, in 10 tosses of a fair coin, you expect 5 heads, but a value as large as 8 is not surprising. In the million tosses we do not expect to be as close as 3 (as we were in the 10 tosses with 8 heads) from the expected value, but it is *percentagewise* that we come closer and closer—probably! The misunderstanding comes when you do not watch where the *n* is—it is in the denominator and when it is there, probably the differences between the number of actual successes and the expected number of successes *divided by* the *n* will decrease as *n* gets larger and larger. But if you talk about the difference between the number of observed successes and the expected number of successes, then it can grow indefinitely large with larger and larger *n*. In this it resembles the earlier Stirling approximation (Table 9.7-1).

Because of its central role in the proof of Shannon's theorem, let us illustrate the theorem by an experiment. Let the probability of an event (success) be

$$p = \tfrac{1}{10}$$

In N Bernoulli trials, what is the probability of k successes? The k successes can occur in any k of the N trials, namely

$$C(N, k)$$

different ways; therefore, the probability for the k successes (and of course $N - k$ failures) is

$$C(N, k)p^k(1 - p)^{N-k} \tag{9.8-3}$$

The expected number of successes is

$$pN$$

In Figure 9.8-1 we have plotted horizontally k/N so that the distribution of (9.8-3) is centered at the same place, namely p, the expected value of a single trial.

To compensate for the compression of the horizontal axis, we plot N times the function (9.8-3), namely

$$NC(N, k)p^k(1 - p)^{N-k} \tag{9.8-4}$$

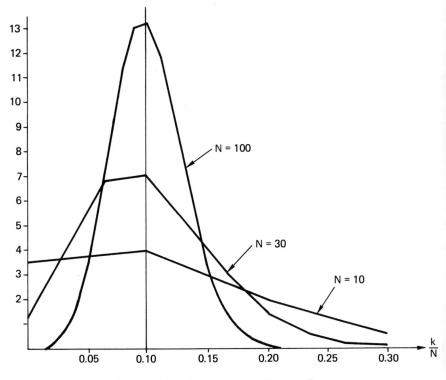

FIGURE 9.8-1   LAW-OF-LARGE-NUMBERS EXAMPLE

Thus the area under the curve is held constant. Figure 9.8-1 gives the distribution for $N = 10, 30, 100$. We see the peaking up of the distribution near $p = \frac{1}{10}$ and the falling away of the probability at places far away from the neighborhood of $p = \frac{1}{10}$. In Figure 9.8-2 we have shrunk the vertical axis and have given the cases $N = 100, 300, 1000$. (Only a few points are plotted and the curve for $N = 1000$ would, in fact, be very smooth indeed if we plotted all the points.)

Thus we see how, as the number of trials N increases, the distribution centers around the expected value p, and the variance decreases like $1/\sqrt{N}$. At $N = 1000$, for example, a deviation of k/N of as much as 0.05 is very unlikely indeed. The probability of being at all far from p can be made as small as you please by picking a sufficiently large N.

We are going to use this theorem when we encode a message in a very large extension. We can expect that the distribution of the difference between the number of actual errors in the transmission of the block of symbols and the expected number of errors, when divided by N, will get to be a very narrow spike indeed—provided the N is large enough. Always probably!

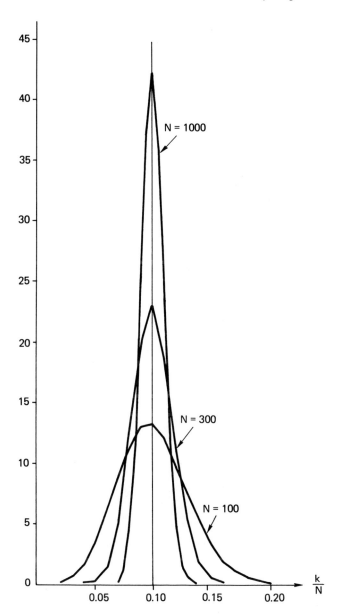

FIGURE 9.8-2   LAW-OF-LARGE-NUMBERS EXAMPLE

Exercise

9.8-1   Make similar plots for $p = \frac{1}{2}$, $N = 5, 10, 20$.

10

Shannon's Main Theorem

10.1 INTRODUCTION

In Chapter 6 we introduced the concept of entropy and in Section 6.8 proved that there are encoding methods which come abritrarily close to the entropy of the input. In particular, we showed [equation (6.8-2)] that by a suitably large extension of length n we can achieve the inequalities for the average code length L_n

$$H_r(S) \leq \frac{L_n}{n} < H_r(S) + \frac{1}{n}$$

Thus the encoding process can be done arbitrarily well, and the entropy $H_r(S)$ provides the limit on what can possibly be done.

We next looked at the channel itself, and defined a channel capacity C, equation (8.1-1). The present chapter will prove the fundamental result that even in the presence of noise, we can get arbitrarily close to the channel capacity. More specifically, we can get arbitrarily close to the rate, and keep the reliability of sending messages through the channel arbitrarily close to 1.

We will prove the theorem for the binary symmetric channel, since in this case the proof is easiest to understand, and it also provides the most common model used in practice. We will merely indicate how the underlying ideas can be extended to prove the theorem for more general channels. The rigorous proof in the general case is complex in all its details and does not shed much more light on why the theorem is true in general.

10.2 DECISION RULES

Suppose that we are at the receiving end of the channel and have received the symbol b_j. Which a_i should we assume was sent? That of course depends on the channel, that is, on the $P(b_j|a_i)$, and also on the source probabilities $p(a_i) = p_i$.

To get a feel for what is involved, consider the particular channel where we have the channel matrix $P_{i,j} = P(b_j|a_i)$:

$$
\begin{array}{c}
 \\
 \\
a_1 \\
a_2 \longrightarrow \\
a_3
\end{array}
\begin{array}{ccc}
b_1 & b_2 & b_3 \\
 & \uparrow & \\
 & | & \\
\begin{pmatrix} 0.5 & 0.3 & 0.2 \\ 0.2 & 0.3 & 0.5 \\ 0.3 & 0.3 & 0.4 \end{pmatrix}
\end{array}
\qquad (10.2\text{-}1)
$$

Let $d(b_j)$ be the result of the *decision rule* we will use when b_j is received. Even if we have a uniform input and all the $p(a_i) = 1/3$ for the source alphabet, the three sets of rules for this channel

$$
\begin{array}{lll}
d(b_1) = a_1 & d(b_1) = a_1 & d(b_1) = a_1 \\
d(b_2) = a_1 & d(b_2) = a_2 & d(b_2) = a_3 \\
d(b_3) = a_2 & d(b_3) = a_2 & d(b_3) = a_2
\end{array}
\qquad (10.2\text{-}2)
$$

are each defensible—arguments can be made in favor of each one. Note that we are here considering one symbol at a time, not runs of symbols.

In the general case there are s rules (one for each received symbol) each of which may have any one of the q input symbols, so there are in total

$$q^s$$

possible decision rules for picking an a_i when a b_j is received.

To settle the question of which set of decision rules to adopt, we shall invoke the widely used *maximum-likelihood rule* of statistics. This rule says that you should "take the symbol that is most probable, given that you have observed what you have." In mathematical terms we require (given equal frequency of the use of the input symbols, which is the reasonable way to use a binary symmetric channel)

$$d(b_j) = a^*$$

where a^* is defined by the conditions

$$P(a^* | b_j) \geq P(a_i | b_j) \qquad \text{for all } i \qquad (10.2\text{-}3)$$

In words, given that you have received b_j, no other a_i is more probable than is a^*. These are not the channel probabilities. To get to them we use Bayes' theorem on each side of this inequality:

$$\frac{P(b_j | a^*)p(a^*)}{p(b_j)} \geq \frac{P(b_j | a_i)p(a_i)}{p(b_j)}$$

Under the assumption of the uniform probability of the input symbols, we have $p(a^*) = p(a_i)$, and we get

$$P(b_j | a^*) \geq P(b_j | a_i) \qquad (10.2\text{-}4)$$

for all i. Thus we now have the maximum-likelihood condition (10.2-3) in the form used in defining the channel.

We will use this rule *even when* the source alphabet is not equally likely. This is not optimal in general, but—like giving away the optimality of Huffman encoding and using Shannon–Fano encoding—what we give away will not cost us too much in the long run. We will still be able to obtain the desired result. This indicates a certain robustness of the final theorem—it is not a delicately true theorem. We can deviate fairly far from the best possible at various stages and still find that the theorem can be proved.

The maximum-likelihood rule is still not unique, as we can see from our example (10.2-2). In the example for the channel (10.2-1), clearly for the maximum-likelihood rule we must take

$$d(b_1) = a_1$$

But given b_2, we can pick any one of the following three:

$$d(b_2) = a_1$$
$$d(b_2) = a_2$$
$$d(b_2) = a_3$$

as our rule. We will have finally, by the maximum-likelihood rule,

$$d(b_3) = a_2$$

Thus there are three possible maximum-likelihood rules (10.2-2) for this channel.

What is the probability of error using this channel and this decision rule? If we write the probability of an error as $P(E|b_j)$, then we have, since $P(a^*|b_j)$ is the probability that the symbol a^* we pick was the source of the received b_j,

$$P(E|b_j) = 1 - P[d(b_j)|b_j] \qquad (10.2\text{-}5)$$

as the probability of making an error given that we have received b_j. The *average error* P_E is given by

$$P_E = \sum_B P(E|b_j)p(b_j)$$

This may be written as, using (10.2-5),

$$P_E = \sum_B p(b) - \sum_B P(a^*|b)p(b)$$

Using Bayes' theorem (Section 7.3) we can reverse the conditional probabilities to get to the channel probabilities [remember that all $p(a) = 1/q$]

$$P_E = 1 - \sum_B P(b|a^*)p(a)$$

$$= 1 - \frac{1}{q}\sum_B P(b|a^*) \qquad (10.2\text{-}6)$$

Let us calculate this for our channel (using the underlined rule). From

$$\frac{1}{3}\begin{pmatrix} \underline{0.5} & 0.3 & 0.2 \\ 0.2 & 0.3 & \underline{0.5} \\ 0.3 & \underline{0.3} & 0.4 \end{pmatrix}$$

and using the formula (10.2-6), we have

$$P_E = 1 - (\tfrac{1}{3})(0.5 + 0.3 + 0.5)$$
$$= 1 - (\tfrac{1}{3})(1.3) = 0.5666\ldots$$

10.3 THE BINARY SYMMETRIC CHANNEL

We now prove Shannon's main theorem for the binary symmetric channel. For a single binary digit we have the standard diagram

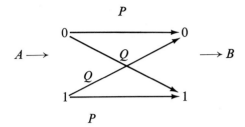

Note that P = the probability of correct transmission. We naturally assume that $Q < \frac{1}{2}$, since if $Q \geq \frac{1}{2}$, we merely reverse the 0 and 1 at B.

For the nth extension of the channel (Section 8.2), we send n binary digits. For example, for the third extension (octal code) we have for single-error-correcting code (maximum-likelihood detection)

Messages	Unused	Received
000	001	000
	010	001
111	011	010
	100	011
	101	100
	110	101
		110
		111

No errors: P^3

1 error: $3P^2Q$ (correctable)

2 errors: $3PQ^2$

3 errors: Q^3

$$P_E \simeq Q^3 + 3PQ^2 = Q^2(Q + 3P)$$

If $P = 0.99$ (99% reliable), we get

$$P_E \simeq 3 \times 10^{-4}$$

We see that the Hamming distance is in this case the maximum-likelihood detector. In general, for white noise the minimum Hamming distance provides the maximum-likelihood detection. In the case of two message points of the same minimum distance from the received symbol, we simply give up, or else toss a coin and guess (we will be right half the time). In the case of more than two message points the same distance away, we can still guess.

For the nth extension of the binary symmetric channel, we see that we have a uniform channel. How we use the channel in practice may be another matter.

10.4 RANDOM ENCODING

Now consider sending n binary digits in a block. There are 2^n possible messages, but if we are to protect against a large number of simultaneous errors, then the admissible messages must be picked very far apart using the Hamming distance. At this point in the text we do not know how to do this in general, so we shall resort to *picking them at random* with replacement. This is the same as picking each code word by tossing a coin for each bit of each word. We can also imagine an urn with all 2^n possible sequences of n 0's or 1's on slips of paper. We pick M slips, replacing them after each draw, to form an alphabet of M symbols, where we are careful to pick *only*

$$M = 2^{n(C-\epsilon_1)} \qquad (\epsilon_1 > 0) \tag{10.4-1}$$

messages. Written in the form

$$M = \frac{2^{nC}}{2^{n\epsilon_1}}$$

we see that $1/2^{n\epsilon_1}$ can be made as small as we please by picking a suitably large n; we take an arbitrarily small fraction of all possible messages. (And we risk getting duplicates!)

We picture these sequences as message points in an appropriate n-dimensional space. The probability of an error in any one position of the block of letters is Q, and we expect nQ errors. We consider a sphere about the chosen message point with a radius of size nQ. Now consider slightly increasing this sphere by a *relative* amount ϵ_2. The radius is now (see Figure 10.4-1)

$$r = (Q + \epsilon_2)n$$

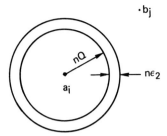

FIGURE 10.4-1 SENDING END

(r is the radius and is *not* the number of symbols or the radix, and ϵ_2 is so small that $Q + \epsilon_2 < \frac{1}{2}$). The actual size of ϵ_2 with respect to ϵ_1 will be determined later.

By the law of large numbers (Section 9.8) there is, for sufficiently large n, an arbitrarily small probability that the received message will fall outside this new sphere. (Since almost all the volume of an n-dimensional sphere is near the surface, it is natural that we are mainly concerned with a shell of thickness $2n\epsilon_2$ centered about the distance nQ.) Thus if we use maximum-likelihood detection, *and* if we can prove that almost surely no two spheres overlap, then we will have the result that the receiver can almost surely know what was sent. The rate of signaling will be arbitrarily close to the channel capacity C, since the probability of any particular random message is

$$p = \frac{1}{M}$$

and we are sending, almost surely, the amount of information

$$I(p) = \log\left(\frac{1}{p}\right) = \log M = n(C - \epsilon_1) \qquad (10.4\text{-}2)$$

bits of information per symbol. Thus ϵ_1 is determined from the desired closeness to the channel capacity.

We must invert the picture in the n-dimensional space and look at the problem from the receiving end (see Figure 10.4-2). The sphere is now to be drawn about the received symbol b_j. We begin with the obvious statement that we have an error if either the correct symbol is not in the sphere, or else if there is at least one other possible sent symbol in the sphere. Therefore,

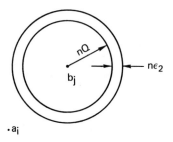

FIGURE 10.4-2 RECEIVING END

the probability of error P_E is given by

$$P_E = P\{a_i \notin S(r)\}$$
$$+ P\{a_i \in S(r)\} \times P\{\text{at least one other code word is in } S(r)\} \quad (10.4\text{-}3)$$

where $\in$ means "is contained in" and $\notin$ means "is not contained in." Since $P\{a_i \in S(r)\} \leq 1$, we can simplify (10.4-3) slightly by dropping this factor:

$$P_E \leq P\{a_i \notin S(r)\} + P\{\text{at least one other code word is in } S(r)\} \quad (10.4\text{-}4)$$

The probability that at least one other code word is in the sphere is certainly less than the sum of the probabilities for each code word other than a_i being in the sphere. We will now multiple-count those cases where several code words fall in the selected sphere about b_j. For example, if there were two other code words besides a_i in the sphere, it is a single error but we will now count it twice. Thus we can write (summation over $A - a_i$ means all of A except a_i)

$$P\{\text{at least one other code word is in } S(r)\} \leq \sum_{A-a_i} P\{a \in S(r)\}$$

where the summation is over the $M - 1$ code words not sent. We now have, for (10.4-4),

$$P_E \leq P\{a_i \notin S(r)\} + \sum_{A-a_i} P\{a \in S(r)\} \quad (10.4\text{-}5)$$

In words, the first term is the probability that the sent word is not within the sphere about the received word (equivalently, that the received word is not within the sphere about the sent word). The second term is the sum over all the terms not sent, any one of which might be in the sphere of radius r, which is, *relatively* with respect to n, slightly larger than the Hamming distance corresponding to the expected number of errors. We hope that by using randomness the message points will be spread out and that there will be only a very small chance that any other symbol will be in the sphere. This, in turn, rests on the vastness of n-dimensional space; it is very unlikely that any two random points will be near each other in a sufficiently high-dimensional space.

The first term of (10.4-5), which depends only on the single symbol a_i, can be made less (by the law of large numbers) than any preassigned positive number $\delta = \delta(\epsilon_2, n)$ simply by making the block length n so large that the extended sphere of radius $r = n(Q + \epsilon_2)$ covers the distances for all but the arbitrarily small number of possible cases. We have, therefore, for (10.4-5),

$$P_E \leq \delta + \sum_{A-a_i} P\{a \in S(r)\} \qquad (10.4\text{-}6)$$

One way of looking at this is that the first term is the error rate and depends only on the particular code symbol sent. The second term depends on all the other symbols in the code and is related to the rate of signaling, since it contains the $M - 1$ possible code symbols other than the correct one.

10.5 AVERAGE RANDOM CODE

All that we have done so far seems reasonable, except possibly the choice of a random code (although we hope that that is at least made plausible by the earlier use of hash coding—Sections 5.11 to 5.14). It is the sort of thing one would think of in the normal course of research. But the next idea of Shannon's, that we should *average over all random codes* (but what else is there to do?) is not one of those things that comes to mind easily. Of course, once the idea is suggested, it is something to try.

We therefore now average over all codes. We use a wavy line for the average over all the codes. The code words come from the urn one at a time (or else are made up bit by bit by the random toss of a coin) and we chose [equation (10.4-1)] $M = 2^{n(C-\epsilon_1)}$ words. There are M symbols of n bits, so there are in all

$$2^{nM}$$

possible codes we could select. With the random selection all these codes are equally likely; namely, each occurs with probability

$$\frac{1}{2^{nM}}$$

The average, weighted by this probability, gives the probable error

$$\widetilde{P_E}$$

The δ is a fixed constant for all the codes and does *not* depend on the whole code. Hence when we average over all the codes, equation (10.4-6) becomes

$$\widetilde{P_E} \leq \delta + (M - 1)\widetilde{P\{a \in S(r)\}}$$
$$\leq \delta + M\widetilde{P\{a \in S(r)\}} \qquad (a \neq a_i)$$

(10.5-1

To evaluate $\widetilde{P\{a \in S(r)\}}$ $(a \neq a_i)$, we observe that each of the M symbols was selected *randomly* from 2^n possible words. Therefore, the average probability that the $a(\neq a_i)$ which we pick is not in the sphere $S(r)$ is the ratio of the number of sequences in the sphere to the total 2^n (the number of possible sequences of n bits). Let $N(r)$ be the number inside the sphere $S(r)$. Then

$$\widetilde{P\{a \in S(r)\}} = \frac{N(r)}{2^n} \qquad (a \neq a_i)$$

(10.5-2)

But for our binary symmetric channel, this is

$$N(r) = 1 + C(n, 1) + C(n, 2) + \ldots + C(n, r)$$
$$= \sum_{k=0}^{r} C(n, k)$$

Recall that [from (10.4-2)]

$$r = (Q + \epsilon_2)n \qquad \text{and} \qquad Q + \epsilon_2 < \tfrac{1}{2}$$

We can apply the binomial inequality of equation (9.4-6) using $Q + \epsilon_2 = \lambda$, to get

$$N(r) \leq 2^{nH(\lambda)}$$

Hence equation (10.5-2) becomes

$$\widetilde{P\{a \in S(r)\}} \le 2^{-n[1-H(\lambda)]} \qquad (a \ne a_i) \qquad (10.5\text{-}3)$$

Assembling things, we have for equation (10.5-1),

$$\widetilde{P}_E \le \delta + M 2^{-n[1-H(\lambda)]} \qquad (10.5\text{-}4)$$

For a binary symmetric channel, equation (8.5-3), we have

$$1 - H(P) = C$$

From the definition of $H(P)$ we clearly have $H(P) = H(Q)$. Therefore, the exponent in equation (10.5-4) may be written as

$$
\begin{aligned}
1 - H(\lambda) &= 1 - H(Q + \epsilon_2) \\
&= 1 - H(Q) + H(Q) - H(Q + \epsilon_2) \\
&= C - [H(Q + \epsilon_2) - H(Q)]
\end{aligned}
$$

But the entropy function is convex and can be bounded at any point Q by

$$H(Q + \epsilon_2) \le H(Q) + \epsilon_2 \left.\frac{dH}{dQ}\right|_Q$$

where (since $0 < Q < \tfrac{1}{2}$)

$$\frac{dH}{dQ} = \log\left(\frac{1}{Q}\right) - \log\left(\frac{1}{1-Q}\right) = \log\left(\frac{1-Q}{Q}\right) > 0$$

Therefore,

$$1 - H(\lambda) = C - \epsilon_2 \log\left(\frac{1-Q}{Q}\right) = C - \epsilon_3$$

and (10.5-4) becomes

$$\widetilde{P}_E \le \delta + M 2^{-n(C-\epsilon_3)}$$

From (10.4-1)

$$M = 2^{n(C-\epsilon_1)}$$

and

$$\widetilde{P_E} \le \delta + 2^{n(C-\epsilon_1)} 2^{-n(C-\epsilon_3)} = \delta + 2^{-n(\epsilon_1-\epsilon_3)}$$

Thus as long as we pick ϵ_2 small enough so that

$$\epsilon_1 - \epsilon_3 = \epsilon_1 - \epsilon_2 \log\left(\frac{1-Q}{Q}\right) > 0$$

then the average error

$$\widetilde{P_E}$$

can be made arbitrarily small by choosing n sufficiently large.

We have now shown that the average code meets our requirements; hence there must be at least one code that does. Thus we have proved Shannon's result:

Theorem. *There exist codes which are arbitrarily reliable and which can signal at rates arbitrarily close to the channel capacity of the binary symmetric channel.*

That in the past we have had great trouble finding such good codes is another thing entirely. The reason is not far to seek—in the proof we have regularly assumed that we could take the block length n long enough. This "long enough" is, in fact, very long indeed!

The proof of Shannon's theorem requires us to send only very long messages. In practice we do not want to wait until we have built up that long a sequence of binary digits before any transmission can occur. Furthermore, from a practical point of view, random codes give large coding and decoding books, and this is bad. Thus the theorem sets bounds but does not suggest much other than that very good codes must be very long, rather impractical ones.

10.6   THE GENERAL CASE

The proof of Shannon's main theorem in the general case goes along the lines of the special case of the binary symmetric channel. The differences in the proof arise from the question of finding an equivalent metric to the Hamming distance (which was appropriate *only* for a channel with white noise). We also have the problem of counting the number of possible messages that lie within a "sphere" with the new distance function. Finally, we cannot use the simple formula for the capacity of the channel but must go back to fundamentals.

The metric we need is the probability of errors. If the "noise" is not white, then the spheres become ovals, with their longer directions in the directions of the less probable errors, and the shorter in the directions of the more probable errors.

Once a suitable metric is found, we pick the "spheres of equal probability radius" about the received symbols, increase them as before, so that by the law of large numbers when n is sufficiently large, almost certainly the original symbol is inside. We choose the number of messages M so that for sufficiently large n, there is arbitrarily low probability of an overlap of the spheres. Otherwise, the proof is the same as for the binary symmetric channel.

10.7   THE FANO BOUND

In order to prove the converse of Shannon's theorem, that we cannot signal arbitrarily reliably at a rate higher than the channel capacity C, we need an important bound due to Fano. For convenience we use the notation

$$\bar{P}_E = \sum_B P(a^*, b) = 1 - P_E$$

where, as before [equation (10.2-5)]

$$P_E = \sum_{B, A-a^*} P(a, b)$$

Consider the expression

$$H(P_E) + P_E \log (q - 1) = P_E \log \left(\frac{q-1}{P_E}\right) + \bar{P}_E \log\left(\frac{1}{\bar{P}_E}\right)$$

$$= \sum_{B, A-a^*} P(a, b) \log\left(\frac{q-1}{P_E}\right) \tag{10.7-1}$$

$$+ \sum_B P(a^*, b)\log \left(\frac{1}{\bar{P}_E}\right)$$

The equivocation $H(A \,|\, B)$ from equation (7.5-4) is of a similar form,

$$H(A \,|\, B) = \sum_{B, A-a^*} P(a, b) \log \left[\frac{1}{P(a \,|\, b)}\right] + \sum_B P(a^*, b) \log \left[\frac{1}{P(a^* \,|\, b)}\right]$$

Subtracting equation (10.7-1) from this we get

$$H(A\,|\,B) - H(P_E) - P_E \log (q - 1) = \sum_{B,\,A-a^*} P(a, b) \log \left[\frac{P_E}{(q - 1)P(a\,|\,b)} \right]$$

$$+ \sum_B P(a^*, b) \log \left[\frac{\bar{P}_E}{P(a^*\,|\,b)} \right]$$

In order to apply the inequality

$$\log_e x \leq x - 1$$

we must convert this inequality to $\log_2$ by writing it as

$$\frac{\log x}{\log e} < x - 1$$

Apply this to *each* sum. The $1/\log e$ will factor out of each term on the right-hand side. Ignoring the log factor, we get for the right-hand side,

$$\leq \sum_{B,\,A-a^*} P(a, b) \left[\frac{P_E}{(q - 1)P(a\,|\,b)} - 1 \right] + \sum_B P(a^*, b) \left[\frac{\bar{P}_E}{P(a^*\,|\,b)} - 1 \right]$$

$$= \frac{P_E}{q - 1} \sum_{B,\,A-a^*} p(b) - P_E + \bar{P}_E \sum_B p(b) - \bar{P}_E$$

$$= \frac{P_E}{q - 1}(q - 1) \sum_B p(b) + \bar{P}_E \sum_B p(b) - (P_E + \bar{P}_E)$$

$$= P_E + \bar{P}_E - (P_E + \bar{P}_E) = 0$$

Hence we have the important Fano inequality

$$H(A\,|\,B) \leq H(P_E) + P_E \log (q - 1) \qquad (10.7\text{-}2)$$

Note first that we have *not* used any decision rule, although the results depend on it. Second, when do we have equality? Equality occurs when

$$\log_e x = x - 1$$

namely when $x = 1$. This corresponds, since we used it in both summations, to both

$$P(a\,|\,b) = \frac{P_E}{r - 1} \qquad \text{for all } b \text{ and } a \neq a^*$$

and

$$P(a^* \mid b) = 1 - P_E \qquad \text{for all } b$$

The second, however, is included in the first, since

$$\sum_A P(a \mid b) = 1 \qquad \text{for all } b$$

10.8   THE CONVERSE OF SHANNON'S THEOREM

To prove the converse of Shannon's theorem, we use Fano's inequality of equation (10.7-2). We want to prove that the probability of error cannot be kept arbitrarily small if we exceed the channel capacity. That is, we cannot make

$$M = 2^{n(C+\epsilon)} \qquad (\epsilon > 0)$$

for M equally probable original messages. Suppose we try. Then for the nth extension of the alphabet, we have that the change in the entropy

$$H(A^n) - H(A^n \mid B^n)$$

is less than or equal to nC (the channel capacity measured in blocks of n symbols is *defined* as the upper bound). But $p = 1/M$, so

$$H(A^n) = \sum \frac{1}{M} \log M$$
$$= \log M = n(C + \epsilon)$$

We have

$$H(A^n) - H(A^n \mid B^n) \leq nC$$

Rearranging, we have

$$n(C + \epsilon) - nC = n\epsilon \leq H(A^n \mid B^n)$$

Applying Fano's result (10.7-2), we obtain

$$n\epsilon \leq H(A^n \mid B^n) \leq H(P_E) + P_E \log (q - 1)$$

Now $H(P_E) \leq 1$ (from Section 8.5), so using $q - 1 < q = M$, we have

$$n\epsilon \leq 1 + P_E(nC + n\epsilon)$$

or

$$\frac{n\epsilon - 1}{nC + n\epsilon} \leq P_E$$

We can therefore write

$$P_E \geq \frac{n\epsilon - 1}{nC + n\epsilon} \geq \frac{\epsilon - 1/n}{C + \epsilon} \geq \frac{\epsilon}{C}$$

which is independent of n. As $n \to \infty$, P_E is bounded away from 0. Hence the error cannot be made to vanish if the rate exceeds the channel capacity.

As an illustration, suppose that we tried to send at a rate of twice the channel capacity. If we sent every other bit through the channel, we could get them through arbitrarily reliably. For the missing bits, the receiver tosses a coin and is right half the time; thus almost $\frac{3}{4}$ of the message is correct and $\frac{1}{4}$ erroneous.

11

Algebraic Coding Theory

11.1 INTRODUCTION

Shannon's main theorem shows that we can signal at a rate arbitrarily close
to the maximum rate and with arbitrarily few errors. The proof is based on
random encodings which are very long, and in any one long word there will
probably be many errors to be corrected at the receiver. In Chapter 3 we
showed how to design single-error-correcting codes as well as double-error-
detecting codes. We now sketch how to design and implement some multiple-
error-correcting codes.

The idea of a random code is appealing until you think about the terminal
equipment. If the code words are long, then the encoding book must be very
large, since by definition "random" means that there is no pattern and each
encoding must be looked up because there can be no formula for computing
the encoded message from the source information. The decoding book must
be even larger, since although only M selected sequences can be sent, every
one of the 2^n possible sequences of n bits (in a binary channel) must have an
entry decoding the received message. Otherwise we must do a very large
amount of computing to find the proper message to associate with the
received message. Thus, in practice, large random codes are hopeless. (But
remember our discussion of hash coding in Sections 5.11 to 5.14.)

We have, therefore, to look for highly structured codes, and to do this
we need the theory of the algebra of finite fields (Galois fields). The topic of
algebraic codes is vast, and we only touch the surface to indicate some of the

ideas involved in the higher-error-correcting codes. This is not a book for experts who are going to design coding systems ideally fitted to complex situations; the book was organized for those who need some acquaintance with what can be done, and hopefully if a situation arises that requires more theory the reader will at least recognize the possibilities and go to other sources for more details (e.g., Refs. [Bl], [G], [Gu], [MS], [Mc], [PW], [W], and [WJ]). However, it is only fair to warn the reader that in practice we seldom know the noise well enough to justify using many of the more elaborate codes that have been developed (and usually based on pure white noise). Occasionally we do.

We will emphasize binary codes, both because they are most widely used, and because the base r codes are somewhat messier in notation, although the ideas needed are usually not significantly different.

11.2 ERROR-DETECTING PARITY CODES REVISITED

The single-error-detecting parity codes of Section 2.2 used a single parity check over all the positions. If we write a 1 for each position that is checked and a 0 otherwise, we get the matrix (in this case the trivial $m \times 1$ matrix)

$$M = (1, 1, 1, \ldots, 1)$$

Consider an encoded symbol which we will now label c; it is a vector of n binary digits, say,

$$c = (0, 1, 0, \ldots, 1)$$

Let the *transpose* of c, written c^T, be the corresponding column vector. We have (using mod 2 arithmetic, of course)

$$Mc^T = 0 \tag{11.2-1}$$

for every encoded word to be sent. It is important to see why this is so. When inspected, equation (11.2-1) is simply another statement of what the parity check is.

Suppose next that a single error is made in sending the code symbol c. The error changes one binary digit. Recalling that we do our arithmetic modulo 2, the received word is

$$c + e$$

where e is the vector with all 0's except a 1 in the position of the error. Consider, finally, the expression

$$M(c + e)^T = Mc^T + Me^T$$
$$= Me^T \neq 0 \quad \text{(for a single error)}$$

The *syndrome* of the erroneous message (the result of applying the parity checks) in this case is a 1 whenever there is an odd number of errors and a 0 whenever there is an even number of errors, including no errors.

11.3 HAMMING CODES REVISITED

In Section 3.4 we examined a special case of single-error-correcting codes. These codes used the parity checks

$$1: \quad 1, 3, \ 5, \ 7, \ 9, 11, 13, 15, \ldots$$
$$2: \quad 2, 3, \ 6, \ 7, 10, 11, 14, 15, \ldots$$
$$3: \quad 4, 5, \ 6, \ 7, 12, 13, 14, 15, \ldots$$
$$4: \quad 8, 9, 10, 11, 12, 13, 14, 15, \ldots$$
$$\text{etc.}$$

In the further special case of $n = 7$, we write the matrix

$$M = \begin{pmatrix} 0 & 0 & 0 & 1 & 1 & 1 & 1 \\ 0 & 1 & 1 & 0 & 0 & 1 & 1 \\ 1 & 0 & 1 & 0 & 1 & 0 & 1 \end{pmatrix} \quad \begin{matrix} \text{3rd parity check} \\ \text{2nd parity check} \\ \text{1st parity check} \end{matrix}$$

where we have put the parity checks in sequence *from bottom up.*
Again let c be a code word. We again have *for all code words,*

$$Mc^T = 0 \tag{11.3-1}$$

since this is really the definition of an encoded word. In technical jargon the matrix M anihilates every encoded word c. A single error e will give the received message

$$c + e$$

and we will have again

$$M(c + e)^T = Mc^T + Me^T$$
$$= Me^T = \text{the syndrome} \tag{11.3-2}$$

Thus the syndrome of the error *depends on the error and not on the code word sent.*

A close examination of the matrix multiplication (11.3-2) by the error vector (which has a single 1 in it) shows that the syndrome is exactly the corresponding column of the matrix. Thus the columns of the parity-check matrix M are all the syndromes that can appear for any single error.

For *any* parity-check code we can write a parity-check matrix M which has 1's in the places of each row where the corresponding parity check is applied and 0's where the parity check does not apply. We *assume* that the rank of this parity-check matrix M is equal to the number of rows in the matrix (using, of course, modulo 2 arithmetic). For example, the matrix (compare Section 3.4)

$$M = \begin{pmatrix} 1 & 1 & 1 & 1 \\ 0 & 0 & 1 & 1 \\ 1 & 1 & 0 & 0 \end{pmatrix}$$

has only rank 2, since if the bottom two checks are satisfied, the upper one is also satisfied. (The sum of all three rows is 0 0 0 0.) If the rows are not independent, then at least one syndrome digit is determined from the others, and we are not going to get all the different syndromes we want—we will waste capacity.

The encoding process *in the general parity-check case* assures us that

$$Mc^T = 0$$

for all legitimate code words. Thus once more, the error e gives rise to the received message $c + e$ and

$$M(c + e)^T = Me^T = \text{syndrome}$$

The syndrome again depends only on the error.

If there is a single error, then we have the following decoding rule: The syndrome is exactly the corresponding column of the parity check matrix.

Therefore, by comparing the syndrome with the columns of the matrix until we find a match, we can locate the position of the error.

Thus we see that for any single-error-correcting code, given any syndrome we can find the corresponding column of the check matrix M, (the syndrome all zeros means no error).

For multiple-error-correcting codes, the syndrome is exactly the sum (modulo 2) of the correcting codes' columns of the matrix corresponding to the error positions. This correspondence *must be unique* if we are to find the proper columns of the matrix and hence the corresponding multiple errors that induced the syndrome. If a syndrome does occur, and it is not the sum of the permitted number of columns, then there is nothing we can do to correct the errors that have occurred. We can only detect the presence of some errors.

To be specific, in a double-error-correcting code, any possible syndrome that can arise from two errors must be the sum of a *unique pair* of columns of the matrix—there cannot be two different pairs of columns leading to the same syndrome, since if there were, we would have no way of knowing which pair of errors gave rise to the observed syndrome. Nor can a sum of any two columns be some other single column. In symbols we have

$$M(e_1 + e_2)^T = Me_1^T + Me_2^T = \text{syndrome}$$

and the syndrome must be unique for *every pair* of errors e_1 and e_2, as well as for every single error.

The same sort of argument applies to higher error-correcting codes.

Exercise

11.3-1   Discuss the problem of triple-error-correcting code design.

11.4   DOUBLE-ERROR-DETECTING CODES REVISITED

For the double-error-detecting code of Section 3.7, we have the matrix (for $n = 8$) where we have added the overall parity check as the top row of the matrix,

$$M = \begin{pmatrix} 1 & 1 & 1 & 1 & 1 & 1 & 1 & 1 \\ 0 & 0 & 0 & 1 & 1 & 1 & 1 & 0 \\ 0 & 1 & 1 & 0 & 0 & 1 & 1 & 0 \\ 1 & 0 & 1 & 0 & 1 & 0 & 1 & 0 \end{pmatrix}$$

Any syndrome with the first component equal to 1 must have the rest of the components as the syndrome of a single error, with the syndrome all 0's meaning that the additional parity check position is wrong (see the last column of the maxtrix M). If the first component of the syndrome is 0, there is either zero or some other even number, 2, 4, 6, 8, . . . of errors. In the first case the message is correct, and in the second case we do not know what to do since the syndrome is not a column of the matrix M. We can merely note the presence of an even number of errors.

11.5 POLYNOMIALS VERSUS VECTORS

Originally (as we did in Chapters 2, 3, and 10) the code sequences of 0's and 1's were regarded as vectors. The significant step forward occurs when this view is replaced by the view that they are *polynomials*—the digits are to be the coefficients of the powers of the variable (indeterminate) x. Thus the sequence

$$1, 0, 1, 1, 0$$

is now to be viewed as the polynomial

$$P_1(x) = x^4 + x^2 + x$$

In a sense we are using a *generator function* representation of the code sequence of 0's and 1's.

Another example is the sequence 0, 1, 1, 0, 1, which corresponds to the polynomial

$$P_2(x) = x^3 + x^2 + 1$$

The set of all polynomials of a given degree with integer coefficients permits addition and subtraction (which in our case of modulo 2 arithmetic are the same thing!) of any two of them. For example, using the above two polynomials, $P_1(x) + P_2(x) = x^4 + x^3 + x + 1$. Addition is *associative*, $(P_1 + P_2) + P_3 = P_1 + (P_2 + P_3)$. The zero element (0, 0, 0, 0, 0) corresponds to the zero polynomial and is identically zero. Since each nonzero polynomial is its own additive inverse, and the sum of any two polynomials is another polynomial of the same degree (at most), it follows that the set of all polynomials of degree n forms a *group*. Remember that the coefficients of the polynomials can be only 0 or 1.

In Section 2.7 we examined modular arithmetic. One of the purposes of modular arithmetic is to be sure that all the numbers that can arise will fall within a given range. This is accomplished in modular arithmetic by dividing all numbers by the modulus m and using only the m remainders $0, 1, \ldots,$ $m - 1$, which are all less than the modulus.

When we face the class of polynomials we find that the *product* of two polynomials has the degree which is the sum of the degrees of the individual polynomials. To keep the product within the maximum degree less than n (so that the polynomial will be indentifiable with a code sequence), we must similarly reduce the degree. Thus we need a polynomial to use as a modulus. Just as with modular arithmetic where we divide all numbers by the modulus and identify the remainder as the number, so we will now divide all polynomials by the modulus polynomial of degree n. As a result, the remainder will have n coefficients (the degree is $n - 1$), which we can then identify as a code symbol.

We saw in Section 2.8 why we want a prime number as our modulus. For a prime modulus, if the product of two numbers is zero, then at least one of the two numbers is zero. If the modulus is not a prime, it is possible that neither number is zero, although their product is. Similarly, we want a prime polynomial as our modulus—a prime polynomial being one that cannot be represented as the product (in the field of coefficients) of two non-trivial polynomials.

A polynomial of degree n might by chance have its coefficient of the highest power 0 so that the polynomial was really of lower degree. Since we have only 0 and 1 in the field of coefficients, we will use the standard words *monic polynomial* to mean a polynomial whose coefficient of the highest power of x is 1.

But the reader may well ask: "Why do we want to multiply polynomials together?" The answer is simply that we want to introduce as much structure into our theory as we can. Then, and only then, will the codes we finally get be highly structured, and as a result we can hope that the encoding and decoding equipment will also be highly structured (meaning easy to build or program in software). In practice, we simply do not want to face random, or even slightly structured codes.

11.6 PRIME POLYNOMIALS

A prime polynomial is a monic polynomial which cannot be factored into a product of lower-order polynomials. But since our field of coefficients uses arithmetic modulo 2, we cannot be sure of how old familiar results will now appear. Thus we will experimentally explore what can happen—we will avoid going into all the technical details of finite fields to prove how factorization must occur.

For polynomials of degree zero there is only the single, trivial polynomial (if you care to call this degenerate case a polynomial), namely

$$P = 1$$

It corresponds in normal arithmetic to the number 1.

For monic polynomials of degree 1 there are only two polynomials,

$$x$$

$$x + 1$$

both of which are prime polynomials (just as we disregard the use of 1 as a factor in factoring integers, so too we disregard the trivial polynomial 1 as a factor).

For monic polynomials of degree 2 we have four possibilities (each of the coefficients of x and 1 may be 0 or 1):

$$x^2 \qquad\qquad = x \cdot x$$

$$x^2 + 1 \qquad = (x + 1)(x + 1)$$

$$x^2 + x \qquad = x(x + 1)$$

$$x^2 + x + 1 \qquad \text{prime}$$

The fact that

$$x^2 + 1 = (x + 1)^2$$

may come as a surprise at first, but multiplying out the right-hand side, we get

$$x^2 + 2x + 1$$

Since $2 = 0 \pmod 2$, we have

$$x^2 + 2x + 1 = x^2 + 1$$

Is the polynomial

$$x^2 + x + 1$$

a prime? Are we sure? We try dividing by the two lower-degree polynomials. If $x^2 + x + 1$ is composite, these are the only possible factors. Clearly, x

is not a factor. We then try

$$
\begin{array}{r}
x \quad\ 0 \\
x + 1 \overline{)x^2 + x + 1} \\
\underline{x^2 + x} \\
0 \quad 1 \\
\underline{0 \quad 0} \\
1 = \text{remainder}
\end{array}
$$

Yes, $x^2 + x + 1$ is a prime polynomial.

For further practice we examine the eight possible cubics:

$$
\begin{array}{ll}
x^3 & = x \cdot x \cdot x \\
x^3 + 1 & = \\
x^3 + x & = x(x^2 + 1) \\
x^3 + x + 1 & = \\
x^3 + x^2 & = x^2(x + 1) \\
x^3 + x^2 + 1 & = \\
x^3 + x^2 + x & = x(x^2 + x + 1) \\
x^3 + x^2 + x + 1 & =
\end{array}
$$

where we have given the four obvious factorizations and left the others blank.

If a cubic can be factored, then one factor must be of first degree. We have given those divisible by x, so we need only try to factor $x + 1$. We have for $x^3 + 1$,

$$
\begin{array}{r}
1 \ 1 \ 1 \\
1 \ 1 \overline{)1 \ 0 \ 0 \ 1} \\
\underline{1 \ 1} \\
1 \ 0 \\
\underline{1 \ 1} \\
1 \ 1 \\
\underline{1 \ 1} \\
0 = \text{remainder}
\end{array}
$$

Hence

$$(x + 1)(x^2 + x + 1) = x^3 + 1$$

Next we try $x^3 + x + 1$:

```
          1 1 0
    1 1 | 1 0 1 1
          1 1
          ___
            1 1
            1 1
            ___
              0 1
              0 0
              ___
                1 = remainder
```

We see that $x^3 + x + 1$ is prime. Similarly, $x^3 + x^2 + 1$ is prime, since by observation

$$x^3 + x^2 + 1 = x \cdot x(x + 1) + 1$$

Last, we try

$$x^3 + x^2 + x + 1$$

From the experience above we now see how to factor directly. Thus we write

$$x^2(x + 1) + (x + 1) = (x^2 + 1)(x + 1)$$

and it is not a prime.

We have, therefore,

$$x^3 + x + 1$$
$$x^3 + x^2 + 1$$

as the only two prime monic polynomials of degree 3.

We shall not go on finding the prime polynomials of higher and higher degrees. Evidently, for each particular polynomial we need only try lower-order prime polynomials up to half the degree of the given polynomial, and we are beginning to see how to do some of the factorizations in our head. In any case, we are not trying to show how to make the best codes but are content to show how coding theory develops towards higher error-correcting codes which have a good deal of structure in them so that the terminal gear is practical to build in software or hardware.

Exercises

11.6-1 Prove the theorem: If and only if the sum of the coefficients of a polynomial $= 0$ (mod 2), then $x + 1$ is a factor.

11.6-2 Knowing how many polynomials there are of a given degree and how many products of lower-order prime polynomials there are, deduce the number of prime polynomials of a given degree.

11.7 PRIMITIVE ROOTS

We need to make one more digression before returning to error-correcting codes. The nth roots of unity are the roots of $x^n - 1 = 0$. Their explicit form is given by

$$e^{2\pi i k/n} \qquad (k = 0, 1, 2, \ldots, n - 1)$$

Some of these roots, for example $k = 1$, are such that their successive powers generate all the other roots. Indeed, if k is relatively prime to n, this will happen. To prove this result, take the successive powers, $m = 1, 2, \ldots, n - 1$, n, of this root:

$$e^{2\pi i k/n}$$

These powers are

$$e^{2\pi i k m/n}$$

If any two of these were equal, then we would have

$$e^{2\pi i k m_1/n} = e^{2\pi i k m_2/n}$$

or

$$e^{2\pi i k (m_1 - m_2)/n} = 1$$

This means that

$$\frac{k(m_1 - m_2)}{n} = \text{some integer}$$

Since k is relatively prime to n, this means that they have no factors in common and n must divide $m_1 - m_2$. However, $m_1 - m_2$ is less than n, so $m_1 = m_2$. Therefore, if k is relatively prime to n, the successive powers of that root generate all the roots of unity, and it is a *primitive root*.

The reason that primitive roots are important is that a primitive root can serve as a *generator* of the whole set of numbers we need.

11.8   A SPECIAL CASE

The perfect Hamming codes have $n = 2^m - 1$ digits. For the case $n = 7 = 2^3 - 1$, we have the matrix (Section 11.3)

$$M = \begin{pmatrix} 0 & 0 & 0 & 1 & 1 & 1 & 1 \\ 0 & 1 & 1 & 0 & 0 & 1 & 1 \\ 1 & 0 & 1 & 0 & 1 & 0 & 1 \end{pmatrix} \qquad (11.8\text{-}1)$$

We know that any rearrangement of the columns of the matrix M will not fundamentally change the code; it will only affect how and where we find the column corresponding to the syndrome that emerges when a single error occurs.

Suppose that we use the prime polynomial

$$x^3 + x + 1$$

as our modulus. Let a be a root of this polynomial. Thus

$$a^3 + a + 1 = 0$$

or

$$a^3 = a + 1$$

Powers of a that are 3 or higher can be reduced, using this equation, to sums of lower powers. Thus every polynomial in a can be reduced to a linear combination of 1, a, and a^2. Now consider a column 3-vector which has components 1, a, a^2 from the bottom up. We have the correspondence for powers of a beginning with the zeroth power. Note that multiplication by a shifts each component up one position, and that $a^3 = a + 1$ is used whenever a cube occurs, so that only 1, a, and a^2 appear in the vector. For the various powers of a, we have the corresponding 3-vectors

$$1 = \begin{pmatrix} 0 \\ 0 \\ 1 \end{pmatrix}$$

$$a = \begin{pmatrix} 0 \\ 1 \\ 0 \end{pmatrix}$$

$$a^2 = \begin{pmatrix} 1 \\ 0 \\ 0 \end{pmatrix}$$

$$a^3 = a + 1 = \begin{pmatrix} 0 \\ 1 \\ 1 \end{pmatrix}$$

$$a^4 = a^2 + a = \begin{pmatrix} 1 \\ 1 \\ 0 \end{pmatrix}$$

$$a^5 = a^3 + a^2 = a^2 + a + 1 = \begin{pmatrix} 1 \\ 1 \\ 1 \end{pmatrix}$$

$$a^6 = a^3 + a^2 + a = a^2 + 1 = \begin{pmatrix} 1 \\ 0 \\ 1 \end{pmatrix}$$

$$a^7 = a^3 + a = \begin{pmatrix} 0 \\ 0 \\ 1 \end{pmatrix}$$

as we should. Thus we have shown that a is a primitive root of the prime polynomial, since its successive powers generate all the seven possible different nonzero 3-tuples.

If we write the columns of this new matrix in the form (for convenience we are reversing the order of the columns)

$$a^6 \quad a^5 \quad a^4 \quad a^3 \quad a^2 \quad a \quad 1$$

$$\begin{pmatrix} 1 & 1 & 1 & 0 & 1 & 0 & 0 \\ 0 & 1 & 1 & 1 & 0 & 1 & 0 \\ 1 & 1 & 0 & 1 & 0 & 0 & 1 \end{pmatrix}$$

we find that this is merely the matrix M (11.8-1) rearranged. In this new arrangement of the columns, we compare the syndrome we compute at the receiving end with the successive powers of a (which we can either store or generate as needed). When we get a match between the syndrome and a column, then we have that column as the corresponding power of a that matches. (A slightly different, but equivalent, decoding matrix would result if we used the prime polynomial $x^3 + x^2 + 1$.)

How do we encode? Since we want the syndrome $0, 0, \ldots, 0$ to mean no error, we must require that the sent polynomial be exactly divisible by the modulus polynomial $a^3 + a + 1$. Thus we put the message in the positions corresponding to a^6, a^5, a^4, a^3, and temporarily put zeros in the other three positions, corresponding to a^2, a, and 1. When we divide this polynomial by the modulus polynomial, we will get a remainder. If this remainder is put into the last three positions of the polynomial we wrote (or if you wish is added to the polynomial), then the result will be exactly divisible by the modulus polynomial. This, then, is the encoding process—supply the last three positions by using the remainder upon division by the modulus polynomial; thus the whole polynomial is congruent to zero modulo the prime polynomial.

To decode at the receiving end, we simply divide the received polynomial by the modulus polynomial. The syndrome (remainder) that results when it is written as a power of a gives the column where the error occurred. We now have a different way of viewing the earlier Hamming codes. This approach is suggestive of what to do next.

Example of Encoding. Given the code above, let us encode the message

$$1 \ 0 \ 0 \ 1 \ - \ - \ -$$

The message corresponds to the polynomial

$$a^6 + a^3$$

We divide this polynomial by the modulus polynomial $a^3 + a + 1$ to get the remainder.

```
                 1 0 1 0
1 0 1 1 | 1 0 0 1 0 0 0
          1 0 1 1
          ───────
          0 1 0 0
          0 0 0 0
          ───────
            1 0 0 0
            1 0 1 1
            ───────
            0 1 1 0
            0 0 0 0
            ───────
              1 1 0 = remainder
```

Therefore, the encoded message is

$$(1\ 0\ 0\ 1\ 1\ 1\ 0)$$

Suppose there is an error at the underlined place (which is the a^3 place) so that the received message is

$$(1\ 0\ 0\ \underline{0}\ 1\ 1\ 0)$$

We divide the received message by the same modulus polynomial as follows:

```
                 1 0 1 1
1 0 1 1 | 1 0 0 0 1 1 0
          1 0 1 1
          ───────
          0 1 1 1
          0 0 0 0
          ───────
            1 1 1 1
            1 0 1 1
            ───────
            1 0 0 0
            1 0 1 1
            ───────
            0 1 1 ⟶ remainder
```

But this remainder is

$$\begin{pmatrix} 0 \\ 1 \\ 1 \end{pmatrix} = a^3$$

This is the fourth position from the right (which is where the error occurred). We add a 1 in this position to get the corrected message, and then drop the last three places to get the original message.

Exercises

11.8-1   Find the decoding matrix for the prime polynomial $x^3 + x^2 + 1$.

11.8-2   Repeat the encoding and decoding of the example for the message 1010 and an error in the a^2 position.

11.9   SHIFT REGISTERS FOR ENCODING

We have developed the theory of algebraic codes in terms of these codes because they are easy to realize in either hardware or software. The apparent complexity of much of the previous division process for the modular reduction of polynomials can be handled simply by means of *shift registers with feedback paths.* Suppose that we have the 7-bit polynomial code of Section 11.8, and we want to encode the message 1 0 0 1. The encoded message will be a polynomial of the form

$$1 \cdot a^6 + 0 \cdot a^5 + 0 \cdot a^4 + 1 \cdot a^3 + {}^*a^2 + {}^*a + {}^*1$$

(where * means coefficient to be determined) and is to be divisible by the modulus polynomial $a^3 + a + 1$ (the one we used in Section 11.8).

We will first set the unknown coefficients equal to zero and, as before, divide by the modulus polynomial to get the remainder. When we add the remainder $a^2 + a$ to the original message polynomial $a^6 + a^3$, we will have the encoded message

$$a^6 + a^3 + a^2 + a = (a^3 + a + 1)(a^3 + a)$$

and this, as shown, is exactly divisible by the modulus polynomial $a^3 + a + 1$.

How can we do the division process in practice? Imagine the shift register in Figure 11.9-1. The digits of the message are imagined to come from the right, the highest power first, with three trailing zeros automatically supplied. The arrows below the register positions show where the "feedback" occurs.

Encode

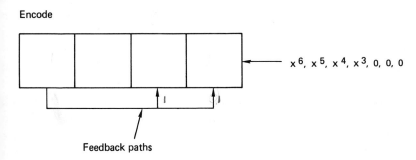

$x^6, x^5, x^4, x^3, 0, 0, 0$

Feedback paths

FIGURE 11.9-1   SHIFT REGISTER WITH FEEDBACK

When there is a 1 in the highest position, it is added to (subtracted from) the indicated positions. We can follow the details in Figure 11.9-2, where we have omitted the early stages, since nothing of interest has happened

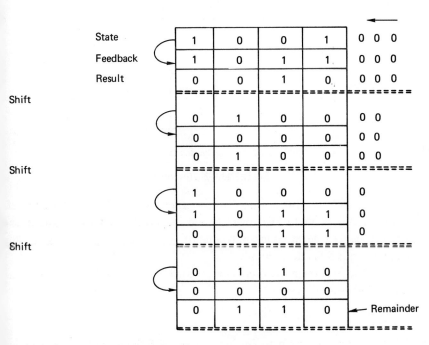

FIGURE 11.9-2   NUMERICAL DETAILS

during the first four shifts until the leading digit gets to the left-hand position. The diagram starts there at the top line. The next line shows the digit fed back and the third row (just above the double line) shows the result of the addition. (We show the adding of 1 in the left position to match the division process in detail; it is not feedback in practice.) The shift occurs at the double line, and we next see the shifted digits. The set of three lines between the double lines gives the details before the next shift. In total there are, in this case, four sets of three lines. The end result is the remainder. A comparison will show how the shift register does the same thing as the division process.

Figure 11.9-3 shows a practical encoder. The digits of the message still come from the right, but now they also go out on the left through the dotted switch. When the remainder is computed, we have all the original message digits sent out and we then change the position of the switch so that we can now shift out the remainder to form the entire coded message (omitting the first digit, which is, of course, always zero). The encoding is that simple!

Shift registers are not hard to build in practice, even with the additional ability to logically add (Exclusive OR) in each position. The rest is similarly easy to build in hardware.

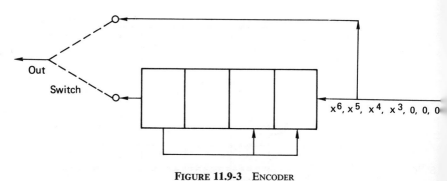

FIGURE 11.9-3   ENCODER

In software it is also not hard to program. We test for the 1 in the left position and if we find it, we logically add the pattern of 1's required by the feedback paths (the modulus polynomial). Then we shift and repeat. The details are not difficult to supply.

Thus the encoding for this code is fairly simple. We next turn to the decoding process.

Exercise

11.9-1   Write a program to encode a message following the model in this section.

11.10 DECODING SINGLE-ERROR-CORRECTING CODES

At the receiving end we do the same as at the encoding end, *except* that we also have to store the message so that we can make the needed corrections when they occur.

After the division process we have the remainder—the syndrome of the error. The all-zero remainder means "the message is correct and therefore send on the first 4 bits."

If the remainder is not zero, it is some power of a, say a^k. How can we find which power? A table lookup might be appropriate for a reasonably short code, but for a very complex one it might require too much storage [although the price of storage is currently (1979) falling rapidly].

Looking back at Section 11.8 we see that $a^7 = 1$; hence $a^6 = 1/a$. We can compute from the syndrome (remainder), which is a^k:

$$(a^6)a^k = a^{k-1} \quad \text{modulo } (a^3 + a + 1)$$
$$(a^6)a^{k-1} = a^{k-2}$$
$$\cdot$$
$$\cdot$$
$$\cdot$$

until we recognize $0\ 0\ 1 = 1$ as the remainder. We then know k.

For example, suppose that we had the message of Section 11.9,

$$1\ 0\ 0\ 1\ 1\ 1\ 0$$

and had an error in the a^2 term. Thus we receive

$$1\ 0\ 0\ 1\ \underline{0}\ 1\ 0$$

The division process will go as follows (simplified)

$$
\begin{array}{l}
1\ 0\ 0\ 1\ 0\ 1\ 0 \\
\underline{1\ 0\ 1\ 1} \\
\quad 1\ 0\ 0\ 1 \\
\quad \underline{1\ 0\ 1\ 1} \\
\qquad\ 1\ 0\ 0 \longrightarrow \text{remainder}
\end{array}
$$

Therefore, we start with this remainder, which is some unknown power of a, say the kth.

$$a^k = \begin{pmatrix} 1 \\ 0 \\ 0 \end{pmatrix}$$

Multiply by $a^6 = 1/a$ repeatedly. This is equivalent to shifting each component down one position. When a 1 is shifted out the bottom, we use $1 = a + a^3$. Thus we have

$$a^6 a^k = a^{k-1} = \begin{pmatrix} 0 \\ 1 \\ 0 \end{pmatrix}$$

until $a^0 = 1$ is recognized:

$$a^6 a^{k-1} = a^{k-2} = \begin{pmatrix} 0 \\ 0 \\ 1 \end{pmatrix} = 1$$

In this case $k = 2$—we need to add a 1 in the a^2 position.

If we shifted out *backwards* we could use the powers of a as a test, and when the match occurred add 1 to the digit being shifted out.

We could also start with the highest power of a and compute down until we get a match. In this case we could shift out forwards.

Notice that in software this needs to be done *only* if there is an error—otherwise nothing need be done beyond getting the syndrome and testing it for all 0's. In real-time coding systems, one must have the capacity to do the computing whether or not is it used.

11.11   A DOUBLE-ERROR-CORRECTING CODE

To illustrate a double-error-correcting code, we need to go to a higher Hamming code with four parity checks and 15 total positions. We examine the polynomial

$$x^4 + x + 1$$

as a possible candidate for the modulus polynomial. Clearly, x is not a factor of the polynomial. If the polynomial is to be divisible by $x + 1$, the sum of the coefficients must be 0 (by Exercise 11.6-1 the old factoring rule still applies here). We have, therefore, only to try as the factor the single irreducible quadratic $x^2 + x + 1$ to find that we have a prime polynomial.

Next, we need to test to see if it meets the primitive condition. We compute the powers of a:

$$1 = \begin{pmatrix} 0 \\ 0 \\ 0 \\ 1 \end{pmatrix}$$

$$a = \begin{pmatrix} 0 \\ 0 \\ 1 \\ 0 \end{pmatrix}$$

$$a^2 = \begin{pmatrix} 0 \\ 1 \\ 0 \\ 0 \end{pmatrix}$$

etc.

We find that $a^{15} = 1$, as it should, and no earlier power equals 1. Thus it is a primitive root and we have the parity-check matrix:

$$
\begin{array}{ccccccccccccccc}
a^{14} & a^{13} & a^{12} & a^{11} & a^{10} & a^9 & a^8 & a^7 & a^6 & a^5 & a^4 & a^3 & a^2 & a & 1
\end{array}
$$

$$
\begin{pmatrix}
1 & 1 & 1 & 1 & 0 & 1 & 0 & 1 & 1 & 0 & 0 & 1 & 0 & 0 & 0 \\
0 & 1 & 1 & 1 & 1 & 0 & 1 & 0 & 1 & 1 & 0 & 0 & 1 & 0 & 0 \\
0 & 0 & 1 & 1 & 1 & 1 & 0 & 1 & 0 & 1 & 1 & 0 & 0 & 1 & 0 \\
1 & 1 & 1 & 0 & 1 & 0 & 1 & 1 & 0 & 0 & 1 & 0 & 0 & 0 & 1
\end{pmatrix}
$$

If we want to correct more errors than this single error-correcting code does, then we must add more rows to the matrix. We will add four more rows, but how?

At present two different double errors can produce the same result for the syndrome, that is,

$$a^k + a^m = a^{k'} + a^{m'}$$

For example, columns a and a^2 give the same syndrome as columns a^{12} and a^{14}. To copy the same columns in any linear rearrangement would get us nothing. We need more. How about using the square of a as a generator? Unfortunately, the two syndromes (let a_1 be some power of a and a_2 be some other power of a)

$$a_1 + a_2 = s_1 = \text{first syndrome}$$

and

$$a_1^2 + a_2^2 = s_2 = \text{second syndrome}$$

are simply related by the equation

$$s_1^2 = (a_1 + a_2)^2 = a_1^2 + 2a_1a_2 + a_1^2 = a_1^2 + a_2^2 = s_2$$

We next try using the cubes for the second syndrome,

$$a_1^3 + a_2^3 = s_2$$

We rearrange this:

$$\begin{aligned}
s_2 = a_1^3 + a_2^3 &= (a_1 + a_2)(a_1^2 + a_1a_2 + a_2^2) \\
&= s_1(a_1^2 + a_1a_2 + a_2^2) \\
&= s_1(a_1a_2 + s_1^2)
\end{aligned}$$

so that

$$a_1 + a_2 = s_1$$

$$a_1a_2 = s_1^2 + \frac{s_2}{s_1} \qquad (\text{if } s_1 \neq 0)$$

Given the sum and product of two numbers, we almost automatically think of the quadratic equation and its roots,

$$a^2 - (s_1)a + \left(s_1^2 + \frac{s_2}{s_1}\right) = 0$$

The two roots give the individual syndromes of the errors.
If there is only one error, then the syndromes are

$$a_1 = s_1$$

$$a_1^3 = s_2$$

and

$$s_1^2 + \frac{s_2}{s_1} = 2s_1^2 = 0$$

The quadratic equation becomes, therefore,

$$a^2 + s_1 a = 0 \quad \text{or} \quad \begin{cases} a = s_1 \\ a = 0 \end{cases}$$

For no errors, we have

$$s_1 = s_2 = 0$$

and the quadratic equation is

$$a^2 = 0 \quad \begin{cases} a = 0 \\ a = 0 \end{cases}$$

Thus for the lower rows of the matrix we use a^3 rather than a as the generator of the columns. The columns are therefore those corresponding to

$$1 \quad a^3 \quad a^6 \quad a^9 \quad a^{12} \quad a^{15} \quad a^{18} \quad \cdots$$

(in reverse order). We get the complete matrix M, therefore,

$$\begin{pmatrix}
1 & 1 & 1 & 1 & 0 & 1 & 0 & 1 & 1 & 0 & 0 & 1 & 0 & 0 & 0 \\
0 & 1 & 1 & 1 & 1 & 0 & 1 & 0 & 1 & 1 & 0 & 0 & 1 & 0 & 0 \\
0 & 0 & 1 & 1 & 1 & 1 & 0 & 1 & 0 & 1 & 1 & 0 & 0 & 1 & 0 \\
1 & 1 & 1 & 0 & 1 & 0 & 1 & 1 & 0 & 0 & 1 & 0 & 0 & 0 & 1 \\
\hdashline
1 & 1 & 1 & 1 & 0 & 1 & 1 & 1 & 1 & 0 & 1 & 1 & 1 & 1 & 0 \\
1 & 0 & 1 & 0 & 0 & 1 & 0 & 1 & 0 & 0 & 1 & 0 & 1 & 0 & 0 \\
1 & 1 & 0 & 0 & 0 & 1 & 1 & 0 & 0 & 0 & 1 & 1 & 0 & 0 & 0 \\
1 & 0 & 0 & 0 & 1 & 1 & 0 & 0 & 0 & 1 & 1 & 0 & 0 & 0 & 1
\end{pmatrix}$$

as the parity-check matrix for double error correction. The syndrome s_1 is from the upper rows and the syndrome s_2 is from the lower rows. The two syndromes, through the quadratic equation, give us the two roots necessary to locate the two errors.

11.12 DECODING MULTIPLE ERROR CODES

For multiple-error-correcting codes there is a simple decoding rule. You might think that we must effectively, as in Section 11.11, turn over the syndrome problem to a computer. For a double error correcting code, the computer must find the zeros of the quadratic. One very simple way to find the roots is to evaluate the quadratic at each position of the stored message as it is being shifted out. If the power of a satisfies the quadratic, then it is a root and is one of the positions to be corrected.

Evidently, we need do this only when there are errors. But in real-time signaling we need to store several messages at the same time. When such a system is in operation, we will be shifting out and correcting one message, computing the corrections of a second message, and working on the first stages of a third. Thus at a minimum there will be two message time delays. And this can be important in the feedback paths of control circuits! It could cause instability problems.

11.13 SUMMARY

In this chapter we have given the argument for why we want a highly structured code: so that we can then encode and decode using systematic methods. We have shown how the division process of dividing one of our polynomials by another polynomial can be implemented easily.

We showed how the syndrome is uniquely tied to the error and is free from the message. We next got down to the necessity of using polynomials modulo a prime (nonfactorable) polynomial. We then saw that the additional condition that the polynomial have a primitive root is necessary so that all the elements can be written as powers of it—sort of going to logarithms.

Finally, we illustrated the methods by devising one particular double-error-correcting code.

We did not attempt to provide all the theory of finite fields necessary to justify all that can be done, nor to create a general theory; we merely showed how a code could be found. The general codes are presented so that special cases can be recognized, or even developed if necessary; more than this would make the book far too long and would not add much to those already available. (See Refs. [Bl], [G], [Gu], [MS], [Mc], [PW], [W], and [WJ].)

A

Appendix:
Bandwidth and
the Sampling Theorem

A.1 INTRODUCTION

This appendix appears to have only a slight connection with the earlier material; certainly the mathematical tools used are completely different. One reason for including it is that in practice the channel matrix (Section 7.2)

$$(P_{i,j})$$

is rarely available. But more important, to send digital information we normally use analog channels that are almost exactly linear. The capacity of analog signal channels is typically measured by "bandwidth"; therefore, it seems necessary in a book on coding and information theory to at least glance at the idea of *bandwidth* and related topics.

The eigenfunctions (the proper functions) of a linear, time-invariant system are the complex exponentials

$$e^{2\pi i f t}$$

Eigenfunction means that the system does not change the form of the function, only the amplitude. *Time-invariant* means that the behavior of the system is not a function of time but only of the inputs. This is characteristic of most current communication systems. *Linear* means that the sum of two functions put into the channel gives the sum of the individual outputs as the output. This is characteristic of most channels *provided* that we avoid over-loading them. The frequency f is measured in rotations (when we do the calculus we use the angular frequency $\omega = 2\pi f$). The independent variable is t, usually time.

A *band-limited function* is a function whose frequencies are all limited to some band. A familiar example is a hi-fi system, which typically will have a lower limit at best of a few cycles per second, say 15 or maybe even a few hundred, and an upper limit of around 18,000 cycles per second. International convention uses the symbol Hz (hertz) for "cycles per second." Radio and television stations are limited to certain bands of frequencies so they do not interfere with each other's broadcasts. Many other systems have a natural limit to their band of frequencies, although in most all cases the band is not as sharply cut off as the theory indicates.

A.2   THE FOURIER INTEGRAL

The Fourier integral is the natural mathematical tool for handling band-limited functions. The Fourier integral represents a function $g(t)$ as a sum of complex exponentials (the eigenfunctions) in the form

$$g(t) = \int_{-\infty}^{\infty} G(f)e^{2\pi i f t}\, df$$

The function under the integral $G(f)$ is called the *transform of g(t)*. It is related to the original function by the interesting formula

$$G(f) = \int_{-\infty}^{\infty} g(t)e^{-2\pi i f t}\, dt$$

which is the same as the original one except for the sign on the i; one integral has a "$+i$" and the other has a "$-i$" term in the exponent.

The Fourier integral is like a glass prism that breaks up a light beam into its colors—frequencies. The function $G(f)$ gives the amount (amplitude) of the frequency f in the original time signal $g(t)$. The integral is simply the properly weighted sum of all possible frequencies; $G(f)$ is the weight at frequency f.

There are positive and negative frequencies to correspond to the pair of functions $\cos 2\pi f t$, $\sin 2\pi f t$, which have the exponential representation

$$\cos 2\pi ft = \frac{e^{2\pi ift} + e^{-2\pi ift}}{2}$$

$$\sin 2\pi ft = \frac{e^{2\pi ift} - e^{-2\pi ift}}{2i}$$

As an example of a band-limited function, suppose that $G(f)$ is zero outside the band (Figure A.2-1),

$$-F \leq f \leq F$$

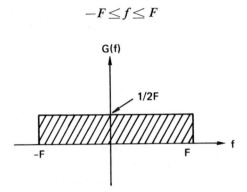

FIGURE A.2-1   BAND-LIMITED FUNCTION

Thus we have

$$g(t) = \int_{-F}^{F} G(f) e^{2\pi ift}\, df$$

Suppose further that inside the band the function $G(f)$ is a constant $1/2F$, chosen so that the area under the function $G(f)$ is exactly 1. We have, therefore,

$$g(t) = \int_{-F}^{F} \frac{1}{2F} e^{2\pi ift}\, df$$

$$= \frac{(1)e^{2\pi ift}}{(2F)2\pi it}\Bigg|_{-F}^{F}$$

$$= \frac{e^{2\pi iFt} - e^{-2\pi iFt}}{2i} \frac{1}{2\pi Ft}$$

$$= \frac{\sin 2\pi Ft}{2\pi Ft}$$

This is the classic function $(\sin x)/x$ shown in Figure A.2-2. It has a *main lobe* about zero of width $1/F$ and *side lobes* of half that width which decrease

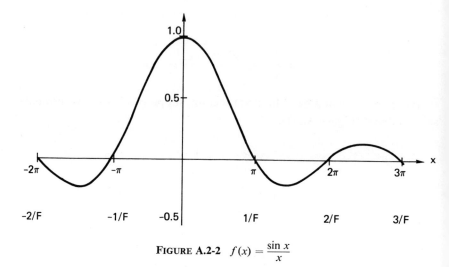

FIGURE A.2-2 $f(x) = \dfrac{\sin x}{x}$

in size like $1/t$. The larger F is (the wider the band), the narrower is the center lobe and the side lobes as well. This suggests that a function can peak up suddenly only if the function has a wide bandwidth.

A.3   THE SAMPLING THEOREM

The famous *sampling theorem* connects the rate of sampling with the bandwidth which is necessary to reconstruct the function from the samples. Before stating the theorem, we need to remind the reader of some of his experiences. When viewing a movie or a TV program, what you see is a sequence of still pictures flashed so frequently that they appear to be moving; typically around 15 to 20 times a second is enough to fool the human eye. However, there are clues to the sampling. For example, when the stagecoach in the "Western" starts moving, the wheels appear first to speed up, then to slow down, stop, go backward, stop, go forward, and so on, depending on the speed. The reason is easy to see. When the stagecoach wheel has turned so fast that one spoke advances to the position of the next spoke, they will appear to be standing still. Indeed, when the spoke gets merely to half the position of the next spoke during one time interval between samples, the wheel will appear psychologically to stand still and to have twice the number of spokes it really has. At slightly faster than this rate the spokes will appear to be going backward! This can be viewed as the consequence of a simple trigonometric identity.

Clearly, any multiples of 2π can be removed from trigonometric sine and cosine functions when the sampling interval is 1 (which we can always have by scaling the time variable). We can also reduce the effective frequency further by taking half-integer multiples from the frequency, since that merely changes the signs of the functions. Thus high frequencies will always appear, because of sampling, to be low frequencies. The highest frequency that can be observed without change is that which has two samples taken in each full cycle. Lower frequencies have no *aliasing*, but higher ones are aliased into lower frequencies, aliased in the sense that *at the sample points* the two frequencies have the same samples.

Once this is grasped, then we can state the sampling theorem. Given the samples of $g(n)$ (at all interger values of n), of a band-limited function $g(t)$, we form the doubly infinite sum

$$g(t) = \sum_{k=-\infty}^{\infty} g(k) \frac{\sin \pi(k-t)}{\pi(k-t)}$$

Inspection of the terms shows that at the sample points, say at $t = k$ the kth term with coefficient $g(k)$ peaks up to the correct value and all other terms have the value zero. Thus the sum has the proper value at this point. There is, of course, the remaining question: "Is the reconstructed function band-limited?" We see from the previous section (A.2) that it is—after the shifting of a $(\sin x)/x$ term it is still band-limited.

Since this is not a mathematics course, we will not try to prove that the series converges (it obviously does at the sample points), let alone that it converges to the right function. Both are true.

A.4 BANDWIDTH VERSUS RAPID CHANGE

From the previous section we see that the bandwidth of a signal is inversely proportional to the width of the main lobe of the function $(\sin 2\pi Ft)/(2\pi Ft)$—it takes a wide band of frequencies to get a narrow spike. We are not in a position (lacking a great deal of mathematical theory) to prove that no shape of the amplitude $G(f)$ in the band can give a narrower spike than the rectangular shape, so we are reduced to making suggestive observations as to why this is so.

It is not rapid change itself that is impossible for a narrow band function; we have only to select any particular frequency, other than zero frequency, and take a sufficiently large amplitude to have as large a change as we want in as short a time as we want. Rather we want a change from one extreme to another, from a maximum to a minimum, or the reverse. This means that at the ends of the interval we want a horizontal tangent. Thus we have, essentially, a $\cos 2\pi Ft$ ($0 \leq 2\pi Ft \leq \pi$), and the transition takes place in time $1/2F$. Again we have the same reciprocal relationship between frequency and rate of change of the signal.

The sampling theorem, of course, is saying the same thing; we must have the necessary bandwidth, and this requires at least two samples in the highest frequency present in order to reconstruct the original signal (assuming that the samples we have go from the time $-\infty$ to $+\infty$).

A.5 AM SIGNALING

Most people know at least a little about AM radios. The AM means *a*mplitude *m*odulation. The frequency of broadcast that you tune the radio set to is called the "carrier frequency" and is a constant frequency carefully controlled by the sending station. All the radio station does is change the amplitude of the frequency they send, and of course in turn that of the signal you receive (see Figure A.5-1). This, however, amounts to a small change in frequency, because the product of two cosines is a pair of cosines each shifted in frequency from one of the original ones (see a few lines later).

The radio receiver, by tuning, filters out all the frequencies that are broadcast except those close to the carrier frequency. Then in one way or another the received signal is "rectified"—meaning that the negative parts are either cut out or else are actually reversed in sign and are made positive. When the result of this is "smoothed" a bit it is, approximately, the original modulation curve that the station imposed on its carrier.

How does this involve the bandwidth? Suppose that the musical note to be broadcast is the pure sinusoid

$$\cos 2\pi ft$$

and that the carrier frequency wave is

$$\cos 2\pi f_0 t$$

where f_0 is very much larger than f. The modulated signal that is sent is the product of the two cosines:

$$(\cos 2\pi ft)(\cos 2\pi f_0 t) = \tfrac{1}{2} \cos 2\pi (f_0 + f)t + \tfrac{1}{2} \cos 2\pi (f_0 - f)t$$

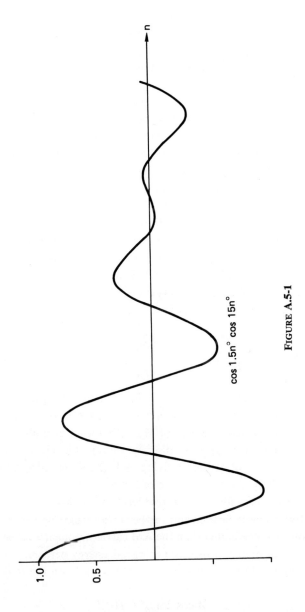

$\cos 1.5n° \cos 15n°$

FIGURE A.5-1

225

Enough information is contained in either of the two terms to reconstruct the original—provided that the carrier frequency f_0 is known (you select the carrier frequency you want when you select the station by your tuning). Thus there are "single-sideband" signaling systems which broadcast only one of the two terms and suppress the other.

Inspection of this formula shows that to receive a band of frequencies of the original signal, you need to receive the same bandwidth (but shifted up by the carrier frequency). Thus it is bandwidth that is necessary to transmit the information—and the wider the band available, the more different signals you can transmit. Put simply, large bandwidth gives high fidelity, and lack of bandwidth will suppress many frequencies and give low fidelity.

The same is true in telephone conversations, although there is no carrier in the simplest cases. The telephone design allows the transmission of frequencies up to around 3600 Hz and pretty well suppresses those above 3600 Hz. This bandwidth gives medium fidelity. Higher-quality phone conversations ("quality" in tone, not in content!) would require wider bandwidth, and it is a fact of nature that bandwidth costs money and effort to achieve. The bandwidth originally chosen for telephones was an engineering compromise *at that time* between quality and cost, and it is not easily upgraded when the installed physical plant is so large.

A.6 FM SIGNALING

Signaling using AM, because of the fading and other properties it has, is not as good as FM (*f*requency *m*odulation). In AM the amplitude of the transmitted signal is modulated; in FM the frequency is modulated, meaning that the information is sent by directly varying the frequency. By using automatic gain control at the receiving end, the amplitude of the signal is kept approximately constant in spite of fading.

If the receiver has a filter (tuner) that lets less and less of the signal through when the frequency is farther and farther away from the carrier frequency (typically this is much higher than the AM carrier frequency), then the energy (or power if you prefer to measure things as energy per unit time) changes correspondingly. Thus loosely speaking, FM works with the signal

$$A \cos 2\pi[f_0 + f(t)]t$$

where $f(t)$ is small with respect to the f_0 of the carrier. Again it is bandwidth that is necessary to convey the information.

By using a much wider band than does AM, the result is that FM has much more ability to suppress noise and more faithfully reproduce the original signal. For the same bandwidth both AM and FM are equally effective.

A.7   PULSE SIGNALING

Typically, *digital signals* are sent as one of two states. One of two frequencies can be used, or one of two voltages (pulses) to signal. In the case of pulses, the corresponding representation in the characteristic modes (the eigenfunctions) of the linear time invariant signaling system,

$$e^{2\pi i f t}$$

is given by a Fourier integral. But a linear system can give various gain and phase shifts to each different frequency. Therefore, the original pulse is apt to have quite a different shape at the detecting end. Further distortion comes from the inevitable "noise" of all real systems.

The wider the bandwidth, the more rapidly the system can change and the more rapidly pulses can be sent down the system. Not that the pulses move faster, but they can be spaced more densely in time. The inevitable distortion of the signaling system must not be allowed to grow too large before detection, reshaping, amplification, and retransmission. By spacing the repeaters sufficiently closely together, the degradation of the original pluse is kept small and hence the reliability is made high.

Sometimes it is the *change of state* of the system that indicates a 1 and no change a 0, rather than pulses for 1's and no (or negative) pulses for 0's.

There are many elaborate systems for pulse signaling, especially difficult are the problems of timing synchronization, and these lead to involved systems. Error detection and correction are often incorporated into the pulse system.

A.8   BANDWIDTH GENERALLY

This appendix is intended to familiarize the reader with several aspects of channel capacity as equivalent to bandwidth. Without the use of a formidable amount of mathematics associated with the Fourier integral, the results can only be sketched. The aim of the appendix is to indicate that in some sense channel capacity as defined in information theory is related to bandwidth, which is the way channel capacity is usually rated in practice.

From Shannon's theorem we would expect that very sophisticated methods of encoding information could achieve great improvements in noise suppression without going to wide bandwidths. It is the complexity of the encoding and decoding that has stopped such efforts on a wide scale, such as for radio and TV. As we have seen, good encoding methods involve very long messages, and this has both severe storage problems and delays to contend with, let alone the processing of the signal. Thus practical signaling systems rarely come near to the ideal of Shannon's theorem. But the appearance of cheap microcomputers and cheap digital storage devices may change matters in the near future.

In TV it is necessary to achieve all the possible changes at each spot on the screen from one picture frame to the next, and this requires very wide bandwidths. But psychological tests indicate that human beings cannot *process* much more than 40 to 50 bits per second, if that much. Even allowing for the fact that various people seeing the same picture will process different parts of the picture, still the disparity between what is done and what seems to be the minimum necessary is almost a millionfold. It is in this way that Shannon's theory is most useful—it points to places where there are possibly large gains and steers the engineer away from places where there can be only small improvements at best.

There is only so much bandwidth in the spectrum of available frequencies that will pass through the earth's atmosphere, and already much of it is assigned to various uses. In a sense bandwidth is a "natural resource" that is definitely limited, not in the sense that the use from moment to moment consumes it, but in the sense that various competing uses of it cannot be made at the same time. From information theory we have a guide to where the bandwidth is used efficiently and where it is being wasted.

Because of the availability of cheap, reliable microcomputers, digital signaling methods which permit easy protection against noise (errors) are of increasing importance, and we have, therefore, neglected analog signaling systems in this brief discussion.

B

Appendix:
Some Tables
for Entropy Calculations

p	$\log (1/p)$	$p \log (1/p)$	$H(p)$
0.00	—	0	0
0.01	6.64386	0.06644	0.08079
0.02	5.64386	0.11288	0.14144
0.03	5.05889	0.15177	0.19439
0.04	4.64386	0.18575	0.24229
0.05	4.32193	0.21610	0.28640
0.06	4.05889	0.24353	0.32744
0.07	3.83650	0.26856	0.36592
0.08	3.64386	0.29151	0.40218
0.09	3.47393	0.31265	0.43647
0.10	3.32193	0.33219	0.46900
0.11	3.18442	0.35029	0.49992
0.12	3.05889	0.36707	0.52936
0.13	2.94342	0.38264	0.55744
0.14	2.83650	0.39711	0.58424
0.15	2.73697	0.41054	0.60984
0.16	2.64386	0.42302	0.63431
0.17	2.55639	0.43459	0.65770
0.18	2.47393	0.44531	0.68008
0.19	2.39593	0.45523	0.70147

p	$\log (1/p)$	$p \log (1/p)$	$H(p)$
0.20	2.32193	0.46439	0.72193
0.21	2.25154	0.47282	0.74148
0.22	2.18442	0.48057	0.76017
0.23	2.12029	0.48767	0.77801
0.24	2.05889	0.49413	0.79504
0.25	2.00000	0.50000	0.81128
0.26	1.94342	0.50529	0.82675
0.27	1.88897	0.51002	0.84146
0.28	1.83650	0.51422	0.85545
0.29	1.78588	0.51790	0.86872
0.30	1.73697	0.52109	0.88129
0.31	1.68966	0.52379	0.89317
0.32	1.64386	0.52603	0.90438
0.33	1.59946	0.52782	0.91493
0.34	1.55639	0.52917	0.92482
0.35	1.51457	0.53010	0.93407
0.36	1.47393	0.53062	0.94268
0.37	1.43440	0.53073	0.95067
0.38	1.39593	0.53045	0.95804
0.39	1.35845	0.52980	0.96480
0.40	1.32193	0.52877	0.97095
0.41	1.28630	0.52738	0.97650
0.42	1.25154	0.52565	0.98145
0.43	1.21754	0.52356	0.98582
0.44	1.18442	0.52115	0.98959
0.45	1.15200	0.51840	0.99277
0.46	1.12029	0.51534	0.99538
0.47	1.08927	0.51596	0.99740
0.48	1.05889	0.50827	0.99885
0.49	1.02915	0.50428	0.99971
0.50	1.00000	0.50000	1.00000
0.51	0.97143	0.49543	0.99971
0.52	0.94342	0.49058	0.99885
0.53	0.91594	0.48545	0.99740
0.54	0.88897	0.48004	0.99538
0.55	0.86250	0.47437	0.99277
0.56	0.83650	0.46844	0.98959
0.57	0.81097	0.46225	0.98582
0.58	0.78588	0.45581	0.98145
0.59	0.76121	0.44912	0.97650
0.60	0.73697	0.44218	0.97095
0.61	0.71312	0.43500	0.96480
0.62	0.68966	0.42759	0.95804
0.63	0.66658	0.41994	0.95067
0.64	0.64386	0.41207	0.94268

p	$\log(1/p)$	$p \log(1/p)$	$H(p)$
0.65	0.62149	0.40397	0.93407
0.66	0.59946	0.39564	0.92482
0.67	0.57777	0.38710	0.91493
0.68	0.55639	0.37835	0.90438
0.69	0.53533	0.36938	0.89317
0.70	0.51457	0.36020	0.88129
0.71	0.49411	0.35082	0.86872
0.72	0.47393	0.34123	0.85545
0.73	0.45403	0.33144	0.84146
0.74	0.43440	0.32146	0.82675
0.75	0.41504	0.31128	0.81128
0.76	0.39593	0.30091	0.79504
0.77	0.37707	0.29034	0.77801
0.78	0.35845	0.27959	0.76017
0.79	0.34008	0.26866	0.74148
0.80	0.32193	0.25754	0.72193
0.81	0.30401	0.24625	0.70147
0.82	0.28630	0.23477	0.68008
0.83	0.26882	0.22312	0.65770
0.84	0.25154	0.21129	0.63431
0.85	0.23447	0.19930	0.60984
0.86	0.21759	0.18713	0.58424
0.87	0.20091	0.17479	0.55744
0.88	0.18442	0.16229	0.52936
0.89	0.16812	0.14963	0.49992
0.90	0.15200	0.13680	0.46900
0.91	0.13606	0.12382	0.43647
0.92	0.12029	0.11067	0.40218
0.93	0.10470	0.09737	0.36592
0.94	0.08927	0.08391	0.32744
0.95	0.07400	0.07030	0.28640
0.96	0.05889	0.05654	0.24229
0.97	0.04394	0.04263	0.19439
0.98	0.02915	0.02856	0.14144
0.99	0.01450	0.01435	0.08079
1.00	0.00000	0.00000	0.00000

References

[A]   ABRAMSON, N. *Information Theory and Coding*. New York: Mc-Graw-Hill, 1963.

[B1]   BERLEKAMP, E. R. *Algebraic Coding Theory*. New York: McGraw-Hill, 1968.

[B2]   BERLEKAMP, E. R., ed. *Key Papers in the Development of Coding Theory*. New York: IEEE Press, 1974.

[B1a] BLAKE, I., ed. *Selected Papers on Algebraic Coding Theory*. Stroudsburg, Pa.: Dowden, Hutchinson and Ross, 1973.

[DG]   DAVISSON, L. D., and GRAY, R. M. *Data Compression*. Strouds-burg, Pa.: Dowden, Hutchinson and Ross, 1976.

[G]   GALLAGER, R. G. *Information Theory and Reliable Communica-tion*. New York: John Wiley, 1968.

[Ga]   GATLIN, L. L. *Information Theory and the Living System*. New York: Columbia University Press, 1972.

[Gu]   GUIASU, S. *Information Theory with Applications*. New York: McGraw-Hill, 1977.

[J]   JAYANT, N. S. *Waveform Quantization and Coding*. New York: IEEE Press, 1976.

[K]   KNUTH, D. E. *The Art of Computer Programming*, Vol. 3, Sorting and Searching. Reading, Mass.: Addison-Wesley, 1973.

[MS]   MACWILLIAMS, J., and SLOANE, N. J. A. *The Theory of Error Cor-recting Codes*. (Elsevier, American ed.) Amsterdam: North-Holland, 1977.

[Mc]   MCELIECE, R. J. *The Theory of Information and Coding.* Reading, Mass.: Addison-Wesley, 1977.

[PW]   PETERSON, W. W., and WELDON, E. J., JR. *Error Correcting Codes,* 2nd ed. Cambridge, Mass.: MIT Press, 1972.

[S]   SLEPIAN, D., ed. *Key Papers in the Development of Information Theory.* New York: IEEE Press, 1974.

[W]   WAKERLY, J. *Error Detecting Codes, Self-Checking Circuits and Applications.* Amsterdam: North-Holland, 1978.

[WJ]   WOZENCRAFT, J. M., and JACOBS, I. M. *Principles of Communication Engineering.* New York: John Wiley, 1965.

Index